Vānaprastha

A Joyous Journey Toward Liberation

Published by
Chinmaya Mission West
P.O. Box 129 Piercy, CA 95587 U.S.A.
Tel. (707) 247-3488
Email: publications@chinmayamission.org
Website: www.chinmayamission.org

First Edition: May 2015, 3,200 copies

Special thanks to Pūjya Guruji Swami Tejomayananda, Swami Prashantananda, Swami Yogasthananda, and Dr. Sajjan Singh for their loving support and guidance.

Grateful acknowledgment to Swami Abhedananda (CM South Africa), Swami Advayananda, Swami Bodhatmananda, Swamini Vimalananda, Brni. Anupama Chaitanya, Br. Piyush Chaitanya, Br. Vineet Chaitanya, , Br. Yukt Chaitanya, Cauvery Bhalla and the team at Chinmaya Archives, Bhuvanesh, Dr. Dilip Rana, Dheepna Benoit, Kishor Ukirde, R. Krishnamoorthy Thatha, Mannu Bhalla, Mithlesh Sharma, Nivedita Naik, Padmaja Joshi, Pranji Lodhia, Ranjana Sharma, Shibani Khorana, Trishna Gulrajani, and many others for their inputs and unconditional help. Subha Pathial, Suresanji (Chinmaya Gardens) and Vishva for photographic support. And deepest gratitude to CCMT for every support.

Author
Meera Seth

Editorial Support by the Mananam Team
Swami Shantananda, Margaret Dukes, David Dukes, Neena Dev,
Rudite Emir, Br. Eric, Rashmi Mehrotra, Arun Mehrotra,
Padmashree Rao, and Aarthi Ramalingam

Design & Layout
Preeti Pahwa

Printed by
Silverpoint Press Pvt. Ltd., Mumbai, India

Library of Congress Control Number: 2011940312
ISBN: 978-1-60827-015-6

THE mananam SERIES
CHINMAYA BIRTH CENTENARY CELEBRATION SERIES

Vānaprastha

A Joyous Journey Toward Liberation

Contents

Foreword

(Based on a talk given by Pūjya Guruji Swami Tejomayananda)

We have to learn the art of living, but alongside we need to learn the art of leaving. That is the focus of the stage of life called vānaprastha.

Today, old age has become synonymous with ailments, loneliness, and complaints. All three result from attachment to the body, to relationships, and to the ego, respectively. So endemic is this attachment that, even at the onset of age sixty, some begin to feel illness creeping up on them, they feel they have become prone to being unwell, and they even imagine that they are losing their memory!

This is because of their fear and their image of old age.

Gurudev initiated the vānaprastha movement in the 1980s and it evolved into the Chinmaya Vānaprastha Sansthan (CVS). The reason Chinmaya Mission started the CVS was to clarify that the age after gṛhasthāśrama is the age to turn inward. Thus, CVS is meant for guiding senior citizens toward the very goal of their life called Self-realization — to declare, "enough of all worldly pursuits!"

Every pursuit has a context. Vānaprastha is when the material context is over. In olden days, estimating the life span of a person to be one hundred years, one's life was divided into four quarters. In the first quarter, called brahmacarya, life was dedicated to discipline and studies. After getting married, for the next twenty-five years, the person led a householder's life in the gṛhasthāśrama, enriching the society. When a person turned fifty, one started preparations for vānaprastha. Thus, by seventy-five years of age, the person became detached enough to renounce all and take sannyāsa.

However, in the twenty-first century, some people begin their married life only when they are in their mid-thirties. As a result of delayed gṛhasthāśrama, when they reach the stage of vānaprastha they are yet householders and worrying about retirement, settling their children, and so on. As a result, their vānaprastha years are spent in endless worrying, almost never thinking of their self-development.

Everything, every investment, is to be left behind on the earthly plane. Even the body will be left here. We will take with us only knowledge and the dharma that we did. Our good and bad karmas, too, will go with us; whatever meritorious practices such as nāma saṅkīrtanam, japa we have done, only those will go with us. We should take care of the body, no doubt, but we must not get obsessed with it.

So Vānaprasthan Sansthan is really meant to guide the senior members of society toward what they need to work on after they attain the age of sixty. By then, with all duties done, it is time to turn the mind toward Self-realization. And, age gracefully! Aging gracefully is when we do what is prescribed for the age. In childhood, students should remain devoted to studies, to knowledge; this is śikṣā. In youth, to their vocation or profession, to serving people with some vow; this is called dīkṣā. And in old age, the attitude to adopt is bhikṣā — being content with whatever life gives you. No more worldly ambitions.

What is graceless aging? When every stage of life is wasted in attachment and worldly indulgence, and when old age is spent in mere worrying with never a thought of God; then life speeds past gracelessly.

Vānaprastha is the period of inquiry, of turning toward God. It is how one should age. It is the path of graceful aging.

Vānaprastha is not the age of helplessness. Elders can take care of themselves and others, too! They have not arrived into uselessness. They have arrived into becoming supportive of and useful to society. Aging is not decaying; aging means maturing for the inward journey. So it is, in fact, the age of non-dependency on things, on beings, and on the ego. It is the birth into empowerment. This is called the art of leaving — leaving the world of dependency on objects and relationships.

Bhagavān Śaṅkarācārya says that even though the śāstras have prescribed many methods of penance to achieve detachment, they are not necessary if you are given to the study of scriptures. With reflection on That, meditation on That, and practice of That, you don't have to do many kinds of severe penance. Remain steadfast in That. The one who has become freed from this elation, depression, and intolerance, freed from life's emotional rollercoaster, freed from the attack of the body, freed of fanaticism at the intellectual level, and freed of the preferences for comfort — that person is a vānaprasthī.

Thus arrive into a life of withdrawal from all worldly occupations and preoccupations and turn the mind's attention to the higher goal.

Vānaprastha is the age of resilience. Don't delve into the past or worry about the future. Just continue and *be,* and remain steadfast in the pursuit of spiritual knowledge.

Hari Om!
Swami Tejomayananda
Head, Chinmaya Mission Worldwide

May 8, 2015
Ernakulam, Kerala,
India

On the occasion of the launch of
Gurudev's Birth Centenary Celebrations

Introduction

We are a vast world of people grouped by geographies and consequent culture. Hence we eat different things or the same things differently. We wear different clothes, we talk different languages or the same language differently, we pray to different gods or the same God differently. We are subject to different economies that determine different outcomes for us. We have different leaders who approach similar problems differently.

In short, we are all the same people, but thinking the same thoughts differently. Vānaprastha is a thought that most of us have in almost every country, albeit differently. Consequently, people all over the globe arrive at the same age of sixty-five to seventy — but differently.

Some societies call the ones who are sixty-five or older, elders, some call them aged, some call them third agers, some call them *budhaoo*, some call them *vṛddha*. We also treat them differently: some depend on them, some exclude them, some disengage from them, and some classify them among the needy and weak. Some reach out to them selectively, as, for instance, to sell insurance.

But vānaprastha does not concern itself with what people think of age. Vānaprastha thinks of the individual, regardless of the culture the person belongs to. Once vānaprastha is entered, culture and country of origin cease to have relevance. Thus, it is a great equalizer.

With this in mind, welcome to *Vānaprastha, A Joyful Journey Toward Realization.*

*

When Bill Gates 'retired' from Microsoft in 2008, he shifted focus and devoted his mind to using the Bill and Melinda Gates Foundation to fight crippling diseases that derail economies and destroy lives, like malaria, HIV/AIDS, and more recently, polio. He focused on the poorest of poor nations, on health, on education, on sanitation, on agriculture, on poverty, on hunger and malnutrition. Gates also invested in innovation in agriculture, education, sanitation, and in techniques to reverse global warming.

Lokasaṅgraha (world welfare) at its best, without a doubt. But there was something else he did; while most pursue golf with a vengeance after retirement, Gates hung up his golf clubs. He said: "It takes up too much time to get any good at it." Gates was rearranging his life. In his own way, he was entering vānaprastha. He decided to devote himself to philanthropy, to saving lives, to putting his wealth into the world in a way that would have a multiplier effect. He would eradicate disease. What was to be had by excelling in golf? That time was up.

The Gates couple, like many of us, had thought that their time for philanthropy would come after age sixty. But their passion for and awareness of global issues began far, far before that, simultaneously with a realization that they had no more personal use for money.

Do we all have a plan for lokasevā (service to the world)?

When Gurudev came down from the hills, he had a plan — to take Vedānta into as many hearts he could. One part of that plan — to resurrect society spiritually — was 'vānaprastha' for those who had graduated from a householder life. This resource pool would resurrect society.

When we read the stories in this book, it might appear that the vānaprastha movement in the Mission began without a warning. And that is true. It did begin without a warning. But it began with a sound intention and a plan that germinated in Gurudev's mind. This book details the gradual unfolding of that plan and how it bloomed.

Some chapters in this book are devoted to examining some research papers that were discussed at a national workshop and some at a national seminar. There is also a whole chapter that goes into the numbers surrounding demographics, population estimates, and projections. These, in fact, are an outcome of Gurudev's initial push to his devotees to pay attention to elders. It has been pointed out twice in this book that Gurudev merely sowed the seed but not once did he say how the fruit should look. That, he knew would be the responsibility of the seed. So the researches and papers that have been written for these workshops and seminars are to be seen as emanating from that same seed. And together, all these define the dimensions of eldercare that Gurudev wished for us to invest in. At the level of the individual, it is vānaprastha; at the level of the collective Mission, it is eldercare.

In 1981, when it began, the vānaprastha movement was most visible in the Chinmaya Mission centers in India, where industrialization, followed by the breakdown of the joint family, followed by rampant neglect of elders, necessitated eldercare. But on closer examination, the diagnosis also revealed that the rot had spread; there was a gradual distancing from spirituality, in some cases starting as early as in school, where even the basic accent on moral values had been replaced by an over-emphasis on performance, material rewards, leading on to material success. Soon the young were displaying an extraordinary indifference, nay, callousness, toward spirituality and religious philosophy.

*

Much of the Chinmaya Vānaprastha Sansthan (CVS) initiative that began in 1981, was India-centric, with research drawn from the West. The West had experienced its own problems with an aging population. There, old age tended to be defined as a state of cognitive and physical decline, resulting in labeling the elder as a burden, a liability. But India that was already overburdened by population, deficits and debts, the growing elder population was bad news. In this din, the words of its roots and ṛṣis, were thus lost. Barely a few knew that vānaprastha is the age of the ascent of man, that societies were nourished by vānaprasthis.

All this means we have an elder population that is marginalized, but growing! When we look at the year 2050 and the 437 million billowing elder population (including a vast majority of the readers of this book), the question is, will this 437 million be scaffolded by systems that ensure care, or will the older population be an abandoned statistic, however huge?

Whatever the statistics say, the fact still remains that we have no plan for human beings after their sixtieth year. This really is at the heart of the problem of why the elderly community in India, is a neglected, uncared-for lot. There is no plan whatsoever, nay, not even a thought.

And the elder? He arrives at sixty-five, unprepared and confused, and is pinned with a label 'Old.' Not just in India, but even in the much coveted Western world, the elder feels marginalized. Medical care is supremely unaffordable even if available. He also finds himself useless thanks to an acute performance orientation that looks at him as an unproductive resource, an orientation that recognizes only gross gains, having failed abysmally to recognize the softer, the subtler benefits. Whereas, Gurudev has sought to show us that every society needs the elder to protect its values.

The religious antagonism of the last two millenia have pushed aside the work of great masters and saints. India lost the teachings of the great ṛṣis who in the past had trained great kings and scholars to know when their pursuit of ambition stops and when one should turn inward. Kings of yore felt the onset of dispassion early in life, and they often handed over power to their young princes, and made off to the forest to reflect and renew.

The loss of vānaprastha, and the consequent despondency, has resulted in a society without any inheritance. If the elder does not know his duty, the youth, too, do not know their rights — their right to a well-built society, pruned by the elders, but only if societies perform their duties to the elders.

Each one of us who is reading this book is lucky to have known, or read about, a Mahātma named Swami Chinmayananda, who spent his life building a path for us to walk on, giving us a scientific understanding of Vedānta. And one of the many marvelous things he did was modernize and revive vānaprastha as a way of life that will put the individual back on the road toward spiritual fulfillment from where he had strayed, strayed because he thought life ended with gṛhasthāśrama, the householder's life. Instead, Gurudev asked, "And who will spiritually resurrect society?" For in the resurrection of society lay the resurrection of man. And this was the role Gurudev conferred upon the elders.

There are innumerable ways in which the elders serve. Some teach, some counsel, some chant, and some pray for world welfare. In the course of this book, the reader will meet many elders who have found a way forward, a path graced with spiritual yearning, inner fulfillment and readiness to be guided by the Guru. What does this do for society? Read on.

Śrī Ādi Śaṅkarācārya no doubt took sannyāsa at a very young age, and his sacrifice was tremendous. Indeed, Śrī Śaṅkara's Mother Aryamba's sacrifice was even greater, for she gave up her life support!

When Lakshmana of the *Rāmāyaṇa* went to bid his mother farewell before leaving for the forest, his mother Sumitra steeled her heart and told him, "Go! Sīta is your mother now!" Guruji says in his lectures, "What mother will give up her motherhood to another?"

Sumitra's sacrifice helped Śrī Rāma's yajña, Aryamba's sacrifice gave us Advaita. The saints and swamis in our midst are the fruit of the sacrifices made by many a parent and grandparent. This book features two such elders, Śrī W. K. Govindraj, father of our Swami Dheerananda, CM Washington, D.C., and Śrī Yashwant Tarkas, the grandfather of our Swami Swatmananda, Ācārya, CM Mumbai. Lives of purity and tapas such as theirs are what come back as fruit that nourishes the Chinmaya Mission and fortify our societies. This is how vānaprastha resurrects society.

Gurudev's mission with Advaita began in 1951 when most of us were not even born. Many of those who worked for him, to establish this Mission, so that five decades later we would have his teachings to nourish us, are today above seventy-five and standing tall and strong, fortified by his teachings. Many of them have seamlessly slid into vānaprastha, like Dr. P. Geervani, like Kshama Metre, like Krishnamoorthy Thatha, like Rudite Emir — silently tilling the ground that Gurudev had walked. We have a duty toward them.

Why did they not choose to live happily ever after in gṛhasthāśrama? Why this vānaprastha? Primarily, it is the urging of the Guru and the scriptures, followed by a choice they made. That is the starting point. The householder life of thirty to forty odd years increases our vāsanās, blurring our goal for this birth. Vānaprastha is meant for us to get in touch with our birth vision, and to do that we need to step off the play-acting we have been doing all these years and now focus on the purpose of our birth.

So is vānaprastha a choice we make only in old age? Vānaprastha is the creation of unencumbered time, regardless of one's physical age. It is a time for freeing oneself from ambition-driven action as well as burdensome relationships and desires. It is a time when the jīva begins the path of unlearning his fifty to sixty years of material dependency and attachments.

And for those who have been following a spiritual path, it would be enormously foolish if after studying Vedānta for thirty-odd years, one came to the threshold of life at age sixty-five and jumped off the cliff of growth into an abyss of self-abnegation. Like Guru Dronacharya, Gurudev has placed the target between the foliage in the forest and commanded that we hit the right eye of the elusive bird. To whimper and complain that our joints hurt or that our progeny pay us little attention is an insult to Gurudev's fifty years of toil. He has armed us with Vedānta: should we not complete the journey?

Vānaprastha is the choice we can make.

I

Before You Drop the Pole

bālastāvatkrīḍāsaktaḥ
taruṇastāvattaruṇīsaktaḥ.
vṛddhastāvaccintāsaktaḥ
parame brahmaṇi ko'pi na saktaḥ.

Childhood is lost by attachment to playfulness. Youth is lost in the quest and attachment to love. Old age is spent in worrying over the past. Alas! No one is interested in the highest Truth, Brahman.

– *Śrī Ādi Śaṅkarācārya,* Bhaja Govindam, Verse 7

Sarla Vaid, like many of us, is an ardent student of Vedānta, studying under an accomplished teacher.

An unusual camp was organized by her teacher at Rishikesh. Sarla, along with six other ladies, enthusiastically signed up. She prepared for her family's needs during her absence, freezing food for their upcoming meals, leaving notes on the fridge, so that she could attend the camp in peace.

Their local Ācārya told them in advance that during the ten-day stay in Rishikesh, only South Indian cuisine would be served, because the cook for that camp was a South Indian. The ladies, who were from North and Central India, laughed off the warning, even making a small joke about vairāgya. Surely the cuisine at the camp could not disturb them!

On her return on day ten, Sarla looked withered. "I got so irritated eating sambar and rice, that my mind had stopped concentrating in class! All I could think of was, today, again, they will serve only sambar. And let me tell you that they served *only sambar* and rice those ten days. On day nine, when Swamiji said that he would like us to stay back for two more days, I knew I would not last!"

Disturbed by her attachment to food at forty-five, Sarla says, "And we talk of renunciation!"

The Ācārya who had designed the camp program had only sought to let them experience the nature of attachment and desire!

This anecdote drives home to us the malady of conditioning. One of the lessons needed in vānaprastha — as we will see later in this book — is unlearning our conditioning. Thus, the subject of vānaprastha is relevant not only at sixty-five but as early as thirty! It is for each one who is on *this side* of the fence, who thinks of vānaprastha as an event, as something that happens to some people, 'other people,' as something that is religious and as something that is a matter of choice.

Vānaprastha is not something that 'happens' to people. It is a way of life that we plan for and commit to, to take our study of Vedānta forward. As for those who are yet to commence their study of Vedānta, vānaprastha is a natural outcome of *viveka,* discrimination.

Perils of a Householder Life. The entire journey of gṛhasthāśrama is often fraught with experiences that are bondage forming, attachment forming, desire promoting — all that could delay or distance us from our objective of knowing our real nature. Those who have established a spiritual practice in their householder lives will encounter many occasions to practice vairāgya, viveka, and so on. But bondage and attachment remain.

Man is a creature of habit. The external world is changing every day, adding new options to its menu of offerings, so that it compels us to remain engaged with variety, even making us dependent on conveniences. Add to this the fact that in modern times, gṛhasthāśrama has come to be the longest among all āśramas — close to forty years.

Consequently, in these sixty years, the householder's life is exposed to temptations, to forming attachment, to developing pride, to forming indelible habits and mind-sets, so that even those with steady spiritual practice can be afflicted, their spiritual sādhanā diluted. Needless to add, those with no spiritual practice would be worse off.

FROM VIṢAYĀNANDA TO BRAHMĀNANDA

Objects and people bring happiness. But this happiness is only a shadow of Brahman's Bliss.

We can employ the material experience to realize the source of uninterrupted joy, just as artha is used for dharma. But we get charmed by objects and people-based joy.

As we grow older, viṣayānanda (joy from objects and relationships) begins to lose its grip in our life through low finances and low energy. As a result, some of us become sorrowful, because we think there is no joy. This is not cause for sorrow, but, in fact, a sign of normalcy! It signals the time to tap the Source of viṣayānanda, that is, Brahman. How wonderful that nature herself prepares us! Let us aspire for Brahmānanda!

How We Age. Age we will. It is non-negotiable. But how are we aging? Joyfully or with alarm? Let us look at our elders. Are they happy? If not, who or what is to be blamed? Perhaps the fault lies in old-fashioned systems, emotions, and tradition. It is common in youth to think older people lead drab, dull lives. How will *we* age?

Gurudev Swami Chinmayananda talked a lot about aging gracefully: "Attach [to the Higher] and detach [from the lower]." Learning to unlearn attachment is disconcerting. But unlearn we must. Of course, detaching will fit poorly initially, but, in time, we will come to see our ability and enjoy the freedom that detachment brings. The young can experiment with detaching to examine their stretch potential.

> "Attach to the higher and detach from the lower!"
>
> – Swami Chinmayananda

We may each be at different stages in our evolution. Some may have found Vedānta or a similar philosophy that explains the Supreme; some may have found devotion; others may have found great joy in serving the community and the nation; and yet others may not have found any of these, yet may be quietly contented with their lot. But many of us will reach that stage where we are called upon to commit time to travel inward. Some will have the mental capacity to engage with that stage and some will not; and some others will likely struggle a bit and yet find a way forward.

This is the stage where the fervor of activity pertaining to home and career and children, admissions, interviews, results, rewards, will calm down, needing no more from us. Not because there are others to do it, but because we have reached a new door which we must now unlock and apply ourselves to a new stage of life. This is nature's indication that we need to shift gears and change direction.

Teaching by Example. When we work feverishly at our career or vocation or other roles, our children watch and learn; likewise, we want them to know what to do when they reach sixty-five. We need to leave for them inspiring examples that become their guideposts in life. For life may go on far beyond sixty-five, when it expects the greatest performance from us.

Are we ready?

When we prepare our lives for the inward journey, the young will watch and know and learn. Preparing for this inward journey occurs simultaneously with reducing the activity in the outer life. This is the beginning of unlearning, the prelude to renunciation when we dare to cut our umbilical cords from the world, to graduate from the ordinary to commence the extraordinary.

The play of māyā is best displayed in gṛhasthāśrama, where we get overwhelmed with the role-playing of partner and parent, provider and partaker. What is worse is that this āśrama is deeply exhausting, even if we bring about some make-believe situations of joy. That it does take its toll is clearly evident from the total helplessness that some householders experience after the purpose of gṛhasthāśrama is accomplished.

There you are, done with your career, your children now married or moving on to their careers. With no more decisions to be made, there you are in midair, like the pole-vaulter who has attained the height to take the leap to the other side. Only, let's say, you are petrified to drop the pole. But drop it you must for gravity will not keep you in the air while you decide! *The decision to make that leap of faith after dropping the pole has to be made on the ground.* It cannot be made midair or later.

Q: How can I start living the divine life?

A: As in life, so in divine life, too. In life, the child learns to walk by walking again; the boy learns to swim by swimming and sinking and swimming again. So, too, in divine life; therefore, there can be only one answer to the usual question: "How can I start living the divine life?" Start by starting!!

The divine life will be yours when you start to *live* it between the frequent falls and start again to *live* after each fall!!

– Swami Chinmayananda

Are we preparing for it?

Like the stage of study and the stage of family, the stage of self-inquiry is also carved out for man; unfortunately, no one saw consumerism coming; no one saw the mesmerizing numbness that the material world would unleash on man, increasing desires.

But consumerism apart, when forty years of gṛhasthāśrama are led without planning for the stage of self-inquiry, then it is not a surprise that man remains in denial even at sixty-five, laughing off the necessity of seeking answers to questions about himself, about divinity, as an exercise for the purposeless!

Attachment — The Silent Invader. When we use an air conditioner, we not only get used to the air conditioning, we also come to believe that an AC *is a necessity*. And soon we use it whether we need it or not. It has become a part of our environment, one of the numerous buttons we switch on as a matter of habit. Gradually, we are no more able to tell if we are warm because of the hot weather or warm because of the absence of an air conditioner.

This is the nature of attachment that we develop — be it filial affection, property, city, or even the bed we sleep on or, as in Sarla's case, cuisine; and its scars are felt in the sixth decade of life.

'Old' always has a ring of the 'decrepit' to it. That is the flaw of an exaggerated emphasis on youth. Many remain in denial because they do not want to be known as 'old' — for the reason that, over time, we have come to give 'old' the meaning of 'irrelevant' and 'unwanted.'

Old is only with reference to time and, hence, to the perishable body, which begins to wear and tear with all that effort at earning, saving, planning, spending, rearing children, staying up late to work, or waiting for a child who has not yet returned home.

Aging is a biological, gradual deterioration of function, characteristic of most life forms and is more appropriately referred to as *senescence,* meaning 'to grow old.' But in many parts of the world, especially today, old is not pleasing.

Lifestyles have also changed. In India particularly, from a situation of scarcity, struggle, and shortages, people have been suddenly catapulted into abundant money. But money has not yet resulted in abundance in quality. With consumerism, salaries have increased in such a way that money has become power. So, by employing money, joy is bought. We have moved from a time when the mind had no grazing field, and was also tethered within the boundaries of social norms, to today when those boundaries have been removed. But the mind has not been freed! Consequently, the mind is unstable.

Unbridled opportunities for usage of money, the experience of vast inheritances without the corresponding humility or wisdom, combined with a great sense of power, along with great disorder in society that leads one to justify the creating of one's 'own world' for peace, has resulted in mindless dependence on the comforts, whatever they be. In fact, the fear of being apart from conveniences is one of the early anxieties of aging among the well-to-do.

For many, gṛhasthāśrama has become so chronically fraught with convenience-dependence, that today this āśrama has become a haven for accumulation, amassing, achievement, and abandon. It is a field of concentrated māyā. Gṛhasthāśrama has become the means, or bait, for reckless living. The speed of this āśrama has grown so disproportionately that a lot of lives have begun to end right here — what we call 'spent force' — on the battlefields of this āśrama so that they do not even enter vānaprastha to know its joys. But, the fact remains that until we have learned to unlearn what saṁsāra teaches us, we have not fully lived the life of man. Unless, of course, a gṛhastha has incorporated spiritual living into his or her daily habits.

And the post-retirement stages of vānaprastha and sannyāsa are for just this completion.

Come, let us look at what Gurudev did (and said) to ensure we age gracefully and commit ourselves to completing his work in our lives. Are we going to leave that undone, unfinished?

HAS YOUR BUS ARRIVED?

A young Mission ācārya was at a bus stand one day holding a copy of the *Rāmāyaṇa.* A young man nearby cocked his head to read its title.

Sensing his interest, she asked him if he would like to see the book. Alarmed, he said, "No, no, these things don't interest me. I am happy in my space!" Then seeing the bus approach, the man said, "If this is not my bus, I will be in big trouble. I am already late for work."

The teacher said, "We may be happy in our space and have everything, but can we be happy even if we do not have it all the time?" The young man caught on and laughed, "Don't worry. My next increment will be enough to pay the EMIs (equated monthly installments) on the bike I am planning to buy. Then, goodbye to bus stops!"

"I am leaving a thought with you," the teacher said as they got onto the bus to occupy different seats. "If you get that bike but one day find that you are unable to pay your EMI, will you be happy?"

"What has that to do with anything?" he asked, a trifle confused. "It has to do with the difference between happiness and bliss, like having money to buy food but not the health to eat it," the teacher replied.

Leaving his seat, he sat next to the teacher, as she said, "Today you need bikes and mobile phones and live from increment to increment to buy them. One day you will retire and there will be no salary to pay EMIs. But these desires will still be there."

"So then?" the young man asked.

"Nothing," the teacher replied. "Texts like this help form what we call vānaprasthavṛttis, the mind-set to be comfortable any which way, where there is neither want nor the drive to possess. And that need not be at ages sixty or seventy; that vṛtti is valuable at thirty, too!"

CONSCIOUS TRANSFORMATION

Plants, trees, animals, birds remain as they are born. They do not have the ability to consciously make changes or decisions, such as, "I am going to do this," or "I will become that."

[Whereas] we can consciously change, consciously bring about our inner and outer transformation. And because we possess this special faculty, we must utilize it to its optimum, which is why we need every kind of education or training, so that we make the best of our lives.

– Swami Tejomayananda, *Graceful Aging*

II

A Star Is Born

The necessary means for attaining liberation are not apparent to the careless man, who is ever thinking of his sons, wife, and wealth, and who is enveloped by the darkness caused by wealth.

~Kaṭhopaniṣad

Every new concept traces back to a cluster of disparate events, each happening over long stretches of time, seemingly unconnected, seemingly innocuous, seemingly of the 'don't-know-where-this-is-headed' kind. What connects them all, if one can trace the dots, is a great man with a great vision, with a determination to execute a thought, with no expectation of applause or approval. The dots will connect with the footprints of this Mahātmā — as he walks each year planting a different seed in a new place, watering an old one, weeding a yet older one, caressing a growing sapling, gazing at a new sprout and breathing life and love into it, for he knows that they are all trees of the same forest. And it is only much, much later that the blur wears off and the idea reveals itself — so that when lesser mortals begin to see the big picture, they will sit back and say, "Aha!"

▲ *1954: Pilgrimage to the Pandava Falls after the havana on the concluding day of the Kaṭhopaniṣad yajña. Leading the procession in front of Gurudev is a young Suryapal Singh, present Trustee of Chinmaya Sewa Trust, Rewa*

So, let us look at those seemingly unconnected events, unconnected humans, unconnected actions, and unconnected decisions that slowly came to a rolling boil almost twenty years after they were all placed on different burners of the same stove. Praised be Gurudev! What foresight, what vision, what a story writer!

R*ewa: The First Stop.* It was close to four years since Gurudev, as the young Swami Chinmayananda, had stepped out onto the plains to share the knowledge he had gained from his Guru, Swami Tapovanam.

At first, the Guru had not been eager to support this plan. He had aggressively demolished it in words that Gurudev would recall many years later: "You can't treat this Knowledge like your newspaper business! It is useless to carry Vedānta to the marketplace!"

Swami Tapovanam was of the view that the secrets of the scriptures should be taught only to the pure of heart and not to all and sundry. Most people were already ensnared by the illusory world and lacked the subtlety to receive holy truths, he said. So Gurudev's plan to go to the plains and teach in the towns and cities was put to rest — at least for the next six months.

▲ *Gurudev at the feet of his Guru, Swami Tapovanam*

By 1951, Swami Tapovanam's tutelage was discontinued; he asked Gurudev to study on his own, with recourse to the Guru when there were any doubts.

And then one day, Swami Tapovanam, of his own, asked Gurudev to go out into the plains, into that same world that Gurudev had left behind, wander there as a renunciate and live on alms from the people among whom he had once sought to build a life. Swami Tapovanam told Gurudev in plain words, "This will rub out your ego!" For he felt that being able to sustain the Knowledge of the Lord even in the midst of a saṁsārī world would be more difficult, albeit good for spiritual discipline.

That was how Gurudev began his journey into the concrete jungle of cities and towns, living as a renunciate, living on alms, yet teaching, lecturing, talking, sharing, and answering questions, all the while allowing the ego to sublimate itself at his Master's feet.

One day, in the fourth year of his journey, an old friend, K. K. Sharma, invited Gurudev to a little hamlet town named Rewa in Madhya Pradesh (then, Vindhya Pradesh). K. K. Sharma was a friend and a classmate from Lucknow University, his friendship with Gurudev going as far back as 1940. While young Balan, as Gurudev was known then, chose to explore Vedānta in Uttarkashi, K. K. Sharma chose to toil for the public services exams and had joined the Indian Administrative Services. In 1954, K. K. Sharma had become the Chief Secretary in the Vindhya Pradesh Government. (This State later merged to form Madhya Pradesh.) Thus, it was he, as Chief Secretary, who invited Gurudev to Rewa.

▲ *Gurudev with old friend K. K. Sharma (on Gurudev's right) and Śrī Shiv Manga Singh, 'Suman,' a poet (on Gurudev's left)*

The town of Rewa is 130 kilometers southwest of Allahabad and about the same distance in the northeast direction of Jabalpur. Until 1947, it was a princely state. The town was not spectacular or known for anything (even though it had a national highway connecting Varanasi to Jabalpur) — it had nothing to boast about, until the then Maharaja of Rewa, Martand Singh, captured the first white tiger, Mohan, in the year 1951, who went on to sire four cubs, needless to add — all white. Naturally, the world sat up and took notice.

But there ended its glory, at least for the time being.

S*adāśivasamārambhām — The Paramparā Invoked.* Rewa's glory runs very deep, so that, in hindsight, it seems natural that Gurudev should select this little town.

In an unusual, yet pleasantly satisfying, twist of historical coincidence, Gurudev's coming to Rewa was to complete the prostration to the paramparā! This is how.

Rewa derives its name from another name for the river Narmada, one of the five great holy rivers of India. The Narmada, or Rewa, is the fifth longest river in the Indian subcontinent and flows east to west, where it surrenders to the Arabian Sea near Bharuch. Legend has it that Lord Śiva once meditated so hard that he perspired profusely and his perspiration collected in a tank, from where it flowed down as a river — the Narmada. Hence, this river is also called Śaṅkarī (daughter of Śiva), and hence has special significance for Lord Śiva's presence here (sadāśivasamārambhām – starting with Lord Sadāśiva).

Years later, when the pioneer Saint Śrī Ādi Śaṅkarācārya was offering oblations to the Sun God while standing in the river Poorna (a tributary of the river Tapti in Madhya Pradesh), a crocodile gripped his leg and did not let go. That was when Śrī Śaṅkara sought his revered mother Aryamba's permission to take sannyāsa. When with a heavy heart she permitted him, the crocodile let go of his leg. Śrī Śaṅkara then set out to find a Guru. He went north, and it was on the banks of this same river Rewa that he met his Guru, Śrī Govinda Bhagvatpāda.

Impressed by Śrī Śaṅkara's self-introduction, yaḥ kevalo'asti paramaḥ sa śivoham asmi (I am Śiva, the divisionless essence of Consciousness), Śrī Bhagvatpāda took Śrī Śaṅkara as his disciple, and the rest is history. Thus, Śrī Ādi Śaṅkara, too, had set foot in Rewa (Śaṅkarācāryamadhyamām – with Ādi Śaṅkara in the middle).

▲ *K. K. Sharma presents his summary of the* Kaṭhopaniṣad *lectures (last day of the* Kaṭhopaniṣad *yajña)*

When Gurudev accepted the invitation of K. K. Sharma and went to Rewa in 1954, he completed the prostrations to the triad with asmadācāryaparyantām (vande guruparamparām) (and continuing up to my immediate teacher — I prostrate). Rewa was thus thrice-blessed.

With Gurudev placing his feet in the town of Rewa, new beginnings for the Chinmaya Mission were etched. That his first talk in Rewa was on the *Kaṭhopaniṣad* is also significant, in light of the fact that the

▼ *Scenes from 1954* Kaṭhopaniṣad *yajña*

vānaprastha activities of the Mission began here, and the *Kaṭhopaniṣad* advises submission to study, the focus of vānaprasthāśrama!

Gurudev's yajña on the *Kaṭhopaniṣad* in English lasted close to three weeks. The unknown little town of Rewa presented a rich audience, mostly of government officers, throughout the twenty-odd days. That the officers attended in deference to K. K. Sharma, their boss, unfolded later, causing much mirth. But later, Gurudev was to learn that, barring a few, several of them did not understand English! (But most still remember him!)

R*an Bahadur Singh: The Second Stop.* Six years later, in 1960, a young man from Rewa named Ran Bahadur Singh took his father for a *Gītā* Jñāna Yajña being conducted by Gurudev in Allahabad. (Ran Bahadur, a postgraduate, was administrating the family property.) The words of the *Gītā,* in Gurudev's voice, washed over him again and again, touching a chord somewhere deep within.

For the next eighteen years, this young man read the works of the great Masters — Ramakrishna Paramahamsa, Swami Vivekananda, Ramana Maharshi — and while he learned a lot, he kept recalling Gurudev, whose words resonated in his heart. Reading those Masters also made him aware that he had duties to perform toward family and children as a gṛhastha. Restless, he tossed and turned between the spiritual and the secular, and when a political career met him on the crossroads, he entered a political career.

However, Ran Bahadur Singh's restlessness only grew, and the tiredness intensified for this Member of Parliament from Rewa. Such restless souls take to Gurudev as iron filings to a magnet. So it was that he sought out Gurudev as often as time would permit, until one day he asked, "Swamiji, why don't you come to Rewa?"

Gurudev shuddered. "NO!" he cried, "No one in Rewa understands English!" Ran Bhadur Singh kept at it, and his persistence was rewarded when Gurudev finally asked Br. Vivek Chaitanya (Swami Tejomayananda's name as a brahmacārī) to go to Rewa.

The Seed Was Sown. That was all it needed — the saṅkalpa of a Mahātmā! Br. Vivek's first *Gītā* Jñāna Yajña at Rewa happened in November 1978. Thereafter, he came to Rewa twice a year and, like a rising wave, a circle of seekers grew around his presence and his talks. Thus was born a Mission Center in Rewa.

That was the yajña prasāda of the 1978 yajña in Rewa.

From then on, yajñas and talks came to be common in Rewa and the name 'Swami Chinmayananda' came to be respected and his presence sought. In August 1981, a group of fifteen men from Rewa decided to attend Gurudev's *Gītā* Jñāna Yajña in Sidhbari.

Accompanying them was Ran Bahadur Singh (the young man who had been following Gurudev relentlessly since 1960), who now also looked after the Chinmaya Mission Rewa. Bhagvati Singh, an agriculturist and a transporter, was also part of the group from Rewa. He offered, at Gurudev's feet, a tract of land measuring 1.25 acres.

Dr. Sajjan Singh, one among the fifteen, recalls: "On hearing the offer, Gurudev went into silence. After some time, he came out of that state and said, rather abruptly, 'Yes, we will take the offer of land and use it for a pitamaha sadan (home for elders).'"

The idea was indeed unique, even surprising, for most of the fifteen men were roughly forty to forty-five years old. A plan for a pitamaha sadan seemed unusual! Dr. Singh continues, "And instantly, Gurudev was outlining the whole idea to us, 'We will invite elders to come and stay there and do their spiritual practices; we will look after them, provide nurses or assistants where needed, and we will have doctors to attend to their health. We will have a common kitchen where we will cook for everyone, people will be in the right environment for study and growth.' And Gurudev went on in that vein, as if he was seeing it all before his eyes!"

Stunningly, *exactly* a year later, 'The Vienna International Plan of Action on Aging' was adopted by the UN's World Assembly on Aging held in Vienna, Austria. That was on August 6, 1982.

And Pitamaha Sadan Rewa was registered a month after this, on September 30, 1982! What a visionary Gurudev was!

The Master and His Master Plan. Bhagvati Singh's donation of land was transferred to Chinmaya Mission under the conveyance of a Trust Deed. A Chinmaya Seva Trust was registered in Rewa in 1982. But before any work could even begin, the government of Madhya Pradesh acquired the gifted land for an industrial estate. However, that did not stop the work. By then, the thoughts about a senior home (as it was being referred to) had grown very intense. The idea was bigger and it had only just begun! The Trust Deed had been carefully worded, and Gurudev had spelled out a three-point agenda with the precision of a cutting tool:

▲ *Dr. Sajjan Singh of Rewa, the heart behind many of the research initiatives*

a. Open a home for the care of elders and the old.

b. Look after the elderly and the old.

c. Create an environment for the moral and spiritual resurrection of society.

While objectives (a) and (b) were evident, the aim of (c) was sudden and enormous. Dr. Sajjan Singh knew it could begin anywhere and the sky was the limit. Suddenly, the surprise they had felt earlier, on being told that the land would be used for a pitamaha sadan, vanished. In its place was a great feeling of 'A-ha!' The pitamaha sadan was not to be just a home for elders. It was an *idea,* a movement, a renaissance. The Master's strokes were unraveling a grand plan.

Gurudev designed the entire pitamaha sadan and declared, "We shall build a Śrī Rāma Temple — and that will be Vanvasi Rāma (the forest-dwelling Rāma)!" These kinds of declarations from Gurudev have always warmed the cockles of many a heart. He knew that the idea and the location had a deep context. Rewa was just 125 kilometers from Chitrakoot, where Śrī Rāma spent a great part of his fourteen-year exile. As the epic goes, the sages Bharadwaj and Valmiki asked Rāma to make Chitrakoot His abode. A vānaprastha pitamaha sadan close to Vanvasi Rāma's abode was perfect and appropriate, according to Gurudev's plan. For that was also a place enriched by venerable Saints such as Atri, Sati Anasuya, Dattatreya, Maharshi Markandeya, and Sarbhanga. Rewa was also a place extolled and praised in the *Rāmāyaṇa!*

And, once again, Gurudev met his vision with the funds needed. "Wherever he went for yajña, he would set aside some of the dakṣiṇā for the pitamaha sadan," says Dr. Singh.

From Pitamaha to Vānaprasthi. Then, a new piece of land appeared on the horizon. Ran Bahadur Singh, the landlord of Laxmanpur (not to be confused with Rao Saheb Ran Bahadur Singh), offered to Br. Vivek three acres of land in his village of Laxmanpur, or Laua, twelve kilometers north of Rewa. Br. Vivek accepted the land, and the necessary modalities were completed for its conveyance to the Mission's Sewa Trust.

On April 13, 1982, Gurudev came to Laxmanpur (Rewa) and laid the foundation stone of the Śrī Raghunathji Temple. Uniquely, the idols to be installed there would be a larger version of those installed at the Sidhbari āśrama. Rewa's pitamaha sadan was, indeed, being prepared for serenity, meditation, and contemplation.

Fittingly, Gurudev had remarked, "It's easier to serve a Vanvasi Rāma than Raja Rāma." For the people who would worship at that place were going to be those who, having completed their householder duties, would now inherit a new vision and a new direction.

Vanvasi Rāma was a sound anchor for the elder, who was gradually losing a foothold in Indian homes, largely owing to the breakdown of the village home system and the joint-family system. With the children moving to cities to build careers away from land and cattle, the elder was in a fix. Land that was the means of livelihood now remained with the elder, while the grown-up youngsters moved to the cities. The elders now could not tend the land, nor did their sentiments (which enslaved them) permit them to sell it. On the other hand, the city-drawn young could not give up their parents or their city lives or career dreams. In some cases, the young wished to sell the village land to afford a city home, and this, while adding grief to the elder, also added distance and angst to the relationship.

In many ways, it is likely that Gurudev felt that the young should make their choices and the elders needed to retire from gṛhasthāśrama. The family home, now the proverbial bone of contention, was delaying the elders' entry into vānaprastha, thereby extending gṛhasthāśrama. The young, too, were unable to lead a successful householder life, as they were struggling to be a part of two households.

▲ *Gurudev with the idol of Vanvasi Rāma*

This could have been the reason why Gurudev, in front of a couple of hundred people in Rewa, presented his concept of a vānaprasthāśrama when he had come to lay the foundation stone for the temple. He did not call it an elders' home (pitamaha sadan) at that time; the term 'elders' home' had an irrelevant and irreverent finality to it, as if it were a parking place where one waited for the end. No, that was not what it was. He told the audience that the place would be a vānaprasthāśrama, a place for getting fulfillment in the here and now, clearly an offer that could not be refused!

God in the Details. The Rewa Pitamaha Sadan was precisely defined and designed: around the temple there would be kuṭiyās (cottages) for the vānaprasthis. They could stay there alone or with their spouses. The āśrama would provide medical help, a library with vast spiritual literature, and a common kitchen that would provide food suited to the vānaprasthis. With Gurudev's precise direction, which is now legendary, the layout was planned: a temple in the middle surrounded by a road on all four sides connecting to the cottages. The dispensary block was to be built near the entrance gate so that visitors

▾ *1982 Gurudev addressing the elders of Rewa*

(from outside the āśrama) to the dispensary had to walk the least. And Gurudev assured them: "When the dispensary block is ready, I will come and inaugurate this place."

He did keep his word. When the dispensary block was ready, Gurudev did come, but in a touching gesture, he handed the scissors to the Maharaja of Rewa, Martand Singh, to cut the ribbon! (Traditionally, a Maharaja is respected as God Viṣṇu's chosen representative on earth.) Later, the lamp inside the block was lit by Gurudev. Following that, on April 13, 1982, Gurudev laid the foundation stone of the temple.

A great moment had been commemorated.

Gurudev, the meticulous planner, sent special artisans from Shimoga (Karnataka) to construct the temple. Two years later, on April 6, 1984, after the temple construction was completed, Gurudev performed the prāṇapratiṣṭhā of the bark-attired stone idols of Śrī Rāma, Mother Sītā, Śrī Lakṣmaṇa, and Śrī Hanumān. Next, Gurudev sent for

▾ ***Clockwise***
Right: *Gurudev performing prāṇapratiṣṭhā of Vanvasi Rāma idol, at the Śrī Raghunathji temple, Rewa*
Below Right: *Gurudev lighting the lamp for the inauguration of the dispensary block, Rewa*
Below Left: *Dispensary block inauguration: Maharaja of Rewa, Martand Singh, cutting the ribbon*

pundits from Kerala to come and perform the temple establishment ceremonies in a manner prescribed by the scriptures. As time went on, the little kuṭiyās, dining hall, and dormitory were constructed and some residents moved in.

A ***Spot Under the Sun.*** In 1954, Gurudev had gone to Rewa on the invitation of an old college friend and had conducted a twenty-day yajña on the *Kaṭhopaniṣad* in English. He was to realize later that, except for a handful of listeners in the audience, no one spoke or understood English. A quarter of a century later, he was setting up a haven for elders — for vānaprasthis — to dedicate all of their time to gaining the Knowledge that would liberate them.

The concept of vānaprastha struck a chord in the people of Rewa. For one, Śrī Ran Bahadur, one of their own and a restless Member of Parliament, had followed Gurudev relentlessly, yearning to be with him. The Rewa Āśrama came up beautifully on the land he had offered to Gurudev. At Rs. 60,000 for a cottage, Ran Bahadur prepared to spend his life in a serene environment where he could leave the cluttered world behind and inquire about his real Nature, as Ramana Maharshi's words had suggested to him way back in the 1960s.

▲ *Swami Prashantananda (earlier: Rao Saheb Ran Bahadur Singh)*

Ran Bahadur moved into the āśrama in 1988. Soon, others who had donated toward the building of kuṭiyās also came to live there.

The chatter of parliamentarians stopped. The noise of everyday pursuits ended.

Ran Bahadur Singh had found his quiet spot under the sun.

JUST A MINUTE

It is important to remember that graceful aging does not suddenly come about in old age — it is a lifelong process.

[...] If no conscious effort is made early in life, although one may attend spiritual camps and graceful aging seminars, inner transformation does not come about easily.

– Swami Tejomayananda, *Graceful Aging*

III

When Lord Śiva Approached Gurudev

Mission Mandhana: 1983

Even while Rewa was warming up to the eldercare idea, in 1982–83, Chinmaya Mission Kanpur came under Gurudev's spotlight.

Twenty kilometers from Kanpur, on the Grand-Trunk Road to Delhi, specifically, on the Mandhana-Bithoor Road, is a tiny town named Mandhana, where people once spoke the most beautifully lyrical language, Awadhi, the dialect of Hindi used by Tulsidas in *Rāmacharitamānasa*. In that little town is a 200-year-old temple of Lord Śiva, which was in the ownership of the Bankhandeśvara Trust. If in April Gurudev was laying the foundation stone at the Vanvasi Rāma temple in Rewa, then in February 1983, just a few months later and 345 kilometers away, the Trustees offered the Bankhandeśvara Mahādev temple, along with the accompanying land, at Gurudev's feet!

The story of the Bankhandeśvara (or Vankhandeswar) Temple must be told, for only then can the events that happened around it be best appreciated. After all, even a blade of grass that moved during these events were movements of Gurudev's thoughts, connected to Gurudev and his plans, the fruit of his labor of love. In hindsight, it seems as if he knew everything that was going on, and that he was instrumental in all outcomes. Today when we look back, nothing surprises, for the events were meant to be.

The story of Gurudev reaching Mandhana is the story of Bankhandeśvara Mahādev. In a landmass of such diversity and vastness as India, a small lamp was lit in a tiny little village called Bagdodhi Bangar, in the little town of Bithoor, eighteen kilometers from the city of Kanpur. There, snug under a thick foliage of bilva trees, stands a small picturesque religious establishment. Inside, stands a very old temple with a Śivaliṅga — which local folk believe was 'self-formed,' or svayambhū. Since Lord Śiva resides as Mahādeva in this temple and chose to dwell quietly in the forest, He came to be called Bankhandeśvara. Local lore has it that there was a time when the cows came here on their own and poured milk on that particular spot. Much later, during some excavations, the Śivaliṅga was found, and devotees built a formal enclosure around it. Thus was born the Mahādeva Temple.

That temple in the town of Bithoor, on the left bank of the Ganges, is considered a holy place for pilgrimage. But the svayambhū appearance of Lord Śiva there should not surprise devotees; for Bithoor is said to be the birthplace of Lava and Kuśa, the sons of Śiva's most dear Lord, Śrī Rāma. Sage Valmiki's Āśrama as well as the place he wrote the *Rāmāyaṇa* are considered to be here.

▲ *The self-formed Śivaliṅga, Bankhandeśvara Mahādev*

Historical facts about the Bankhandeśvara Temple are fascinating and would inspire many to see it. Bithoor is reputed to have been home to many of the freedom fighters of the 1857 rebellion against the British empire, including Rani Laxmibai of Jhansi. Laxmibai — who apparently had her ear-piercing ceremony performed in Bithoor — was so fascinated by this temple that after her marriage, she had an identical temple built in the fort of Jhansi. It is believed that in 1830, Peshwa Bajirao II, the banished Maratha leader, had renovated this temple. His adopted son, Nanarao Peshwa, made this little town his headquarters, and it is said that, along with Tatya Tope (another leader of the Sepoy Rebellion of 1857) and Laxmibai, he had worshiped at this temple.

In 1936, Śrī Ram Chandra Mishra, a devotee from the village, overcome by great love and devotion for the svayambhū Mahādeva, vowed to worship Bankhandeśvara Mahādev (as He was now called) every day, adding, "I may live or die, but the worshiping and chanting of the Lord's name shall continue here always." And with that, he offered to the Lord roughly two-and-a-half hectares of land, and what is more, he transferred the land to the Lord as 'owner' and himself as His trustee! Thus was born the Śrī Bankhandeśvara Mahādev Temple Trust, on May 21, 1936. Two months later, Śrī Ram Chandra Mishra registered the Trust with four other members. The Trust was then reconstituted in July 1976, when respected citizens from the surrounding villages — Mandhana, Bagdodi Bangar, and Vaikunthpur — were also inducted on to the Board.

▲ *Śrī Ram Chandra Mishra*

Śrī Ram Chandra Mishra specified three distinct goals for the Trust:

- Once a year, the Śrīmad Bhagvad Purāna will be narrated in the month of Śrāvaṇa.
- The garden will be maintained at all costs.
- Every day there will be ārtī for Lord Mahādeva, and naivedyam will be offered.

At this writing, for seventy-five years since those goals were stated, the tradition continues to be honored.

Even so, the place began to fall into disrepair. The aging trustees continued to meet and serve the temple, but in 1982 they began to worry about renovating the rapidly crumbling property to make it more comfortable for devotees. With no resources at their disposal, they resolved to meet some NGOs[1] and have them rebuild the temple.

The secretary, Śrī Dayashankar Dubey, mentioned to the trustees that CCMT's founder, Swami Chinmayananda, was coming to Kanpur in February 1983 for a jñāna yajña, and the thought arose, "Why not meet him and maybe request him to help?"

▲ *Annual Bhagavat Saptah*
Top: *Br. Jaidev Chaitanya, 2014*
Bottom: *Sw. Gangeshananda, 2013*

Gurudev's 344th *Gītā* Jñāna Yajña was held at Moti Jheel in Kanpur. Accordingly, the trustees arranged for Gurudev to visit the Bankhandeśvara Mahādev Temple. On February 9, 1983, Gurudev, along with Swami Tejomayananda and a few others, visited the temple and took in the ancestry, history, and other details.

Gurudev had been talking about the concept of vānaprastha and sannyāsa in Indian culture. In several of his talks at different yajñas, he had

[1] Non-governmental organizations

urged elders to reorient their lives and make them delightful, always suggesting that it was their turn to stabilize society. Just the previous year, he had established a pitamaha sadan in Rewa, Madhya Pradesh. Of course, the need for pitamaha sadans was logical and practical, given the changing sociological dynamics in India, but Gurudev had added that the concept needed modernizing.

As a continuation of these very thoughts on enhancing the vānaprastha idea, Gurudev was scheduled to see two places in Kanpur for pitamaha sadans. One of them was the Bankhandeśvara Mahādev property.

The other property that had been shown to him was close to the shores of the Ganga, near Bithoor. That place had the problem of sandy winds in summer, which could be bothersome for elders. Whereas the town housing the Bankhandeśvara Mahādev's Temple lay next to the main road, tucked away in solitude, and with spacious vast tracts for farming, too. There was also a ready supply of potable water — and the ancient Śiva Temple was there as well.

So when the trustees of the Bankhandeśvara Temple suggested that Gurudev take over the temple, Gurudev agreed and asked that a pitamaha sadan be constructed on that property. Thus began a new chapter in the history of the Bankhandeśvara Temple.

Śrī Ram Chandra Mishra — A Word Well Kept. Six months later, Gurudev formally began to oversee the management of the Bankhandeśvara Mahādev Temple and property. Another six months later, in December 1983, a new management committee was duly set up according to law. Śrī Ram Chandra Mishra, the original trustee and caregiver-founder of the temple, formally handed over all the trust papers to Swami Tejomayananda.

With that, the temple and property formally changed hands. The temple was now in good hands, and the original saṅkalpa of Śrī Ram

Chandra Mishra was received, accepted, and honored. Śrī Bankhandeśvara Mahādev would be perfectly celebrated by His new sevaks.

In an unexpected turn of events, just a week later, Śrī Ram Chandra Mishra departed from this world. It seemed as if he had waited for just this handover to take place!

Events like these cause us to stop and ponder.

Gurudev was touched by the service and contribution of Śrī Ram Chandra Mishra and suggested that a photograph of him should adorn the satsaṅga room as a reminder of his commitment and dedication.

Laying Foundations, Building Trust. The Chinmaya Tapovan Trust, Sidhbari, was enlisted to look after and develop the Bankhandeśvara Temple's spiritual activity. Meanwhile, Br. Vinod Chaitanya, who had been an important engineering resource in the initial construction work of the Sandeepany Himalaya (Sidhbari) āśrama, accompanied Gurudev to the planning meetings for Mandhana.

On September 16, 1984, the construction of a pitamaha sadan at Mandhana got its firm foundation, and the lease registry was drawn up in favor of Chinmaya Tapovan Trust.

As was Gurudev's style in many of the construction activities of Chinmaya Mission, Mandhana, too, saw Gurudev roll up his sleeves and sit down to visualize the construction plan. In November 1984, after a week-long jñāna yajña at Varanasi, Gurudev took a detour, went to Mandhana, and drew the limestone outline on the ground for the construction of the pitamaha sadan. And within two months, on February 1, 1985, the bhūmi-pūjā was conducted by Gurudev himself, after his visit to Prayāga (see page 41, Chapter IV). A visit to this confluence of holy rivers is considered auspicious before commencing any work, and that had happened unwittingly!

What a beginning!

The pattern continued. Thereafter, en route anywhere, Gurudev would halt at Kanpur to monitor the progress of the construction activity and, more importantly, remind the people of their commitment to serve the elders of society.

Gradually the people of Mandhana began to get drawn to the Mission's work there, be it the construction of a dispensary or a common kitchen. Love poured in from unexpected quarters, such as young volunteers from the Yuva Kendra who came to perform Viṣṇusahasranāma-arcanā!

How Mandhana Got Its Ācāryas. Most great events have a genesis tucked far, far back in time, and connecting all the dots can take more than a book. Suffice it to say that Mandhana's Ācārya-in-charge had been spotted by Gurudev two decades earlier, and groomed to be the language bridge that Chinmaya Mission would need in Allahabad.

Thus, it was that, in 1967, Pratap Chandra Shukla, a professor of philosophy in Kanpur, met Gurudev at a *Gītā* Jñāna Yajña and became his devotee. Thereafter, Shukla spent all his time translating

▼ *Gurudev during satsaṇga at Mandhana*

Gurudev's books into Hindi and printing them at his printing press. Swami Tejomayananda, who was in Kanpur between 1976 and 1980, had occasion to be present at Śrī Shukla's erudite lectures and svādhyāyamaṇḍalas (study circles), and to see his commitment to Vedānta. So in 1985, when the pitamaha sadan was developing, Swami Tejomayananda appointed Śrī Shukla as Ācārya of the Mandhana Āśrama.

▲ *Swami Subhodananda at the Mahādev Temple*

Within a month, Gurudev called him to Mumbai and, on October 28, 1985, gave him sannyāsa dīkṣā. Pratap Chandra Shukla became Swami Shankarananda Saraswati. He was entrusted with the responsibility of the Pitamaha Sadan at Mandhana. It was indeed an important day for Mandhana.

By 1988, the pitamaha sadan activities needed more supervision and attention, more importantly — momentum. Not too far away from Mandhana was Chinmaya Mission Prayāga, which was conducting a Sandeepany

◄ *Swami Shankarananda*

Vedānta course. Swami Subhodhananda was the Ācārya-in-charge there. Gurudev then requested Swamiji to devote six months of the year to Mandhana. The Mandhana Pitamaha Sadan is considered by devotees to be one of the greatest gifts that Gurudev gave to Chinmaya Mission Kanpur.

In 1991, Swami Shankarananda moved to Mandhana Pitamaha Sadan as a full-time Ācārya. He was joined by Shiv Swarup Agrawal, who was appointed as manager. But who was this Shiv Swarup Agrawal?

From Śiva to Shiv Swarup. An event that took place in 1989 was going to be precious for Chinmaya Mission Allahabad, for it would unravel a larger divine plan. The General Secretary of CM Allahabad, Shiv Swarup Agrawal, was the Chairman and Managing Director of his family's group of industries. A householder who had been serving the Mission since 1976, Shiv Swarup decided to join the two-year Vedānta Course at Sandeepany Mumbai.

When he graduated in 1991, Gurudev met him, as he did with all new brahmacārīs, and asked him the usual question about his future plans. At the end of their conversation, Gurudev said to him, "The Pitamaha Sadan in Mandhana needs great administrative support, and with your years in business and commerce, this place should benefit greatly."

▲ *Shiv Swarup (sitting to Gurudev's left on the floor) and his Kolkata Study Group — with Gurudev 1964–65*

So Shiv Swarup, who had worked for CM Allahabad (before going off to Sandeepany Mumbai), happily arrived at Mandhana

▲ *Swami Yogasthananda (earlier, Shiv Swarup Agrawal)*

and, with his management acumen, gathered the crumbling place together. For three years, he was fully absorbed in understanding the operations and goings-on there. Fresh with his knowledge of Vedānta, he met visiting elders every day, each with a different set of problems. He began to see that people who had lived a reasonably happy life, who had adeptly dealt with the vagaries of life in their youth and middle age, in business and service, were now — in their third age — completely at a loss to understand the twists and turns in life. Lives that were seemingly well-lived had begun to crumble. Their children, once loving and engaging, had now grown into preoccupied adults. Their erstwhile social status that once had people clicking their heels and whipping up a salute for them, did not work for the elders anymore. Money, which came into the bank with regularity earlier, was now a trickle. The elders were unable to comprehend why everything looked different. They each came to Shiv Swarup with their stories, and he now found his days filled with the angst of the elders of the Mandhana Pitamaha Sadan.

Elderly women visitors to the pitamaha sadan talked anxiously about their changed lives. Retired husbands were interfering, energy was low, and housekeeping, which was once a joy, shamefully seemed a pain. Their loving sons were not even calling. Their minds were agitated and restless; and everything was annoying them, just as they, too, were seemingly annoying everyone around them.

Shiv Swarup heard variations of these refrains every day, and he brought out Vedānta to enable him to guide them all. He now knew about the delusion of saṁsāra and saw that an aged body that housed a weaker mind was most unprepared to face the fact that they had not prepared themselves for this phase of their lives. So he counseled them, talked to them, heard their sorrowful stories, and comforted them as much as he could.

Work at Mandhana had waited to gain direction. Some administrative matters begged resolution; he addressed them all. The grassroots work that Shiv Swarup was doing was going to scaffold a great new CM initiative — as we will soon see.

After three years of serving the elders at Mandhana, Shiv Swarup was transferred to CM Allahabad. We will meet him again in Chapter IV, when we reach Allahabad.

TOWARD CONTENTMENT

The food you get by begging is bhikṣā. The idea here is to have total contentment with life as it comes to you — yadṛcchā-lābha-santuṣṭo (from *Bhagavad-gītā* 4:22). In this stage of life [vānaprastha], everything should be accepted as is without complaint.

– Swami Tejomayananda, *Graceful Aging*

IV

Mission Prayāga: The Confluence of Love's Labor

At this stage, we will leave Mandhana and walk to another place, to another time, toward another team of people who, too, were instrumental in aiding the vānaprastha movement. Once again, we see completely disparate people, places, events, and transactions that verily became the building blocks for one grand vision.

That was how Gurudev's vision unfolded — one word here, one direction there, one infrastructure somewhere else — they belonged to the same canvas, the same artist, only created by different strokes at different times.

Prayāga is the place where the three holiest of rivers Ganga, Yamuna, and Saraswati converge. A visit to this confluence is considered necessary for auspicious tidings. Prayāga is today called Allahabad. This chapter uses both names interchangeably.

For the Love of a Son — Attachment Handed Over. Nandkishore Agrawal was a well-known civil contractor and philanthropist of Allahabad, who had brought up his three strapping sons with great care and love, like any good father would. And then life dealt a hard blow when Naveen Chandra, his oldest son, an engineer with his whole life ahead of him, died an untimely death.

▲ *The Śrī Akhileshwar Mahādev Temple, Prayāga*

Gathering all the love and dreams he had for his young son, Nandkishore plowed it all into service; he sought to cope with his loss by setting up a trust in Naveen's name, a trust that would tend to anyone who was in need. Thus came about the Naveen Seva Āśrama Trust (NSAT).

▲ *Nandkishore Agrawal*

Allahabad, known for its eminent personalities, came together in Nandkishore's time of grief. His loss hurt especially more because he was a philanthropist, a naturally compassionate human; hence, his loss was inexplicable. So, when the trust was formed, Śrī Rajarishi Purushottamdas Tandon, Allahabad's most eminent personality, readily agreed to be its chairman. Śrī Tandon was a Member of Parliament (Rajya Sabha) and was also known for his austerity and detachment from possessions. Śrī Tandon ran the trust with remarkable dynamism. Combined with Śrī Tandon's own popularity and the trust's noble aims and objectives, more and more people began to gain from the trust's beneficence.

Nandkishore had a three-acre plot of land that he transferred to the trust. Around the same time, the municipal corporation of Allahabad wanted to establish a home for the destitute in Allahabad. So they gave Nandkishore a similar piece of land on the bank of the Yamuna for a period of twenty-five years for such a home.

His tireless, dispassionate work showed how deeply his mind was committed to the memory of his son. Since he had already donated a three-acre plot to the trust, Nandkishore invited the social welfare department of the state government to set up a school for the mentally challenged children of Allahabad. The government accepted and started the venture. However, for various reasons, the school did not run as planned, and Nandkishore set up a regular school instead for the poor children of Allahabad. (Later, this very school would be embraced by the Chinmaya Vidyalaya fraternity and receive the 'Chinmaya' prefix to its name, to dedicate itself fully to nourishing Gurudev's vision for education.) The new school ran very well, dedicated as it was to the memory of a son so deeply loved. So much had Nandkishore immersed himself in the work that he did not see time pass, his body age, and his environment change. It was as though he wanted nothing else but this work. The trust had become his son Naveen. But, remarkably, as time passed, his personal pain was healed by the very act of giving. His own pain was sublimated in the pain and the needs of the many, and he began to see suffering as just another shared condition of the world, and not his personal experience. His love for his son was no more singular, but had grown into a love of the collective.

On June 24, 1983, Nandkishore Agrawal stood with palms folded, before Gurudev, in the conference room of NSAT. A certain tiredness washed over him as he prepared to speak. He was handing over the only thing left in his life to which he had been attached — the memory of his oldest son, Naveen Chandra. The trustees who sat around the table must have felt Agrawal's surrender in the finality of his decision: to hand over the trust that he had dedicatedly nourished for over thirty-two years, applying it toward the care and sustenance of the tired, the meek, the frail, the disabled, the needy, the hungry, the ill, and the homeless. Nandkishore admitted that he was tired. In handing the trust over to Gurudev, he was handing himself over into the hands of Gurudev. All that he seemingly had now was the trust, and its accompanying assets such as the school. Those, too, he wished to hand over.

Gurudev, Swami Chinmayananda, was a special invitee to that meeting, along with some of the office bearers of Chinmaya Mission,

Allahabad. There before him stood Nandkishore, a mature soul wrapped in an aged body, palms joined, and looking at the only face in that room that would ever move his heart now. "Take this," he beseeched. "I had constituted this trust in 1951 in memory of a loved son. This body has aged and cannot now manage the trust's affairs. I request Pūjya Swamiji to take it over."

Gurudev looked at the faces of the trustees around the table. Sincerity shone on their faces, too. All that Nandkishore stood for, worked for, resonated with the values of the Chinmaya Mission. Gurudev nodded, "I will," he said, taking into himself the love of a father, the love of a son, the love of a people; and breathed into the Naveen Seva Āśrama Trust (NSAT) his acceptance.

There now remained a small detail — creating a new legal entity (since the old one had been handed over to Gurudev), appointing its new governing body, and then naming it afresh.

Gurudev appointed Br. Vivek Chaitanya (now Guruji Swami Tejomayananda) as the vice-president of the new organization. Śrī Shiv Swarup Agrawal, who had worked with the Chinmaya Mission since 1976, was appointed general secretary. (He would later run the Pitamaha Sadan in Mandhana.) Four of the old trustees were also retained.

It was Gurudev's view that Naveen's name must be retained in the new organization's name. He wanted that respected.

Thus was born CNSAT, Chinmaya Naveen Seva Āśrama Trust, one more rose in the bountiful bouquet of service trusts.

CNSAT — Tracing the Dots. Over the next four years, until around 1987–88, CNSAT grew in stature and vision, adopting the activities of the Chinmaya Mission. It continued its erstwhile service to the underprivileged via a food kitchen, a dispensary, and a shelter.

Alongside it ran the grassroots activities of Bala Vihar, Study Groups, Jñāna Yajñas, and a few Devi Groups.

CNSAT worked vibrantly in step with Gurudev's mission, adopting his vision as its own. In 1985, CNSAT hosted 'Sandeepany Prayāga' a three-year Vedānta Course in Hindi, with Swami Subodhananda as Ācārya-in-charge.

A Sandeepany on the premises always augurs well for a growing institution, for it brings with it the direct blessings of the paramparā, which strengthens its foundation and its work. Thus enriched, CNSAT was greatly energized for its next event, the week-long 16th National Spiritual Camp, held in 1987, in which sixty delegates participated.

Gurudev had made a saṅkalpa some years ago to build a Śiva temple on the premises. Being a cantonment zone, permissions were being awaited, but Gurudev performed the bhūmi-pūjā at Śrī Nandkishore's request, and during the National Camp of 1987, Gurudev laid the foundation stone for this most beautiful temple.

▼ *The Śrī Akhileshwar Mahādev Temple, Prayāga*

Śrī Nandkishore passed away some years later, and as things went, the permission for the temple construction (from the development authorities) came only in late 2004. The temple was ready by 2009 when Pūjya Guruji Swami Tejomayananda, along with Swami Subodhananda, performed the prāṇapratiṣṭhā of the Śrī Akhileshwar Mahādev idol.

(Meanwhile, the Registrar of Societies of Uttar Pradesh issued a certificate approving the change of the name to CNSAT, Chinmaya Naveen Sewa Āśrama Trust, with effect from February 23, 2006.)

Chinmaya Mission Prayāga flourished on NSAT's premises, amid plush fruit gardens and a shelter for cows. After all, with its location in Uttar Pradesh, home of Kṛṣṇa, a gośālā was part of all the resident traditions of the temple. In fact, Kanpur derives its name from Kanhaiyapur, or town of Kanhaiya — Kṛṣṇa!

Steadily shaped by its activities, NSAT would soon be instrumental in developing and launching a great new grassroots activity for the Chinmaya Mission — Chinmaya Vānaprastha Sansthan, or CVS — an institute for teaching the art of detachment from all this and attachment to That. This initiative was akin to a 'Third Age University,' to help man look ahead into a life of new beginnings. How that came about was itself aided by a series of events, key among them being the transfer of Shiv Swarup Agrawal from Mandhana to Prayāga. Shiv Swarup had earlier been posted at Pitamaha Sadan

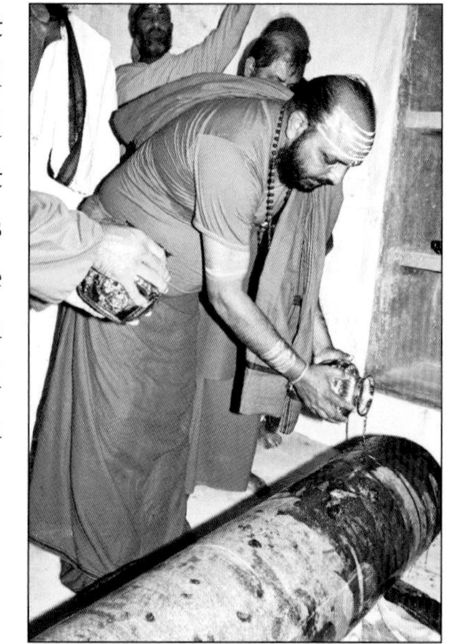

▸ *Swami Subodhananda, preparing for the prāṇapratiṣṭhā ceremony (consecration) of the Śrī Akhileshwar Mahādev idol. Swami Tejomayananda is to his left (partly hidden)*

Mandhana, where he had developed such alertness and awareness about the mind of the elder that, when he was transferred to Prayāga, not too far away, these very memories and experiences with eldercare became the skills that would fuel the CVS activity.

CNSAT, and CM Prayāga, too, were strategically located in the land of erudite scholars. The ground was fertile for ideation and more.

Thirty Men and the Third Age. Shiv Swarup Agrawal's baggage held more than his personal effects. He had brought with him the memories of his innumerable dialogues with the elders at Pitamaha Sadan Mandhana — their difficulties, their confusion, and their painful shocks at life's unasked-for offerings. Even if they were not prepared for their third age, he knew that they still needed help.

Looking around Allahabad, that amazingly erudite city, Shiv Swarup had a thought. If its learned people came together, they could apply their learning and wisdom toward the greater good of the anchorless elders.

Shiv Swarup's business family was well connected with the literati of Allahabad. Now in charge of CM Allahabad, he felt that it would be good to invite the literati to come visit the place. He was encouraged by Swami Shankarananda, who had been the Ācārya at CM Kanpur, and by Dr. Sajjan Singh, who initiated a discussion on vānaprastha lifestyle,

▶ *Guruji Swami Tejomayananda, along with Swami Subodhananda, performed the prāṇapratiṣṭhā (consecration) of the Śrī Akhileshwar Mahādev idol*

based on a paper he had presented at the International Congress of Gerontology at Acapulco, Mexico, in 1989.

So invitations went out to thirty eminent citizens of Allahabad, and on December 4, 1995, on the lawns of CNSAT, thirty men and women presented their thoughts: 'Empowering Our Elders.'

They were all well-known, highly respected pillars of the Allahabad society. They also knew each other, either through the interdependency of their work or through their natural respect and reverence for each other's integrity and dedication. And then, of course, they were also the people who had either met, known, or heard Pūjya Gurudev, Pūjya Guruji, and other Ācāryas of the Mission.

Among the thirty stalwarts were four vice chancellors of renowned universities; businessmen, doctors, lawyers, educationists, officers of the Indian Administrative Service and Provincial Civil Service; medical practitioners; and the then-retired Chief Justice of Allahabad High Court, Śrī Amitav Banerji. These prominent scholars heard the Chief Justice propose the idea: 'Should we not be empowering our elders?'

Banerji's proposition to the eminent audience was singular: Scientific excellence had decreased early mortality and increased longevity, so that now the population of elders was growing. What could be done to empower that segment of the population so that they did not regard themselves a burden to society, so that they did not see their retirement from their professions as a retirement from living, so that they were rendered most self-sufficient emotionally?

The group came up with a meaningful answer: a specially designed curriculum that would add joy and purpose to the twenty to thirty years of post-retirement life, which medical science had now found possible to give mankind.

PRAYĀGA'S GIFT

The Ayodhyakānd of *Tulsi Rāmāyaṇa*, refers to Prayāga as Prayāgraj, the king of holy places.

In his talks on *Rāmacharitamānasa*, Guruji gives the literal meaning of Prayag as: prakṛṣṭaḥ yāgaḥ yatra — where the highest yajña, Jñāna Yajña, is conducted, that is Prayāga. Here is the complete bio-data:

Prayāgraj's minister is Truth. Shraddha is His wife, Madhava (Lord Nārāyaṇa) is his best friend! His treasury is filled with dharma ārtha, kāma, and mokṣa. His army is all other holy places, for they destroy the evil thoughts in man. His throne is the spot where Ganga, Yamuna, and Saraswati meet.... And who serves this tīrthakṣetra? The great sadhu purushas! (*Ayodhyakānd Doha* 104)

This is where Śrī Rāma meets Sage Bharadwaj with a warm embrace, and the sage, completely overcome, says, "Today all my tapasyā has borne fruit." For having given up the world, they had submitted to a life of austerities in the forest. And the reward was? Brahman!

Coincidentally, Shiv Swarup and Swami Shankarananda had found a news item in the United Nations news bulletin that talked about a unique entity called 'University of the 3rd Age.' Commonly called U3A, this concept, which was growing in parts of Europe and Australia, aimed to educate and stimulate the people who had retired from active work life and who were in what they now referred to as the 'third age.'

The 'third age' concept corresponded with the Vedic third āśrama of man, vānaprastha; and both Shiv Swarup and Swami Shankarananda found that intriguing. What was more, hundreds of U3As were functioning in these countries, with terrific results that empowered the elders.

Clearly, the growing population of elders in India was becoming a stark fact. Medical care was within reach, and life was longer. If a longer life span was also going to be healthy, then inner health had to be accessed during the aging years. Clearly, there was a greater need to create purpose in the lives of the elders. Gurudev would have intended the vānaprasthāśrama to be such a time of purposeful living. Arriving at this thought, CNSAT committed itself to enabling the spiritual evolution of the elders.

Prayāga, as Allahabad was known in Vedic times, denoted 'place of offerings,'[1] the confluence of three sacred rivers: Ganga (representing Bhakti), Yamuna (representing Karma), and Saraswati (representing Jñāna) — the three suggested paths to attain Śiva. Prayāga, now was where the efforts at Pitamaha Sadan in Rewa and Mandhana merged — a holy confluence indeed!

Nandkishore Agrawal would have approved heartily!

EARN THEN TURN

In gṛhasthāśrama when we say 'earn,' it does not mean only money. As a gṛhastha, we can earn wealth for ourselves, society, the community; we can earn name, fame, power, and much more. But in vānaprastha, we must also 'turn.' Turn toward that land of immortality from whence you have come. That Paramātma is the real source of your origins. That is where you have to go back. So turn now. Turn.

– Swami Tejomayananda, *Graceful Aging*

[1] http://en.wikipedia.org/wiki/Allahabad#cite_note-Dubey2001-14

V

The Vānaprastha Thought

Three Missions, One Vision

Like every work of creation, any major event has a warm-up phase that leads to a stage of consolidation when different people, equipment, skills, and ideas slowly come together through divine intention. The same happened in the case of the vānaprastha idea. Three locations offered themselves for Mission activities almost simultaneously, yet disparately — Rewa in Madhya Pradesh; Mandhana and Allahabad in Uttar Pradesh.

The vānaprastha thought progressed like a wave, starting in Rewa, moving to Mandhana, and then to Prayāga, to unleash a movement that would see another of Gurudev's visionary programs find elegant, rational expression. In each of these three cities grew different events surrounding eldercare, which enabled a larger cause. All three centers grew in parallel, developing toward Gurudev's vision.

Remarkable parallels are seen in all three cases. All three centers were born on land donations from elders, Rao Saheb Ran Bahadur Singh at Rewa, Śrī Ram Chandra Mishra at Mandhana, and Śrī Nandkishore Agrawal at Prayāga — all three elders who, having endured saṁsāra, had arrived at a desire to detach from the worldly life. Again, the donations from all those three elders came in the same year, 1983. And all three elder donors came to Gurudev and offered their properties to him. It is hence not surprising that all three sowed the seeds of vānaprastha activity in their locations — and that all three developed one common grassroots activity that Chinmaya Mission would commit itself to.

Thus, three Mission Centers converged toward Gurudev's vision for eldercare.

Synchronicity and the Vienna Convention. In August 1981, when fifteen men from Rewa, Madhya Pradesh, met Gurudev in Sidhbari and offered him a piece of land, he had directed them to work on caring for elders. Even as Gurudev recommended using the donated land to develop a pitamaha sadan, the UNO was likely nurturing the same idea, for twelve months later, on July 26, 1982, the Vienna International Plan of Action on Aging[1] was adopted by the World Association on Aging.

The Vienna Convention reiterated its commitment toward the aging population in the world, underscoring in its resolution several points that were unassailable:

- [The Convention] solemnly reaffirms its belief that the fundamental and inalienable rights enshrined in the Universal Declaration of Human Rights apply undiminished to the aging; and
- [The Convention] solemnly recognizes that quality of life is no less important than longevity, and that the aging should therefore, as far as possible, be enabled to enjoy lives of fulfillment, health, security, and contentment in their families and communities, and appreciated as an integral part of society.

---

[1] www.un.org/es/globalissues/ageing/docs/vipaa.pdf

The International Plan of Action also included these resolutions:

- To develop and apply, at the international, regional, and national levels, policies designed to enhance the lives of the aging individuals and to allow them to enjoy [in] their advancing years, peace, health, and security.
- To study the impact of aging populations on development and the impact of development on the aging; to fully realize the potential of the aging; and to mitigate, by appropriate measures, any negative effects resulting from this impact.

Different Centers, Different Strokes. Particularly in India, the period between 1984 and 1994 saw strong growth of the ideas which Gurudev had inspired at different places. It will be valuable now to examine how the ideas took root, and then, led by the devoted sevaks, converged toward Gurudev's vision.

When the fifteen elders from Rewa who had met Gurudev in Sidhbari (see Chapter II) tried to build a different project, Gurudev firmly pulled them back, saying, "Only pitamahas!" Many were men in their fifth decade of life and hence rightly poised to relate to the aging population. They were neither helpless nor hopeless. Fit in body, mind, and spirit, and already endowed with the attitude of service, these men were aware of others in their twilight years, such as their own parents and in-laws.

Dr. Sajjan Singh, for example, was a medical practitioner in Rewa, who, in the course of attending to family healthcare, had seen the sociological patterns change. The call of a growing economy had grown louder than before, and he observed that the younger generation was more outward looking — seeking interests outside tradition, careers outside family businesses, outside home towns, outside the home country, and raring to go out and explore. That the economies worldwide were accelerating, and aggressively at that, thanks to technology, was good; but it was slowly alienating the elders. As a doctor, Singh was naturally focussing on the state of the elders.

The team at Rewa was coming to grips with the fundamental issue of aging, but the care of the elderly had to go beyond the obvious. Singh, therefore, got together sixty of the elders of the village and decided to talk to them directly about the help and support they needed, and the gaps they experienced. "Tell us how we may serve you?" was the mantra that Singh adopted, using this to do primary research at Rewa. (More in Chapter VI.)

Mandhana, on the other hand, became the lab where Shiv Swarup Agrawal met and spoke to the elders. He also met their families and witnessed the truth of the refrain from Śaṅkara's *Bhaja Govindam:* "Seek Govind, O fool! When the appointed time comes, grammar rules surely will not save you."

As elder after elder met him, Shiv Swarup grew more and more anxious for them. In contrast, Śrī Śaṅkara had the forthrightness to be blunt, even cruel to the old man, addressing him with these words in the *Bhaja Govindam*: "vārtāṁ ko'pi na pricchati gehe" (verse 5), referring to old age, when no one even asks after the elder. He even chided the old man for being caught up in wife and son, saying, "kā te kāntā kaste putraḥ," "Who is wife and what is son?" (verse 8), and cautioned him, "vṛddhastāvat cintāsaktaḥ parame brahmaṇi ko'pi na saktaḥ," "This is how old age passes away by thinking over many things" (verse 7), concluding with a lament, "But there is hardly anyone who wants to give thought to the supreme Brahman."

And Shiv Swarup recalled Śrī Śaṅkara's words: "Strength has left the old man's body; even then attachment is strong and he clings firmly to fruitless desires." (*Bhaja Govindam* 15)

Shiv Swarup had seen all these signs that Śrī Śaṅkara painted in the *Bhaja Govindam* in many elders. He had learned at Sandeepany, at the feet of revered teachers, how ephemeral worldly pursuits were;

yet, when the elders wept at his side, he felt their pain. Each elder was a storybook of unique experiences.

Shiv Swarup knew he had to help them. (More in Chapter VI.)

As for Prayāga, it became the confluence where the experience of Mandhana met the research of Rewa. By then, Rewa had worked with the department of social welfare of the government of India. Subsequent to its National Workshop in 1989, the Rewa team asked the Awdesh Pratap Singh (A.P.S.) University in Rewa to collaborate with Chinmaya Mission. What came out of this, we will see in the next chapter.

That was what Gurudev had wanted. He had sown the seed, but he wanted the devotees to tend to the field and nurture the crop; even strategize the direction this vānaprastha thought would take, as further narration in the book will show.

Why Pitamaha? Gurudev's vision was to light the lamp of spirituality, of divinity, in every life and to keep it lit in every stage of life, so that at no stage was man at risk of being deluded and losing his past efforts into the sacrificial pit of saṁsāra.

Not that Gurudev denounced enjoyment. Not in the least. He believed that human life was a school of experiences that taught, that honed, that shaped, that sculpted the Man of Perfection. But what he cautioned everyone about, time and again, was getting attached to an experience.

From attachment arises desire and from desire wrath ... from delusion to failure of memory, loss of conscience and utter ruin (*Bhagavad-gītā* 2:62–63), because:

> *The self-controlled man, moving among objects with his senses under restraint, and free from both attraction and repulsion, attains peace.* (*Bhagavad-gītā* 2:64)

SEEKING THE ONE

From the very moment he set eyes upon Gurudev, Śrī W. K. Govindaraj was attracted to him. Thereafter, he regularly attended Study Groups in his area in Secunderabad. In 1967, after a personal meeting with Gurudev, he began the Chinmaya Vidyalayas.

Once at the height of his devotion, when Śrī Govindraj told Gurudev that he saw him as his family deity (kula daivam), Gurudev said, 'SEE ME IN EVERYONE.'"

Today, Śrī Govindraj lives a life of a vānaprasthi at Tiruvannamalai, seeking that One in all.

Śrī Govindraj's life of sacrifice is what gave our Mission Swami Dheeranan-da, CM, Washington, D.C.

Thus, the *Gītā* Jñāna Yajñas of Gurudev aimed to 'Teflon coat' his devotees so that they could wade through life detached from its ensnaring offerings. But the one segment of society that he was beginning to notice was the elderly — those who had, during the British era, lost touch with their Vedic heritage and the spiritual tradition of India; for that was the overwhelming nature of foreign rule: the obliteration of all inquiry, all pursuit. Those elders who had bravely held their families bound together, were themselves rudderless. In their late sixties and seventies, when they had done all that they could possibly do, including transferring their properties to their children, they stood on the crossroads of life wondering where they had gone wrong. For the world of relationships — be it with humans or with things — looked vastly different from what they knew it to be. And they wondered if they had failed somewhere.

Some who were predisposed to joy found the emptiness all-consuming. Those who were predisposed to sorrow were worse off. Their emptiness was resoundingly unbearable. *"How much longer do we have to live?"* they seemed to wonder.

But the beauty of this entire movement lies in how Gurudev only sowed the seeds and did not tell the sevaks how the fruit should look. The seed he sowed was care for elders. The fruit? Amazingly, the people in whose hands he placed the plow and sickle and tilling implements took it many steps further and produced just the movement that Gurudev heartily approved: *empowerment of elders.*

Let us look at how this panned out across Prayāga, Mandhana, and Rewa — places that Gurudev nurtured with the greatest care. When Rewa began to examine why Gurudev first forbade them from looking at any other project than the pitamaha activity, they arrived at an uplifting solution: *Yes, we will be very happy to look after the old, but they should also know how to look after themselves.*

Rewa was clear that it was returning power back to the elder.

Then came Prayāga with the combined power of Mandhana — not very different from Rewa's agenda, but with Shiv Swarup's Mandhana experience, there was an all-round consensus that there was now a greater need to create purpose in the lives of the elders.

Gurudev had deliberately talked of pitamaha sadans that would simply care for the neglected elders. Likely, he wanted the workers to develop ownership for the idea. Sure enough, as we see, his initial idea germinated and grew to become 'Empowerment and Purposefulness.'

Shall We Make a Kuṭiyā for You? Why Gurudev thought of a pitamaha sadan specifically is difficult to say. But if we scroll back to Sidhbari–1981, when fifteen elders from Rewa met him, we see the thought beginning then. Gurudev had gone into an unusual silence when one of them, Bhagwati Singh, offered a handsome donation of land. When he came out of his silence, he said, "The land will be used for the care of elders, for a pitamaha sadan." Two years later, in 1983, at Kanpur, when the Bankhandeshwara Trust offered him another piece of land, Gurudev once again thought of a pitamaha sadan. Thereafter, we see all energies trained on this original thought.

PITAMAHA DIWAS

Committing to His Feet

Small celebrations in small towns may seem like small events for the big city dweller. But in Rewa, May 8 is a day of contemplating and calling to mind that one Guru who gathered them together with an entreaty to lift themselves up by themselves!

Every year the 8th of May is celebrated as Pitamaha Diwas in Rewa. This was a fallout of the 1985 elders' convention held at Rewa. The very next year, 1986, the volunteers went from door to door and called the elders to the āśrama. They garlanded the photograph of Gurudev, chanted Gurustotram, and offered a Viṣṇusahasranāma arcana. They then discussed about father-son relationships as it was in the old days and where it stood then.

A pitamaha diwas is a good idea. At Rewa it was the beginning of a sense of purpose. The purpose of committing to a Mahātmā who came to their pretty land far back in 1954 and taught the *Kaṭhopaniṣad*. From there, they derived a reason to commit to the scriptures, offering themselves to Gurudev.

Gurudev was involved in so many projects that to list them all is impossible. Wherever one looked, there was a project manager whom Gurudev had appointed to nurture something: schools, rural development, Bala Vihar, Sanskrit research, cultural revival, books, Jñāna Yajñas, Sandeepany institutes of Vedānta — the list is endless. And each area of work was intricate and intense, and called for Gurudev's attention.

Amid all that, he circled 'pitamaha sadans' in red and kept it on his mental desktop. And this we see reiterated in many letters he wrote to Mission members and devotees.

Consider his letter in June 1986 from Kenya, right in the midst of a world tour, to Swami Tejomayananda: *Sidhanath Kapoor … I think I met him in Kanpur. … He will be very useful for our pitamaha sadan activities.* Or again in August 1987 to a generous devotee, Chimanlal Mehta: *Your kind letter and cheque. I am endorsing it to the Chinmaya Tapovan Trust, who is renovating an old Śiva temple in Kanpur around which we are building a pitamaha sadan. Your amount will go into the temple funds.*

Or Gurudev's letter to B. D. and Krishna Seth in Normal, Illinois, in June 1988, when B. D. was recovering from knee surgery and likely was restless, missing Mission work:

> In your restless enthusiasm, don't vigorously run about before the operated knee settles down. … When you return to Kanpur, you can go and serve at the old age home and temple in Mandhana.

It is natural for devotees to want Gurudev or Guruji all for themselves and sometimes to feel anxiety when it seems as if the Master has

▾ *Satsaṅga Hall, Pitamaha Sadan Mandhana, Kanpur*

forgotten their work. But he never forgets! In another letter, this one to Krishna Seth, B. D.'s wife, in 1989 (mindful of B. D.'s open-heart surgery), Gurudev gently inquired:

> Again [there is] a camp in Kanpur, Mandhana, ... from Feb. 19th to 25th. On the 26th, we do the prāṇapratiṣṭhā of Śiva liṅga in the temple, now fully renovated at Mandhana. ... When are you returning? Shall we make a kuṭiyā for you at Mandhana?

Every letter one reads from the archives drives home how much, how very much, he loved his devotees, that he could never stop thinking of them.

Could it then be that the pitamaha sadans were an outpouring of his great love for his aging disciples, who were caught in the crossroads of a changing society? Why then should he, in the midst of a global world tour, write to Swami Tejomayananda about the human resources that he could deploy on pitamaha sadan activities? Again, consider the letter that Gurudev wrote in December 1989 from Allepey to Sita Juneja (now Swamini Gurupriyananda) in Delhi, a letter with just two sentences, one inviting her to attend Mahā-śivarātrī celebrations, and the next, ... *when you go to Kanpur, try to reach our pitamaha sadan at Mandhana and find what we can start there to help the middle-class villagers.* A whole letter just for this? And three weeks later in a letter to Sain Dass Bhalla in New Delhi, Gurudev said:

> I am sure Śrī and Smt. Khosla will take interest in our pitamaha sadan at Mandhana, Kanpur. It is a few kilometers behind IIT Kanpur.

Undeniably, Gurudev gave every project of his this very same attention — love, care, and enthusiasm. Aptly he is called "utsāhavardhakaḥ, one who encourages and is himself very enthusiastic" — the Good Shepherd watching over our shoulders, anticipating our needs, creating resources, and teaching all to manage and evolve through love and service.

Om Jīrṇa-mandiroddhārakaya Namaḥ! Gurudev is adored as "jīrṇa-mandiroddhāraka," the restorer of old, dilapidated temples, as well as the restorer of temples in the hearts of people. Putting devotion back in barren hearts was akin to rebuilding the house of the Lord and giving Him back His esteemed place in the life of a jīva.

In a unique coming together of events, Gurudev's desire to restore self-respect to his older devotees and other elders of society and empower them with renewed purpose through the establishment of the vānaprasthāśrama, found uncanny synergy with the restoration of one temple and the construction of two new temples.

The vānaprastha activity brought purpose into the lives of the elders, and was akin to the temple restoration process, because innumerable elders found their destination at the feet of the Guru and God through the efforts of the Chinmaya Vānaprastha Sansthan — the initiative that began with pitamaha sadans and culminated in a system of education — as will be seen in a subsequent chapter. After all, the restoration of bhakti and the building of jñāna in those weary hearts was the work of a jīrṇa-mandiroddhāraka!

▲ *1983–84: Śrī P. C. Shukla offering Pūrnakumbha to Gurudev in Mandhana. Br. Vivek looks on*

Gurudev was offered the Bankhandeshwara Temple at Mandhana by the sage-like Ram Chandra Mishra (photo, see page 28, chapter III) and his colleagues on the temple's Board of Trustees —

this, when they had given up all hope of being able to look after the temple, owing to paucity of funds. They asked Gurudev to restore the temple to its old glory and continue worship there, for Ram Chandra Mishra had sworn one day in 1936 that he would see to it that worship of Lord Śiva in this temple never stops. Ram Chandra Mishra took one step toward Gurudev and Gurudev took the remaining steps!

Likewise, Nandkishore Agrawal handed over to Gurudev the trust he had formed in his departed son's name, at a stage when Nandkishore's youth had left his body and interest had left his mind. The Naveen Seva Trust was a veritable temple in the name of his son, Naveen Agrawal, which he had tended to for thirty-two years. Here, too, Gurudev had laid the foundation stone for the Akhileshwar Mahādev Temple in 1987, while the construction itself was in 2009, with prāṇa-pratiṣṭhā being done by Swami Tejomayananda.

▲ *At home in Mandhana with Bankhandeshwara*

Vanvasi Rāma was installed by Gurudev himself at Rewa, with the desire to bring to the hearts of the elders the vairāgya and surrender that Śrī Rāma of Chitrakoot displayed.

But in all three centers, innumerable little temples were restored in the hearts of all the elders who submitted to study and practice, lighting the lamp of vānaprastha in their hearts.

The journey to Self-realization had begun!

AND A RETREAT FOR ME

Chinmaya Uparati — A Spot of Heaven

Rewa is the place where the story of Chinmaya Mission's vānaprastha activity began in 1982, and then, during one of his visits, in 1986, Gurudev found a spot of heaven!

Fifteen kilometers to the south of Rewa is a place called Govindgarh, which has a lake with a tiny island owned by Maharaja Martand Singh of Rewa. Because that place had such beautiful surroundings, a satsaṅga was arranged in the Maharaja's Lake Rest House situated in the middle of the lake. There, seated under a peepal tree on a raised platform, was Gurudev, surrounded by devotees. A cool breeze was blowing and the moment was idyllic. There was a pause, as if Gurudev was feeling the peace around him. Then he said to no one in particular, "It would be nice to have a kuṭiyā here. Whenever I feel like resting, I can stay here. No one will be able to disturb me!"

▲ *Path leading to lake*

▼ *Govindgarh Lake*

And then his eyes fell on Rao Saheb Ran Bahadur Singh, the president of Chinmaya Mission Rewa. "Can we get a piece of land here?" he asked him. Rao Saheb said, "I will convey Gurudev's wishes to Maharaja Martand Singh since all this land belongs to him."

Gurudev left after the jñāna yajña and uncharacteristically kept inquiring about the land in Govindgarh.

At an opportune time, Ran Bahadur Singh approached Maharaja Martand Singh of Rewa. The Maharaja, being himself a scholar and of benevolent disposition, ever wishing to support spiritual and charitable causes, agreed promptly to the request.

▲ *Chinmaya Uparati*

Maharaja Martand Singh was the erstwhile Maharaja of the princely state of Rewa and, as a Lok Sabha member, he spearheaded a number of

▼ *Chinmaya Uparati front view*

developmental works, including bringing the railways to Rewa! When the Pitamaha Sadan in Rewa was being inaugurated, Gurudev had accorded him the same respect that his people gave him, asking him to cut the inaugural ribbon. So it was that on November 28, 1988, Maharaja Martand Singh gifted 1.27 acres of land — another small island on the lake — to the Chinmaya Seva Trust, Rewa. It was mound-shaped, covered by a jungle of trees, thorns, and shrubs. Gurudev was informed about it by Rao Saheb Ran Bahadur Singh through a letter. And promptly came a handwritten letter from Gurudev, giving a sketch of the kuṭiyā to be built there, which he later named 'Chinmaya Uparati.'

On June 10, 1992, Maharaja Martand Singh performed the Bhūmi Pūjā, and soon, funds started to arrive from Gurudev.

The approach to the little island was the biggest problem during the kuṭiyā construction as it was surrounded by water and it was a desolate jungle far from any habitation. Various animals, including carnivores, used to visit the place, particularly in the summer when there was no water in the hills. In addition, there was no one to look after the construction. It was difficult for the Mission to manage the place from Rewa.

"Fortunately, two young men, Pankaj and Sheshmani, came forward to help us," says Dr. Sajjan Singh of CM Rewa. "They belonged to Govindgarh, hence it was easy for them to manage. The entire construction material had to be transported by boat, and it took forty minutes to reach the spot." There was a need for a watchman to stay guard there all day and night. Babulal, an old man, a hunter by profession, took this on, undeterred by the fact that tigers often visited the place at night.

Finally, a two-bedroom kuṭiyā, furnished with an attached modern bathroom, a verandah on two sides, a kitchen, a pūjā room, and a storeroom, were completed in 1993. Separate attendant's quarters were also constructed.

Destiny intervened. Pūjya Gurudev attained Mahāsamādhi on August 3,[2] 1993. However, his itinerary for 1994 (later recovered from his briefcase) showed that he had planned a four-day stay at Chinmaya Uparati.

"We did feel badly that Gurudev could not visit the place," says Dr. Sajjan Singh, "but we feel his presence even now: His pādukās are placed in the pūjā room."

In summer, when the water in the lake falls, the island is approachable on foot, via a strip of land. During the remaining part of the year, it is approachable by boat, and boats are always available there, since the fisheries department maintains them.

End note: 'Uparati' is defined by Śrī Ādi Śaṅkara as: *pratyāhāra*, the withdrawing of the self (*Vedānta-sāra* ślokas 18–20).

BEING DEVOTED TO THE LOTUS FEET OF THE LORD

'Conquer the mind' means purify the mind. Lord Kṛṣṇa says, "When the mind keeps brooding over sense objects and pleasures, it gets attached to them. But when the same mind meditates on Me, it becomes one with Me."

Therefore, the bhikṣu refuses to get bothered or angry by what people do or don't do. His only goal is to cross over the ocean of saṁsāra by being devoted to the lotus feet of the Lord. That's all!

– Swami Tejomayananda, *Graceful Aging*

[2] August 3 has been designated the official Mahasamadhi date, even though it was August 4, in India, when Gurudev attained Mahasamadhi.

VI

Researching the Elderly Life
Rewa and Mandhana

We will now see the efforts laid out by Rewa and Mandhana separately between 1984 and 1999, yet together heading for the same goal, empowerment of the elder.

R*ewa Researches Eldercare.* The seed of vānaprastha was sown as early as 1983. In the ten years that followed, Gurudev energized the seed by his mere presence on one level, and his encouragement of new research ideas on the other.

The three centers — Rewa, Mandhana, and Prayāga — worked on their own assigned tasks and on their pieces of land. The teams at Prayāga and Mandhana were headed by Shiv Swarup Agrawal, who began in Mandhana and, after three years, moved to Prayāga where he applied his Mandhana experience. With his background in Vedānta at Sandeepany, Shiv Swarup honed his expertise in eldercare, and with the combined strength of knowledge and experience, he approached the assignment at Prayāga.

There he was joined by Prof. P. C. Shukla (later, Swami Shankarananda), who had gained firsthand experience in eldercare and management at Rewa. Shukla had worked there from 1985, soon after setting up the pitamaha sadan. It may be recalled that Shukla had been present at the meeting with the village elders in Rewa — a meeting that sought to inquire into their condition.

Meeting the Village Elder (November 1985). Unknowingly, Rewa had chanced upon the right road. The seed first sprouted in Rewa in a most unusual way. The pioneer team, who had met Gurudev in Sidhbari (1981), along with Dr. Singh, was committed to the idea of eldercare, but an additional thought came to them: They agreed that they would be very happy to create a nurturing environment for the elderly; however, the elders *should also know how to look after themselves.*

So, in November 1985, they called a meeting of the elders from the Rewa district and the surrounding areas of Satna, Sidhi, and Shahdol. Śrī Gorey Lal, an Indian Administrative Service (IAS) officer and the Director of the Social Welfare Department of the government of Madhya Pradesh, was also invited. Faculty members from the departments of medicine and preventive and social medicine of the Rewa Medical College also participated. Importantly, these two departments would get to hear, in a focused way, what elders experienced but had never vocalized until then.

Groups were formed to discuss the various sources of the problems faced in old age. The village elders shared their understanding and experiences: While India had traditionally adopted the joint-family system, that 'social-given' was disintegrating in the 1980s. In the joint-family structure, the health of old and young had been taken care of, work had been shared and enjoyed, and familial roles and traditions had been typically respected and valued; grandparents had been looked up to and treated with care. But now, in its delight with consumerism, Indian society had first given up the joint family and, next, the elder, as though elders ceased to be people after they had retired, and their children had married.

In that meeting in 1985, Chinmaya Mission redirected the spotlight on the elder.

The meeting with the elders was attended by 114 people, including the resource persons. The key focus areas defined and addressed at that meeting were:

Elders and Their Health
Elders and Their Social Relations
Elders and Their Families
Elders and Their Financial Status
Elders and Their Spirituality

Research revealed how worse off the 'village elder' was compared to the 'city elder,' owing to very poor infrastructure in the villages. Very simply, even primary healthcare was absent, and, as a consequence, awareness of health management of elders was nonexistent. Many difficulties that elders faced in villages were directly related to their financial status. Once they were incapable of adding to the family income, they were seen as a strain on resources; and if they also fell ill, as was prone to happen with advancing age, then elder abuse took place as well.

The Rewa team saw the intense need for spiritual education for the elders so that they could come to see their age-related situation in a positive light. Spiritual education was thus recorded as a significant must-have in the solution for eldercare.

To the seventy elders from the regions of Rewa, Singh said, "We want to serve you. That is why we would like you to come visit us, so we can talk together and find out how we may serve you."

The elders arrived at the meeting, intrigued by the call. Dr. Sajjan Singh also invited the very learned Mr. Buch, the director of social welfare from Bhopal. Having formed the elders into groups to enable study of their maladies, Singh said to them, "We are going to try to help you with suggestions on how to look after yourself in old age, and how you can, in fact, do all this successfully and happily!"

Never an Old Age Home! The assembled village elders were mostly retired people — people who had once left home to earn for the family or fight for the nation. That spine which had held up society all these years had now become bent with age and anxiety.

As Singh spoke to them and told them about the elders' home coming up in Rewa, he began to hear their protesting voices: "We will not go to an old age home. No matter the hardship, we want to stay with our children and grandchildren." Why? Cultural bonds, and then the stigma attached to parents not staying with their children. Ironically, it was this stigma that had played a pivotal role in keeping society together, keeping families together, keeping homes ringing with chatter, and tradition passing from grandparent to grandchild, generation after generation.

On the other hand, the educated, city-bred elders did think positively about staying at a pitamaha sadan if it offered a solitude that was enriching and yet wholesome. But the village folk would not negotiate tradition.

The Social, the Financial. Sajjan Singh pondered over the sources of the problems of the elders. Clearly, he could see that there were physical conditions which the elders brought upon themselves by not attending to ailments which they preferred to classify as 'owing to old age.' Then there were maladies at the level of relationships with the family and society — those were the biggest — as they governed both mental conditions and social relations.

He wondered if all those difficulties had to do with not being prepared. In almost all cases, it was observed that the elders realized they were at a new stage of life, and yet had not seen it coming. They had worked until the very last minute as householders, not once thinking about the changes ahead. But then, that was the lot of gṛhasthāśrama — if it was not children, then it was work, or health, or recreation, or education, or yet another preoccupation.

THE POWER OF THE NAME

HEMANTINI BHATIA

When at thirty, Hemantini Bhatia mentioned to her father her desire to know God, he said to her, "If this desire gets intense, go only to one person please, Swami Chinmayananda."

Hemantini met Gurudev when she was in her forties. Her interest grew and along with her husband she began to study Vedānta under a Brahmacārī. But she was yet hungry. So, in 1993, Gurudev told her to do the Dharma Sevak Course. Oh! Hemantini cringed. How could she, with children and family? She was in her fifties then.

It was when she was in her late seventies, that Hemantini enrolled for the Sandeepany Vedānta Course in Mumbai. Her ācārya was Pūjya Guruji! It was the two most amazing years, she says. The naam was planted in her ears in her thirties and the naam had guided her to her eighties! Every day of these fifty-plus years she sees as having been guided by Gurudev.

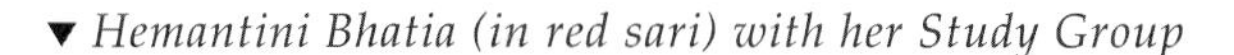

▾ *Hemantini Bhatia (in red sari) with her Study Group*

She looks back at her journey all these years and wonders about the ways of the Guru.

Here are some letters he wrote her when she was struggling to enter vānaprasthāśrama:

Feb 1992, Sidhbari
[...] I am so very happy to hear that you are taking classes and trying to guide others toward what you now understand and enjoy.

You had your time. At your age, you must be able to stand apart without getting yourself involved in the family bickering. Let them fight it all out themselves. You will live peacefully in one corner. Advise if they come and approach you. Love them in spite of their mental brutalities. Desire and attachment create disturbances.

Love
– Chinmayananda

And a year later, again...

July 1993, Chicago
Your letter crying with your woes. It made me laugh. Śrī Bhatia had a successful open-heart surgery. Sons are in Uganda and London. Why should you get worried over them? Leave them alone at His feet and be at ease in yourself at your seat of study & contemplation.

Love
– Chinmayananda

At eighty-three, Hemantini Bhatia continues to teach out of her Matunga apartment, blessed and guided by Gurudev.

The other concern was the finances: Even those who had enough and earned a pension tended to skimp on necessities in a bid to save for a 'rainy day.' This made their lives more difficult than it needed to be, thus leading to a bigger spiral of anxiety for the future.

Many of the elders assembled there were artisans and farmers. One might think that for those people the loss of finances was not likely because their land would continue to produce. Dr. Singh said, "No doubt, but when health fails and they cannot work, they become a burden on the healthy members of the family! Even in that situation, the village elder will pick up a *khurpi* (sickle) and cut grass to feed the cattle, so that he can be productive in some manner."

The plight of the farmer-elder was thought-provoking. For he did not retire at sixty like his white-collared counterpart in the city did. Nor did he have access to compulsory savings like provident fund. A farmer 'retired' only when it was physically impossible to work. He then handed over the capital assets (land) and the goodwill to a son, brother, or other family member. Thereafter, somebody else would reap the fruits of his years of labor. Despite that, the beneficiary considered that elder a burden on resources, for the elder then had to be fed, clothed, and cared for.

That was the painful paradox of the agrarian majority in India. And the Indian farmer believed: *Uttam kheti!* "The best profession is farming, because it keeps you fully dependent on God!" Therefore, everything was Hari icchā (will of God)!

From Icchā to Icchā Śakti — from Will to Willpower. But tradition itself was straining at the seams. More and more elders were experiencing the throttle of dependency with increasing severity because they saw their dependency as a burden.

For the next four years, the Rewa team worked at enabling the people to use their beliefs to empower themselves more. Applying

One man, a lifetime of research

Some papers presented by Dr. Sajjan Singh on aged and aging until 1999:

- **Coping with Aging the Ancient Way.** Paper on living by the prescriptions of the āśrama system. Presented at the International Symposium on Gerontology and the VIII Conference of Association of Gerontology (India) New Delhi, March 1994.
- **Spirituality, the Basis of Quality of Life (QOL).** Presented at National Seminar on Community Psychology at the A.P.S. University, Rewa M.P., March 1999.
- **New Horizons on Aging — From the Time Bound to the Time-less:** Paper on meditation as a means in vānaprastha to qualify for sannyāsa. Presented at the International Conference of Geriatrics and Gerontology, New Delhi, November 1999.

the insights gained from their small-group meeting discussions, a number of camps were conducted to help the village elders see that 'Hari icchā' (equivalent to 'what God proposes') had to be transformed into icchā śakti, one's own will power; that resigning to fate was very far removed from the will of the Lord; that purposelessness was faulty. The purpose of life was reaching the Lord Himself.

The Sample of Seventy. From the sample of seventy elders who attended that meeting, the Rewa team gleaned a certain perception about the life of the elderly — of what it meant to be over sixty-five in India — that, with age, an individual's gross needs blur and the subtle needs assert themselves: the need for patience, care, love, respect, and attention. Add to this the gentle drone of three kinds of anxieties: regrets over past actions, anxieties over the future, and feelings of restlessness that seize the present.

Dr. Singh's team readily saw that all such anxieties came from the world outside through the mind. To help elders look past the world, and look within, required a strong spiritual discipline, which would then support physical wellbeing. Once again, the indicators pointed to robust attention to spiritual growth. *The more one reaches 'third age' with little or no spiritual leaning, the more the difficulty that is felt in the body and mind — probably because spirituality is the raison d'être for human birth, and if sixty years are lived without attention to that, the inner self agitates.*

Reorientation Program — More Research. A Prelude to the National Workshop. While health, mental and physical, social relationships, and financial challenges were amenable to discussion, the fifth focus of that meeting — spiritual growth — brought on confusion and doubts, along with the inhibitions that arise when talking about spirituality.

The group assembled, talked, argued, and debated. A broad outline was drawn of a program that would enable the elders to reorient themselves to their 'third age.' This was the foundation of the five-day camp known as Vṛdhāvasthā Samadhan Śibir (or camps for getting comfortable with old age). Śrī P. C. Shukla (introduced in Chapter II) was the main architect of the course.

That foundational camp was to later evolve into a very enabling meet for elders as many

▲ *Dr. Singh spent a lot of his time on research and conferences.*

Contd. from previous page

- **Efficacy of the Program of Graceful Aging for the Aged: An Evaluative Study.** Paper presented along with Prof. R. S. Singh and D. S. Baghel at Workshop of the Dept. of Psychology, Utkal University, Bhubaneshwar, Orissa, 2007. Based on the 'Art of Graceful Aging' camps held by CVS, in which the efficacy of the program was evaluated using psychological testing.

GURUDEV'S MESSAGE FOR THE NATIONAL WORKSHOP, 1989

Many are the old, getting older and getting more and more confused at their growing sense of inner inabilities and physical infirmities. The younger ones, though loving, have their own lives to follow, and so are compelled to remain in their field of work. Thus, even when they are well-off financially, elders feel neglected and uncared-for — and this is a voiceless sorrow for many.

To give them a clubhouse atmosphere to live in, where they are looked after, kept very cheerful, mentally engaged in the wonderland of spiritual thoughts, with ▶

more such camps came to be held. By 1985, the Rewa team, through more such camps, was gleaning more and more understanding about elders and how to help them help themselves. Dr. Singh had learned a lot from his interactions with the Rewa elders, and in January 1986, he presented his study in a paper titled, 'Medico-Social Survey of Elders in Rewa District of Madhya Pradesh in Rural and Urban Areas,' at the Annual Conference of the Geriatric Society of India. This study covered the experiences of many families, and the problems that elders faced.

Ten months later, based on that same study, Dr. Singh presented another paper, 'Problems of Elderly in Rural and Semi-Urban Areas of Rewa District, Madhya Pradesh — A Strategy for Action,' at the Round Table Discussion on Care of the Elders organized by the Indian Medical Association, at IMA House, New Delhi. This was a follow-up program to the 'International Conference on Health Policy, Ethics, and Human Values' held in New Delhi the same year.

Papers like these cannot be written without first-hand, primary research on the target segment. The more the teams probed, the more they learned about the management of elders.

By 1989, the team felt that they had gained a lot of expertise through first-hand research and their own analysis. The conclusions needed to be taken to a wider audience, an intellectual community, so that action points could emerge. Thus was born the idea of a National Workshop.

Economic and Demographic Reality: A Quick Glance. Dr. Singh studied the numbers for the elders in the world population against the corresponding figures for developing countries and developed countries.

In 1989, according to the 1981 census, 6.5 percent of the world population was above 'age sixty.' Given medical breakthroughs and better living conditions (and, importantly, the absence of major wars), that percentage was only bound to increase, and rapidly at that. A United Nations report (1989) projected that by the year 2100, 2.5 billion people (or a quarter of the world population) would be over sixty years of age. The UN report startled the team's efforts back in 1989. And since the time of their findings, new data have emerged.

The number of older persons has tripled over the last fifty years; that number will more than triple again over the next fifty years.

As for the oldest old (those eighty and over), in 1950, they numbered fewer than 14 million worldwide. In 2000, this same segment had grown to 69 million. In the year 2050, this segment is estimated to grow to

their food and medical needs [provided], would be the greatest service to our today's community.

This is a new demand thrown by the changing social conditions in India. The old may not work as the young can. But they have a wealth of experiences gathered in the life span lived [so far], and this rich treasure is readily available for the young muscles to strive in all productive and creative fields.

To bring them — young and old — together for a meaningful discussion for planning our future is a sacred function.

I am glad Chinmaya Seva Trust, Rewa, is now trying to achieve this difficult task under PITAMAHA SEVA.

Jai Jai Jagadeeshwara!
Love,

– *Swami Chinmayananda,*
Śivarātrī Greetings,
Bombay, 1989

380 million — two-thirds of whom are women. This 'eighty years and over' segment is growing faster than any younger segment.

In relative terms, the UN places this segment in 2000 at 'only slightly more than 1 percent of the total human population,' adding, that 'this proportion is projected to increase almost fourfold over the next fifty years, to reach 4.1 percent in 2050.' And alongside, the base on which this 4.1 percent is expressed, is on the increase. The rise in percentage of a growing base means many things, including a fitter elder community. Therefore, we are forced to think — have we planned at all for our elders?

The (Rewa) National Workshop team was acutely aware of the needs of an expanding elder base. Previously when Gurudev had said, "Eldercare and nothing else!" the team members had whispered a rhetoric — "We will care for elders, by all means, but they, too, must look after themselves."

And when they sat and stared at the reams of research data on the table, they realized how right they had been, even if unwittingly. That was when they restated that very rhetoric with emotion, "It would be difficult to cope with such numbers [as published by the UN] unless the elders themselves are prepared to change their attitude to old age." A stunning statement had been made.

National Workshop on Eldercare (November 1989) — Helping Elders Help Themselves. The Chinmaya Seva Trust of Rewa (the land donated by Ran Bahadur Singh was then committed to a trust) approached the Awadesh Pratap Singh University, Rewa, and sought its collaboration on a workshop on 'Welfare Awareness and the Productive Utilization of the Aged Component of Human Population.'

These may be very stony, clinical words to express what we otherwise call 'respect.' Gurudev, for his part, said in a message of appreciation (see box page 57) "The old may not work as the young can. But they have a wealth of experience gathered in their life span lived (so far), and this rich treasure is available for the young muscles to strive in all productive and creative fields."

What Gurudev said demands reflection. Human beings study trends in many sectors and industries to know what to anticipate, or forecast what will be, say, the buying behaviors if a soap is changed from pink to blue; in productivity exercises, operations and methods are examined minutely to know how productivity can be increased. Yet, mankind has not yet learned to interpret effectively the experiences of the elders or apply them toward his own learning. Humankind continues to commit new mistakes, mistakes that are taking their toll on the social intelligence and spiritual health of the younger generation, and thus on civil society at large.

As Gurudev stressed upon the wealth of experience with the old, which the young could avail — that experience can be used both to correct their future actions, as well as correct or modify those trends that pose roadblocks to productivity and creativity.

In essence, Rewa's National Workshop was an attempt to understand the projections for 2050 and the mind-set needed to deal with it. For, the survey had shown that elders held a rather bleak outlook on old age.

It is extremely important to examine the kind of people who participated in this workshop. Each one presented a paper on a distinct aspect of 'third age,' and what each of them said can fill a book. But going by the sheer credentials of these participants, we can see:

- Rewa's commitment to conducting a meaningful and valuable workshop.
- The importance given to this subject by the intellectuals of Rewa society.

It is a matter of great pride that people of such caliber came together to focus on elder management and that the small Rewa team gathered such momentum among them to urge venerable IAS officers, district collectors, deans of universities, heads of departments, and the joint director of the Ministry of Welfare to come forth and contribute.

National Workshop Ripple Effect: More Leads to Even More. The Workshop had seen robust participation and each of the participants had presented well-researched papers on key subjects (see box, page 61). That the population of the elderly was increasing drew mixed feelings — a definite joy that the elderly could expect to live longer, yet, pain that increasing awareness and self-sufficiency was not going to be an enthusiastic process. In India, at that juncture, social problems were already rampant. The breakdown of the joint-family system did not seem half as bad as the consumerism that was gnawing away at human sensitivity.

The workshop had examined demographics; the participants were alarmed to see the future present an inverted pyramid, in which the apex (now reversed) would be young people and adults, while the flat wide bottom (now inverted) would constitute the elders, thanks to a sure drop in birth rates.

The National Workshop recommended:

- Repositioning the elder as one worthy of respect
- Empowering the elder through education and training
- Providing psychological support to deal with old age

In short, the focus of the Workshop was to reposition the status of the elder members of society as being worthy of respect and attention, and lead them toward a happily empowered life.

FACULTIES AND PARTICIPANTS AT THE NATIONAL WORKSHOP

- Department of Anthropology, Lucknow University
- Professors of Psychology:
  - University Campus, Hardwar
  - Awadhesh Pratap Singh University, Rewa (M.P.)
- Professor of Applied Math, Applied Sciences and Humanities
- Department of Sociology:
  - Madurai Kamraj University,
  - Rani Durgawati Vishwavidyalaya, Jabalpur (M.P.)
  - Principal, Govt. Sanskrit College, Rewa (M.P.)
- Department of Community Medicine:
  - Kempegowda Institute of Medical Sciences
  - Pt. J.N.M. Medical College, Raipur
  - Shyam Shah Medical College, Rewa
  - Director of Global Conference on Aging
  - Śrī Shyam Sunder, Shyam Institute of Public Cooperation and Community Development
- Department of Criminology & Forensic Science, University of Sagar, M.P.
- Departments of Ophthalmology, of Medicine, and of Physiology — S.S. Medical College, Rewa (M.P.)
- Department of Environmental Biology, Awadhesh Pratap Singh University, Rewa (M.P.)

- Department of Pharmacology:
  - Shyam Shah Medical College, Rewa
  - Ayurvedacharya, Ayurved Medical College, Rewa
- Department of Ancient History, Shyam Shah Medical College, Rewa
- Government of India, Ministry of Welfare

A *Very Conscientious Focus.* Clearly, the quality of participants that the Workshop attracted created the right kind of ripple effect. A few years later, in 1993, the Vice Chancellor of the Awadhesh Pratap Singh University, Rewa, Professor J. S. Rathore (one of the key collaborators of the National Workshop) convened a meeting of people who had made an impact on the key result areas of the workshop recommendations in July 1993.

The members felt that the immediate and direct need was for an orientation program for the 'above fifty' to be organized and made accessible in more and more towns and cities. Further, they agreed that the University's Psychology Department was poised to collaborate with the Chinmaya Seva Trust, Rewa, along with the Red Cross and the Rotary Club.

Vice Chancellor Rathore had specifically invited those people whose work would make a difference to society, whose jobs already involved or included the elders of the society; hence, directly involving these stakeholders was a very intelligent move.

At that meeting were present the heads of key organizations who managed or monitored elder life, such as the Pensioners' Samaj, the joint director of the Panchayat and Social Welfare Department, the head of the university's Psychology Department (to ensure that the efforts were directed to the needs), the head of Community Medicine from Rewa's medical college, and many other experts. The names and titles of those who participated indicate the level of interest and importance given to that program. A seven-day program was drawn up and the first of its kind was held in October 1993. That program, held in the evenings to facilitate the office-goers, examined the physical, financial, mental, intellectual, and spiritual needs of the individual.

Sixty people participated in the seven-day program. It was this program that was later enhanced by Swami Shankarananda (Śrī P. C. Shukla) to relaunch later as the five-day Vṛdhavāsthā Samadhan Śibir, or the 'Art of Graceful Living.' Thirty-three such camps were held by the Mission in collaboration with Awadhesh Pratap Singh University's Adult Education Department, in Rewa, Satna, Sidhi, and Shahdol districts of M.P.

Welfare State Versus Welfare Society — The Enabling Vānaprasthāśrama. At the meeting that the Professor J. S. Rathore, Vice Chancellor of Awadhesh Pratap Singh University, Rewa, convened in 1993, he directed the spotlight on the rapid increase expected in the 'above sixty' segment. Calling India a graying country, Rathore pointed to the sixty-plus population, which then stood at almost 7 percent of total population. Rathore's anxiety was not ill-founded, for the total population itself was increasing rapidly.

Typically, fingers tended to point to the State to ensure welfare, but Rathore wondered if that approach was tenable, given the large size of India's population. The 'welfare state' was a good option for smaller nations like Sweden, he said. Yet, if it were supplemented by a 'welfare society,' the entire fabric and complexion of Indian society, he thought, could be pleasing, considering India's social and traditional background, and the fact that almost three-fourths of older people lived in the villages.

Rao Saheb Ran Bahadur Singh, the Vice Chairperson of the Chinmaya Seva Trust, pondered on that concept. The combining of the 'welfare state' and 'welfare society' appealed to him, not so much because he was a Member of Parliament but because he, as a Vedāntin, saw clearly how the adherence to varṇa-āśrama was beneficial to all. What the ṛṣis of yore had prescribed, held, in its fold, perfect directions for a perfect lifestyle in every stage of a human's life.

Rao Saheb Ran Bahadur Singh was of the view that in his 'third age,' a person should look after his or her mental and physical health by taking up service in the spirit of sādhanā. This, he said, contributed greatly to his wellbeing. Therefore, the need of the hour was to reinterpret the vānaprastha lifestyle in the modern context. The reorientation program was headed in that direction.

SANNYĀSA — TURNING TO THE SOURCE

In India, we find that even the river Ganga, which flows from Gaumukh to the Bay of Bengal, after a short time, turns toward its source and returns to the ocean. Vānaprastha is like this turning toward the source, which becomes sannyāsa. If one revels in learning, has a disciplined resolve, and is content with whatever he gets in life, then such a person alone ages gracefully and comes to revel in the supreme Brahman.

– Swami Tejomayananda, *Graceful Aging*

Meanwhile at Prayāga

Shiv Swarup Agrawal remained in Mandhana for three years before he was transferred to Prayāga in 1994. The property at Mandhana was functioning mainly as a home for elders facing varied problems or those who had nowhere to live.

Prayāga (also now known as Allahabad) was an administrative center and a renowned center of education in the time of Emperor Akbar (1556–1605). Shiv Swarup felt it would be a great place to touch for wisdom, meet some educationists and intellectuals, and then draw on their knowledge to design Gurudev's vision: a center that would empower the elders.

Seeing how erudite the city was, Shiv Swarup was confident of getting a variety of ideas for an empowerment center. He spoke with Swami Shankarananda, who was in Mandhana, invited him to the meeting of 'thirty eminent citizens,' and along with Dr. Sajjan Singh (the Rewa team leader), they agreed to form an organization for solving the problems of the elderly. They would not establish yet another old age home, but form a Vānaprastha Sansthan that would focus on the needs of elders.

▲ 'Triveni Sangam' by Puffino – Own work. Licensed under CC BY-SA 3.0 via Wikimedia Commons – http://commons.wikimedia.org/wiki/File:Triveni_Sangam.JPG#mediaviewer/File:Triveni_Sangam.JPG

Until then, Shiv Swarup had seen that Mandhana was just functioning as an old age home, and the elders there believed that they were old, helpless, with no purpose or use. Shiv Swarup did not want to affirm that disillusionment, but to establish an institution founded on higher principles, a place where people would be empowered and would learn to take charge of themselves. Old age homes didn't solve any problems. They only reinforced and confirmed to the elders that they were the problem.

Shiv Swarup's mantra resonated with that of Dr. Sajjan Singh's in Rewa: Elders must be empowered sufficiently to solve their own problems. The mantra worked!

At Allahabad (Prayāga), a pitamaha sadan did come up; many elders arrived and were given accommodation. But Shiv Swarup called it a sevā āśrama. The residents were old, but that did not make the āśrama an old age home. With the coming of Shiv Swarup to Prayāga in 1994, Gurudev's vision began to take shape.

Prayāga, like Rewa, had examined the same research figures on demographics, and the Allahabad literati concluded that there was an urgent need to formulate a curriculum to train the elders in self-empowerment, purposeful living, and psychological comfort to receive life in their third age with joy and purpose.

At first, they contemplated a university, but Shiv Swarup felt that the concept would not work in India. Instead, he formulated plans for a 'Chinmaya Institute of Gerontology,' which was adapted to Chinmaya Vānaprastha Sansthan, or CVS.

Chinmaya Vānaprastha Sansthan. Thus was born the Chinmaya Vānaprastha Sansthan which was conceived as an institute for the onward education and evolution of the people who choose to enter their sixties in a planned, structured manner. The word 'vānaprastha' is the Sanskrit equivalent for what the West calls the 'third age.'

Śrī Amitav Banerji, a retired Chief Justice of the Allahabad High Court, the most senior and much revered in that group of citizens, was asked to draft a scheme of administration for this proposed institute.

▲ *Śrī Amitav Banerji, ex-Chief Justice, High Court Allahabad*

Banerji proposed that the Chinmaya Vānaprastha Sansthan (hereon CVS), should be an institution aimed at improving the lifestyle of elders to make their third age happy, healthy, and purposeful; the curriculum would follow the gerontology approach prescribed for vānaprastha. Banerji felt that it was time to form a dedicated team that would focus on the needs of the elders — to provide answers and direction for them and make the third age a much-awaited, inspiring, and aspiring journey. This was the prime endeavor of CVS.

Banerji anticipated the need for informal courses that would address lifestyle issues related to stable health (such as desirable attitudes toward food consumption and fitness); that would address sociocultural issues (such as expectations of, and relationships with, family and society); and that would enable working toward satisfaction and striving for detachment. Thus, the elders would also begin their spiritual journey, that is, understanding their relationship with the world and its Creator.

Both Shiv Swarup and Banerji had noticed that while the women's lives remained almost unchanged when their husbands retired, it was the men who folded up into an armchair of boredom and sedentary inactivity instead of exploring life and devoting themselves to all that they could not do when they were working to earn for the family. They could see that both men and women experienced different needs with age; they would need to plan training activities for both genders.

The proposal found great support and was approved in principle in February 1996. Swami Shankarananda was entrusted with the responsibility to develop a course, test-run it, evaluate feedback, and then review the course material.

Thereby Was Born Vṛdhāvasthā Samadhan. Swami Shankarananda set to work in great earnest, and, in three months, by the end of June 1996, he had a draft course ready, which he called 'Vṛdhāvasthā Samadhan' — loosely translated, 'Facing the challenge of old age.' Before long, the course was retitled 'The Art of Graceful Aging' — not because the third age was a challenge, but because it had to be communicated that one needed to enter the third age artfully.

After everyone had seen the contents of the course and thoroughly discussed it, it was decided to launch it formally through a camp. On August 11, 1996, the former (late) Chief Justice of India, Śrī Rangnath Mishra, inaugurated the first ever educational course for the elderly in India, entitled 'Vṛdhāvasthā Samadhan Śibir' at the Āśrama of CNSAT. It was a residential camp and was attended by forty-three delegates from different parts of India.

▲ *Śrī Ranganath Misra, ex-Chief Justice of India, with Shiv Swarup Agrawal*

It was a good sample size for evaluating the course. Over the four days, Swamiji himself conducted the entire course which covered sociology, psychology, financial planning, and spiritual awareness. His talks were later published as a textbook for CVS, titled, *An Introduction to Gerontology*. The Hindi original was titled *Jara Vigyan Praveshika*.

The feedback from the delegates was overwhelming and encouraging. That affirmed that the course was extremely successful — far more than what Swamiji had expected! Soon, other Chinmaya Mission centers wanted camps to be held in their regions. And, before long, the course spread all over India.

▲ *Delegates lining up for a CVS camp*

Central Chinmaya Vānaprastha Sansthan — A Consolidated Grassroots Activity! In the first quarter of 1998, it was formally decided that vānaprastha activities were core to all that the Chinmaya Mission did. Guruji, Swami Tejomayananda, declaring vānaprastha as a grassroots activity (alongside Bala Vihar, Yuva Kendra, and so on), decided that an apex body named Central Chinmaya Vānaprastha Sansthan would be set up, headquartered in Prayāga, and that it should automatically become germane to every CM center.

▲ *CVS Camp Kolhapur, 2002; Chief Ācārya Swami Purushottamananda lighting the lamp. Shiv Swarup Agrawal is behind Swamiji, in white*

The objectives of CVS would be:

- To strive to improve the quality and lifestyle of senior citizens through learning and service.
- To learn, through training, the prevention and management of geriatric diseases through a holistic approach; to tackle financial, social, and psychological issues of the aging

population; and, above all, to understand the aims of the third and fourth stages of human life and the means of achieving them.

- To engage in selfless service of society utilizing the energies, experiences, and expertise of senior citizens.

Some subsidiary goals were also listed, two of which were expressly in the nature of education — the conducting of regular day and postal courses on vānaprastha; and the holding of camps, lectures, and seminars on related subjects. The rest were activities conducive to eldercare and welfare. Concurrently, in 1998, *Vanprasth*, an English quarterly magazine for senior citizens, was launched. The journal has continued its journey uninterruptedly since then.

▲ *Participants of Vānaprastha Camp Sikkim, 1999*

▼ *All three come together: Second from left: Sw. Prashantananda, Sw. Yogasthananda, and Dr. Sajjan Singh*

The CVS is a core outcome of the vānaprastha initiative of the Mission, arising out of the early moves made by Gurudev at Rewa, then Mandhana, and then Prayāga.

▲ *Śrī Shiv Swarup (extreme left), Swami Shankarananda and Dr. Singh (in blue trousers)*

In 1999, Prayāga organized a national seminar. That seminar presented some of the most thought-provoking papers on eldercare and deserves appreciation for delving deep into the area of eldercare. Consequently, this is the subject matter of the next chapter.

LONG FOR GOD

Sant Tulsidas writes that in old age one should feel sad that his life has passed by without knowing God. He asks, "When will I have love for God and dispassion for the world?" ... [S]uch a mind comes only by God's grace. Therefore, invoke God's grace through sincere prayer.

As vānaprasthis, when we are firmly rooted in the conviction that we must get established in Brahman, we will rightly and determinedly live a life that harbors all proper means to achieve this goal. A life that is adorned with such a goal naturally ages gracefully. ... [W]e must concern ourselves with how to get such a mind that longs for the right things in life at the right time.

– Swami Tejomayananda, *Graceful Aging*

VIII

1989

Rewa's National Workshop

Rewa had researched the condition of elders to identify and understand the underlying problems. And from this, Rewa derived the objectives for its National Workshop, held in November 1989:

- To formulate strategies for better utilization of elders' skills — through plans, forums, and agencies, if necessary
- To explore and exploit existing research in medicine, psychology, and sociology to enable better aging (and also to appraise the needs of aging)
- To organize a forum for the exchange of views and information on spiritual and other aspects of geriatrics
- To formulate steps and plans that government can adopt for eldercare at national, state, and local levels

If such formulation and ideation was to be fruitful, they had to address five aspects of aging:

- Sociocultural
- Religious or spiritual
- Physical (health)
- Psychological (mental)
- Ecological

▲ *Swami Purushottamananda (in the center) at Rewa's National Workshop*

But uniquely, in and through all their research, everyone was tending toward the traditional, ancient values. That was when they consensually wrote a focus statement: "Interpret ancient values in the context of modern life." For they faced the statistic of an increasing life span, thanks to ever-improving medical facilities and scientific breakthroughs that said:

- A majority of the aging population will be in developing countries.
- The number of the 'very old' (eighty and over) will be on the increase.

Pre-1989 global research indicated that by the year 2020, worldwide, there will be more than 100 million people older than age eighty. But for India, the 1981 census had placed the 'sixty and over' count at 4.3 million, while projecting that, in 2001, the number would be a staggering 76 million! In parallel, the Population Division, Department of Economic and Social Affairs, United Nations, said: *Over the first half of the current century, the global population sixty or over is projected to expand by more than three times to reach nearly two billion in 2050.*

The same report quotes: "By then, 33 countries are expected to have more than 10 million people sixty or over, including 5 countries with more than 50 million older people (eighty and over): China (437 million), India (324 million), the United States of America (107 million), Indonesia (70 million), and Brazil (58 million)." This confirmed that a majority of the aging population will be in developing countries.

Hence, strategy for eldercare had to be formulated soon. But before that, there needed to be a fundamental fact-finding method that would enumerate the problems facing elders, followed by avenues for attitudinal change needed from elders themselves, as well as from the government and other stakeholders in society. This then became the anvil of the National Workshop.

This chapter carries the summaries of the main perspectives for elder welfare put forth by six eminent thinkers during that workshop. It is to be kept in mind that these observations are peculiar to the Indian society, although similarities may exist with others.

Spiritual Perspectives in Welfare Awareness and Productive Utilization of the Elders

by Rao Ran Bahadur Singh (now Swami Prashantananda)

Rao Ran Bahadur Singh, then the Vice Chairman of the Chinmaya Seva Trust, Rewa, linked the socioeconomics of each social strata to their degree of spiritual orientation. Drawing from the experience of the West — since India lost its spiritual accent, more recently during and after the British rule — Singh observed:

> Old age in the Western culture is a time of failing physique leading to reluctant restriction of activities that [once] gave pleasure. It is also a time of anguish and loneliness because the progeny moves away, leaving an emotional void. ... The social strata of our country that enjoys the advantages of education, wealth, and influence has traditionally imbibed the mores and methods of the West. And so, here too, this class of people have almost a similar replication of old age life as in the West.

Exemplifying their disillusionment due to modern socioeconomic changes, Singh made a stunning observation:

> [T]he wealthy person of the coming age cannot escape this scenario of money becoming helplessly useless in bringing the children back [home] or rejuvenating the old body. And this happens at the end of a lifetime devoted to amassing money. ... The very foundation of lifelong beliefs is wiped away.

Then, focusing on the spiritual needs of elders, he said:

> In today's world, spirituality is ... considered to be the twilight zone, bordering [on] the unknown. ... [However,] spirituality is the net profit earned in terms of happiness, when toils and efforts of an average life are deducted from the gross income of fame, money, and family. In times to come, this net profit will progressively diminish. ... The real profit would only be gained by an inward journey. And such a journey can only be profitably undertaken in a quiet and stress-less ambience.

Historical Perspective

by Prof. R. K. Varma

Prof. R. K. Varma, Head of the Department of Ancient History, Awadhesh Pratap Singh University, Rewa, traced the advent of the āśrama system, especially the birth of vānaprastha in civilized society and how it was lived. He said, "The problem of old age and the adjustment of elders in society has been the problem ... since time immemorial."

As civilized society grew, the family institution evolved, and once life expectancy increased, then began the problems of old age and social adjustment. He pointed out that, "In India, too, in the Ṛg Vedic period, old people were considered to be a burden,"[1] but then it was a society ridden with contradictions, and ancient thinkers were alive to this change in social order and devised remedial steps, he remarks later. As he explained:

> It was considered that each individual must fulfill his aspirations without inhibition in a regulated manner .... Thus, the system of āśrama-vyavasthā was devised during the later Vedic period.

[1] Vedic Index Part I, 351–352, referred to in pg. 5 of National Workshop printed report.

> This system regulated society and the life of the individual in a manner that eliminated conflict between young and old, father and son. It was a system in which each contributed to the welfare of society. In the beginning, there were only three āśramas — brahmacarya, gṛhastha, and vānaprastha. Vānaprastha and sannyāsa āśrama were kept together, but later, sannyāsa āśrama was separated from vānaprastha. This was considered necessary because it is very difficult to change the way of life all of a sudden.

Thus, we see that vānaprastha āśrama prepared the individual mentally and physically before sannyāsa, or total renunciation. Varma goes on to say:

> [E]ven after entering vānaprastha or sannyāsa āśrama, the elderly persons were part of the society. They acquired knowledge through tapas and acted as guiding guardians, besides working for their own salvation, or mokṣa. They moved from place to place, imparting the benefits of their realization, unmindful of their own comforts. They followed the highest ideals of *niṣkāma karma.*

And here, Varma makes an important point: "It was the duty of the gṛhastha to look after the elder's worldly needs."

Pointing to the joint-family system as one of the most important institutions that developed in ancient India, coming into existence in the Vedic period, Varma said:

> [These] joint-family system[s] provided security and a sense of wellbeing to young and old alike. ... It looked after the essential needs of each member of the family, and every member was supposed to work according to his capacity. The elders had a respectable place in the family system.

It was this family system that provided for the elder. And this, according to Varma, was why the problem of 'old age' insecurity was almost nonexistent. He adds, "They [elders], for their part, looked after the welfare of the family and spent time on the attainment of mokṣa."

Varma alludes to the breakdown of the joint-family system, which was both a unifier and a custodian of cultural values, as the cause of social problems. This would explain why the elder remains disintegrated.

Varma presented the psychological aspects of aging at the micro level of the elder, and the sociological aspects of aging at the collective macro-society level. Examining the aging process as one where the harmony between mind and body is disturbed, Varma says:

> The body [deteriorates] faster and the mind is not able to adjust with the changed conditions [of the body]. Thus, the conflict within starts and disbalances the harmony. Desires persist, which is the cause of all suffering. Buddha ... had preached the message of self-abnegation. Similarly, the other thinkers propounded the theory of detachment and niṣkāma karma, which can be practiced while living a normal life as a householder. Every individual nearing the age of retirement must prepare himself mentally .... But it is only possible if one remembers that the ultimate aim of one's life is mokṣa, and real happiness lies not in the pursuit of desire, but 'wantlessness.' Dharma, artha, kāma, mokṣa — these are the four puruṣārthas which complete one cycle. After having followed the trivarga [dharma, artha, and kāma], one should concentrate on the fourth, mokṣa, which can be attained through knowledge or unflinching devotion, with complete detachment. Standing at the crossroads, it is high time we pause and think about where lies the solution to old age — in materialism or in adhyātma (spirituality)?

Dr. Sajjan Singh, Managing Trustee, Chinmaya Seva Trust, Rewa, was the one at the helm of conducting the primary research during the first Rewa camp for the sixty rural elders. It was there that he saw the disturbing images of elder life and understood their struggles, and what CM Rewa could do for the vānaprastha movement.

Singh emphasized, "Health forms a major component of welfare awareness and upon it depends, to a large extent, the productive utilization of the elder population." Singh, a medical practitioner, knew the human body's response to different initiatives. He explained:

> The control and effects which the various endocrine glands (ductless glands) produced on the various physiological functions of the human systems was hailed as a major breakthrough in the field of medical research. Undoubtedly, it was so since it explained the many unexplained aspects of various diseases. However, the real controller ... would be in an ascending order ... the mind, the intellect, and finally Consciousness itself, which we refer to as the spiritual Spark within.
>
> Thus, the concept of a healthy mind as a precondition to a healthy body is being accepted by modern medical science. The applicability of this as a preventive measure for various medical and psychological maladjustments cannot be overemphasized.
>
> ... The mind is, at any given time, under the influence of the three moods (guṇas) — rājasika, tāmasika, and sāttvika — in different proportions. The mood of sāttvika, when predominant, gives us a peaceful, alert, and vigilant mind. The aim should be to achieve this by the various techniques (sādhanās) of karma yoga and meditation.

The aim of this [National] workshop is to create this awareness in the elders ... as well as [in others] ... since, if the process is started in ... adulthood, it will be smooth and ... effective. ... This approach is bound to be conducive to a productive utilization of the elders without any conflict or competition with the younger generation or society as such.

Changing Social Status and Role of Elders in Modern Society

by Prof. P. C. Khare

Whether the period after retirement is short or long, varies, depending on an individual's physical and mental degeneration — was the view of Prof. P. C. Khare, Principal of the Government Sanskrit College, Rewa. He said, "[P]reventive and curative [medicine], healthy environment, and rising standards of living ... [have shown that] people do not show signs of old age [until] seventy to seventy-two in developed countries."

That being so, some do continue to work, but this time of life also coincides, for many, with children being settled and key debts paid, so that one can devote this time to growing spiritually.

Khare pointed out that in pre-industrial societies, the joint family was an important social institution. Elders occupied a high status not just in the family but also in the community. Since it was a predominantly agrarian society, the elder "provided guidance in matters relating to ... cultivation, crops, and [treatment of] cattle diseases, and so on," and, as we know, often even in forecasts about the climate and rain.

In his paper, Prof. Khare emphasized that the elder's advice and opinion was sought during natural calamities, to settle property disputes (since land was a key family asset), as well as to exercise control over the conduct of family members in the community.

Another speaker, Prof. J. S. Rathore, in his paper on 'Ecological Perspectives in Welfare Awareness and Productive Utilization of the Elderly Component of Human Population' corroborating the latent values that Khare addressed, said that modern education lacked the singular ability to convey culture to children, which the elder of the past did with aplomb and least resistance from the young. Rathore also reiterated that, "Destruction of homely togetherness is perhaps the most serious ecological disaster." For in a society's pursuit of material growth, where development correlated with material acquisitions, the primary victim of neglect was the elder, who was both infirm and unproductive.

Such an elder, in the pre-industrialized era, had been valued as the epitome of good human values, while also being respected as the custodian of spiritual conduct.

Khare said, "In modern times due to advancement in medicine, healthy environment ... [and] rising standards of living, and so on, three main demographic trends have resulted: ... reduction in fertility rate, ... significant reduction in mortality rate, and ... increase in life span." He expressed the consequences of the changing demographics as a "ratio of active to dependent population."

Khare said:

> Old age dependency, which is the proportion of population above sixty years, has been increasing. ... [T]oday it presents a challenge before planners, medical, and social scientists. ... Old age should normally be the phase of life full of contentment, peace, and pleasure. [The] elderly ... expect complete freedom and facilities to enjoy their rest and leisure in the manner they like. ... [T]oday there are a few elderly ... in our society who feel emotionally happy, economically secure, and socially [content]. The twin process of industrialization and urbanization has rendered the joint family unworkable.

In contrast, Khare examined the urban nuclear family organization, which had no room for elders:

> They are no longer the heads of household [spanning] two or three generations. [Instead, they] feel ... neglected and no longer wanted, which affects their psychology adversely.

Such was the social change that damaged the status of the Indian elder. In the 1950s, the elder was a fountainhead of seniority, counsel, advice, and authority, and the object of love, respect, and care. But the twenty-first century presents a situation that is diametrically reversed. If anything, the elder is quiet and sad — and, as a result, unwell, too.

Khare also made a sharp observation about the workplace:

> Industrialization tends to decrease rather sharply the extent to which old people can take part in the economic life of society. Changes in technology, in work methods and techniques, are ... factors which account for the difficulties .... In modern societies, the emphasis is given to skill, energy, and physical fitness, resulting in the feeling that elders are useless.

In short, the social transformation of the elder, from a much revered and strong authority and guide of families, to one who had no role in modern family life, was the anvil of Khare's social perspective.

Aging — A Psychological Perspective

by Dr. Lal A. Singh

Dr. Lal A. Singh, Professor and Head of Department of Psychology, Awadhesh Pradap Singh University, Rewa, minced no words in his presentation. He said, "The term 'aged' evokes mostly [a] negative image in the

Western world, such as slow moving, unchanging, conservative, poor learner, uninteresting, rocking chair, decaying and dying person."

That 'old age' was pegged to the age of retirement (sixty or sixty-five) was seen by Dr. Singh as a faulty parameter. He said:

> The onset of 'aging' [based on chronology] has little to do with physical [health], social [evolution], or developmental base. A better assessment of 'aging' can be [based on psychology], with syndromes of change in feelings and attitudes, failing sensory-perceptual capacities, work efficiency level, decreased memory or intellect, loss of interest in things, and enhanced emotionality or involvement.
>
> The onset of aging may be at the age of forty-five years in one person of the same culture and group and at the age of seventy years in another.

Singh listed and elaborated on a variety of psychological issues related to aging — which he classified as 'normal aging,' 'abnormal aging,' and 'successful aging,' according to different psychological functions in different groups and cultures — and urged attention to them as pointers for underlying causes. To name some: psychosomatic disabilities, somatic-psychological disabilities (deteriorating mental functions due to organic changes); varying emotional states and their assessment and control; changes in sensory perceptions; cognitive changes in intellectual functioning and in work efficiency;

WHAT ONE THOUGHT CAN DO

Gurudev's initiative in 1981 opened the floodgates of research. The work of these thinkers and scholars at the National Workshop of Rewa are a valuable asset of Chinmaya Mission's vānaprastha teams.

personality problems (decreasing self-worth, regressive tendencies, self-preoccupied states, psychological shocks and their aftereffects); and problems triggered by organizations (caused by rapidly changing perception of success, growth, modernity, which distance the elder from younger, abler family members and consequent loss of psychological security).

The problems related to 'environmental psychology,' in situations where the elder must "exist in an environment largely planned by and for younger persons," are more pertinent to begin with. As society modernizes and technology takes over, older, familiar ways of working are replaced by new, unfamiliar methods that alienate the older generation if they are not included in the change. The call is for societies to be sensitive and inclusive of the elder.

WHY ME? WHY DON'T *YOU* AGE GRACEFULLY?

Some people complain that nowadays, no one follows values anyway, so why should I? Try; see if you can live such a life! But also be ready to pay the price when the time comes!

Values themselves have never lost their relevance in society. ... [E]veryone respects values — the only difference is that now most people respect values in others, but don't strive to live these values themselves. They want and expect to see values and virtues in others. They may be corrupt themselves, but they respect loyalty in others. Even the criminal wants only that accountant who is reliable and loyal!

– Swami Tejomayananda, *Graceful Aging*

IX

Prayāga's National Seminar

1999

The National Seminar on 'Multigenerational Relationship in the Indian Context,' which was held in Allahabad on November 20–21, 1999, was the result of the changing face of Indian society, especially the Indian family.

Change, Change Everywhere, but No Change Management. Change in one part of society invariably prompts change in another part of the same society. The industrial revolution that began in the late eighteenth century (first, as a series of small innovations and then continued steadily into the nineteenth and twentieth centuries) saw "a revolution which, at the same time, changed the whole of civil society" (Friedrich Engels). Significant among the changes were an increase in population, improvement in living conditions, followed by a series of industrial and agrarian revolutions, and consequently, healthcare also improved by the nineteenth century. This improvement was mostly in the form of reduced infant mortality rates, but as a consequence, there was an increase in child labor — a function of the fact that the entire population was inexperienced with the industrial system. What also gained currency was the migration of labor from the villages to the urban centers. As the young bodies were subjected to long working hours, neglect, violence, and low pay, they were exposed to untold dangers and developed industrial diseases. As a result, many died before the age of twenty-five.

At the dawn of the twentieth century, there was a steady exodus of workers, as young as sixteen or eighteen years of age, from villages into the urban cities. Some came under the pretext of higher education, but most migrated to work. Back in the villages, the homes got emptier, and with only the arduously slow postal system to depend on, there were no timely means to stay in touch with family. The erstwhile agrarian family now noticed a change in the family dynamics. Whereas earlier the father passed on farming to his son, now the son worked on machines in the city factories, and the father continued to till the land. He was unable to hand over his work to his son.

And the son? His city home was not even a home, just a corner of a room where the worker slept, hung up his clothes, and counted his daily wages. Happiness had been accorded a new definition: money. And this new definition came with an overwhelming weariness that dulled the mind: it grew impatient and gradually — unhappy as well. The migrant was working harder, eating poorer, and living a less fulfilled life; while initially he went home eagerly during vacations, gradually his visits home became infrequent and hurried. The parents who had aged by then noticed that, and the silence in their hearts became deafeningly loud.

That unfortunate trend was what Śrī Amitav Banerji — ex-Chief Justice, High Court Allahabad, and the President of the CVS course — also noticed. "It is contrary to the traditions, norms, and culture [of this country]," he said in his welcome address. What he had also sensed from his encounters with the attendees at the CVS course was the lack of care that elders were getting. If anything, neglect was rampant. This is especially visible in India, where respect and sensitivity for the elder citizen has not yet become a national concern. As a result, the elder grows more frightened with age, is unable to travel without help, and does not have even a dependable dial-in service that will attend to him in the event of criminal attack or health emergency.

With an increase in the population of elderly citizens, Banerji saw that the elder was between the devil and the deep sea — unnoticed by the government, neglected by the society, and inadequately cared for by the family system. It was clear to Banerji that the elder had to be liberated from his limiting idea that he was unable and incapable. It was equally clear that the consequences of neglect would damage the fabric of society irreparably.

A Society for All Ages. Sometimes, small aspects of life change. And these changes startle the world enough to have the United Nations (UN) discuss them. Demographers around the world would not have thought that medical science would change in such a way that living conditions and longevity would cause startling shifts in the proportion of young, old, and very old. After both world wars, as peace returned, so did optimism and a general sense of 'life is good.' Work progressed, and health received a lot of attention. By the 1960s, longevity was contributing to population increases. Around the world was a growing passion for bringing respect and attention to the situation of elders.

In 1982, the 'Vienna International Plan of Action on Aging' was adopted by the World Assembly of countries in Vienna,

VIENNA INTERNATIONAL PLAN OF ACTION ON AGING, 1982

Strengthen the capacities of governments and civil society to deal effectively with the aging populations, and to address the developmental potential and dependency needs of older persons.

Austria. The Vienna Plan, as it was sometimes called, was the first instrument to set the direction for global policy-making on aging. This plan brought minds together to formulate and take ownership of an issue that was poorly addressed until then — the aging population. And in doing so, the plan aimed to:

> Strengthen the capacities of governments and civil society to deal effectively with the aging populations, and to address the developmental potential and dependency needs of older persons.

That plan was adopted in the form of a resolution called 'The Proclamation on Aging' by the General Assembly of the UN in its 47th Session, October 1992. The General Assembly urged the international community to dedicate substantial resources toward this goal, and declared the year 1999 as the 'International Year of Older Persons' (IYOP). The declaration was made by Kofi Annan, the UN Secretary General at that time. The theme declared by the UN for the IYOP was 'Toward a Society for All Ages' — urging all segments of society to engage with each other, and calling for solidarity, respect, and exchanges between the generations.

First Gurudev, Then Vienna, Then a Flood of Thoughts. It began in 1981, when Gurudev earmarked a gift of land for a pitamaha sadan at Rewa, where elders would be cared for, respected, healed, and encouraged on a spiritual path. One year later, the UN adopted the 'Vienna Plan on Aging.' A gentle current had been set up. Even as the Rewa National Workshop of 1988 created a churn of feelings, a little further away, plans were afoot for the organization of a National Seminar on 'Multigenerational Relationships' at Prayāga. Historians, scientists, politicians, philosophers, economists, sociologists, and gerontologists came together to address the need for a sustainable solution for older persons in the times to come.

That seminar was held in Allahabad on November 20–21, 1999, where numerous erudite members of learned society spoke on the subject in the Indian context.

National Seminar — Much More Than That. The interesting feature of a seminar like this was the fact that these erudite minds were going to present observations about the same society of which they were a part. And seeing it from the inside, they also brought clarity about what they observed.

The Organizing Committee was chaired by G. Khare, the ex-Chairman of the Railway Board of India, who had just retired after serving this mammoth organization for thirty years. And on the very day that he returned to his home town, Allahabad, he ran into Amitav Banerji. Banerji, delighted at meeting an old friend, said, "Now that you are also back, come and work with me on Chinmaya Mission's work with elders." Khare did not even think twice. If something was good for Banerji, it was good for him, he reasoned. That was how he initially became involved in the CVS course, and then, in 1999, as the chairman of the National Seminar.

CCVS Central Chinmaya Vānaprastha Sansthan, had roped in institutions from Allahabad whose opinion would make a difference, such as Allahabad University; G. B. Pant Institute of Social Sciences (which became a part of Allahabad University in 2005); Allahabad Medical Association; and Allahabad Management Association. Their eminent spokespersons presented papers on topics such as:

- Role of religion and spirituality in aging gracefully
- Changing values and emerging trends in society
- National policies and societal support
- Comprehensive care of the elderly
- Research, education, and training of elders

PŪJYA GURUJI SWAMI TEJOMAYANANDA'S MESSAGE ON THE OCCASION OF THE NATIONAL SEMINAR

Human society is based on relationships, since man cannot live in total isolation. These relationships form the many units of society and are called families. Taking the life span of man into account, we find that generally there exist three generations together at a given time [in a family]. ... Relationships restrict every person's freedom to some extent, giving rise to conflicts at times. As such it becomes necessary to evolve a value system based on which the family members can live together in joy, peace, and harmony. Then alone the prosperity and happiness of the whole society is also assured. The importance of a value system should be recognized by all because, with the passage of time, a generation gap is created between any two generations that can create a major problem if not handled carefully. ... Various civilizations have tried in the past, and are still trying, to deal with the issue of multigenerational relationships. ...

... [I]n olden days, [the] relationship between parents and children was based on reverence, obedience, and discipline. Those virtues were more prominent than the demonstrative love and friendship which are observed in modern times. The reasons for this change in attitude could be smaller family units due to industrialization, urban living, and increased contact with Western countries, among other factors. Here, the question is not as to which attitude is right or better, but the important point is how to synthesize multigenerational relationships in a manner that will ensure harmony in family life. This issue will have to be examined and dealt with by all generations more seriously than is being done now. When two generations take rigid stands, then conflict is certain. Such a situation can be avoided by mutual understanding in a cordial atmosphere. This can be done. We can. We must.

The intention behind that seminar was to home in on the real issues, examine practicable ways forward, and then explore the means to implement them as well, with sustained enthusiasm. CCVS and its supporters were already circling one wish repeatedly: that the seminar vociferously place before the government and other well-meaning policy makers, the need to set up a national-level institution on gerontology for training and research, with special emphasis on happiness and contentment in old age.

In his presidential speech, Swami Tejomayananda asked a poignant question: "Is it possible that the elders present here, who have solved so many problems in their lives, are unable to solve their old age problems? Just as a student prepares ahead for a project or an exam, in the same way, one ought to prepare for old age before its onset. And, just as Brahma (the God of Creation), faced the relentless demands of creation stoically, we, too, can keep Nārāyaṇa in the forefront of all thought and action!"

National Seminar — Graceful Aging and the Governance. An initiative so huge would reap results only if backed by the government, felt the speakers, and this reflected in each section they addressed.

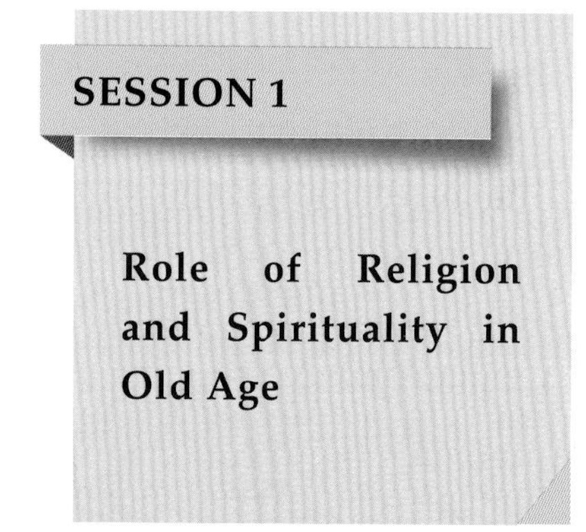

The response to this section was tremendous as many papers were sought to be included. In his paper 'Spirituality — the Basis for a Quality Life,' Dr. Sajjan Singh, a medical practitioner, leaned on Vedānta as his foundation, and sought to establish that improvement in the quality of life calls for every relationship to be based on one common factor — spirituality.

Dr. Ramjee Lal, Reader in Psychology from Kushinagar, presented 'Vipassana Meditation' as a means to remedy sociopsychological problems. Vipassana meditation, he held, enables one to banish likes and dislikes, the cause of inner agitations. This naturally leads to a happier state of being, he proposed.

> Older persons who are victims of abuse are not likely to discuss it with those outside the family, as they are very often dependent on those who abuse them.
>
> *– Anupriyo Mallick at the National Seminar*

Akbar Husain and Nazli Pervez of Aligarh Muslim University, explained several meditation techniques for healthy aging and alleviating psychological, emotional, and physical problems. Pervez stated that meditation brings the individual closer to God, and the experience of a better life is the concurrent result.

SESSION 2

Changing Values and Emerging Trends

Dr. H. S. Vidyarthi, former Head of the Department of Education, Degree College, Soharatgarh, wondered if advancement in education, urbanization, and modernization were throttling the softer values such as respect, care, and sensitivity, and rendering the young incapable of nurturing ways to deal with age-related situations.

Elder Abuse: Dr. Anupriyo Mallick examined 'Elder Abuse in Family: Strategies for Prevention and Intervention.' Mallick defined elder abuse as "nonaccidental act or omission which undermines the life, the physical or psychological integrity of an elder or that which harms the development of his personality or undermines or damages his financial security." His view was that more than one kind of abuse usually coexists in every case.

Interestingly, Mallick points out that the nature of abuse varies according to the stage of development of the country. The nature of abuse he encountered in India was physical — food deprivation and financial abuse (wresting away an elder's wealth by cunning). For instance, in a bid to have early access to an elderly mother's wealth, greedy children were known to declare her mentally unstable and then seek to institutionalize her. Sadly, the law allows wealth to be passed on to the next generation when the elder is declared mentally incompetent.

> The condition and status of elders, as it presents in any society, is deeply rooted in the view that the young hold of the old.
>
> *– D. S. Baghel*

Perception of Elders: In his paper titled 'Youth Perception of Elders,' D. S. Baghel's observations are as poignant as they are eloquent in expression. In one simple summary, Baghel says: "Once, mortality rates were high and consequently the number of people reaching old age was very few. As a result, those who did manage to live till old age were revered, seen as worthy of respect and held a special status in society. With increasing life spans and hence more people living into their seventies, it was likely that the view of the young toward the old was changing." In this context, Baghel pronounced yet another stunning statement: "The condition and status of elders, as it presents in any society, is deeply rooted in the view that the young [or those not so old] hold of the old. This does speak volumes for the prevailing angst that elders the world over feel.

Baghel conducted a survey of 447 people between the ages of twenty and forty; among them, 64 were from the rural parts of Rewa and 383 from urban Rewa. He administered to them a questionnaire of ten questions that pointedly addressed their perception of elders, such as: Elders are a burden on family; eldercare is the responsibility of the government; shelters should be provided for elders outside the home; elders are of no use to society; the advice of elders should or should not be considered; and so on.

Considering the wide disparity in the sample sizes, the numbers do not conclusively confirm that there are emerging rural and urban differences. But both groups show similar skews in their views and to nearly the same extent. What is noteworthy is the disparity in the percentages in the category of urban and rural respondents who were 'Not Sure.' For example, while 75 percent of rural respondents AGREED that elders were NOT a burden and should not be in old age homes, 55 percent of urban respondents also AGREED but 21 percent were unsure. This points to a confusion or uncertainty among the urban population under age forty in regard to the values presented in the questionnaire.

As early as 1999, Baghel had mooted the idea of using media to canvass respect for elders and urged that sociology and family welfare be introduced into the school curriculum.

It must be reiterated that the research done by the scholars and thinkers who presented papers at the National Seminar would not have come to light had not Gurudev sown the seed of the need for eldercare. This is why we call him a visionary!

Retire, Not Tire — Road to Rural Renaissance: Dr. T. Karunakaran, Vice Chancellor, Mahatma Gandhi Gramodaya Vishwavidyalaya, Chitrakoot, made one of the most interesting observations that working people should contemplate. He said that the new millennium would see, even in the first decade, "tens of thousands of planners, technocrats, scientists, administrators, and professionals like doctors, lawyers, and educationists, retiring but not tiring."

Such resourceful people, he said, "... would retire with a feeling that, during the period of their service, they could not deliver their best to fulfill the needs of the nation." He continued, "Such immense resources would sadly waste away, 'settled' in some urban colony, counting rosaries, playing cards, or entangled in some petty family problem."

Karunakaran had echoed what many others were thinking back in 1999. And those were the kind of minds present at the National Seminar; they represented the unspent forces wanting to make a difference.

In the new millennium, more professionals will retire but not tire. And these people will regret that they could not give their best to the nation.

Can the nation enable this resourceful gray bank to nationalize itself and help catalyze the much needed rural renaissance?

Karunakaran placed before the august audience this question: *Can the nation enable this resourceful 'gray' bank to nationalize itself and help catalyze the much needed rural renaissance?*

The brain drain of rural India had taken place when the rural youth had begun to rapidly migrate to the cities. The cities educated and empowered many of those erstwhile rural citizens, but forgot to return to rural India some of the gains of urbanization. Karunakaran was calling for a reconstruction of rural India — to return to its villages what was lost owing to government apathy and lack of professional help.

The resources needed to empower and enable the elder community lay sadly unused and Karunkaran was calling for a renaissance by elders, for elders!

ELDER ABUSE

A WEAKENING OF SOCIAL PRESSURE TO CARE FOR ONE'S RELATIVES

Dr. Anupriyo Mallick presented four theoretical perspectives of elder abuse:

- Psychopathology: Abuse occurs due to pathological behavioral problems inherent in the abuser.
- Interpersonal Relationships: Lack of trust or mutually respectful relationship is lacking between the elder and his/her spouse and/or children.
- Social Learning Theory: Abusive behavior is a recurring phenomenon within the family. Replication occurs as a result of observed conditioning.
- Situational/Environmental Stress: Examples include accommodation problems, nonavailability of social-care facilities and health assistance (Eckley and Vilakazi, 1995).

An important reason that Mallick attributes to the prevailing situation in countries like India, which are socially bereft of administrative order or policy, is *'weakening of social pressure to care for one's relatives.'* Mallick also observed, "Financial and psychological abuse seem to be far more prevalent than physical abuse [in India]. One of the reasons why physical abuse is rare is because age is still venerated, and societal pressure against individuals who abuse their parents or other elders is strong."

There was a time when social life revolved around family. Social life comprised festivals, weddings, and various ceremonies that were designed for recreation. In the last thirty years, the social scenario has changed in India. Recreation in the new millennium now involves movies, TV dinners, vacations, parties, and weekend getaways. The social infrastructure has not evolved commensurate with lifestyle changes [thereby creating hurdles for the young on whom the elder is dependent]. Nonavailability of social-care facilities and on-call health assistance also lead to environmental stresses on a young person, who is no more able to sustain both a career and eldercare.

The frustration and stress on young people is thus a function of the absence of dependable social infrastructure. And social changes have led to changes in tradition, for instance, the disappearing norm of a 'live-at-home daughter-in-law' who cares for the elders, for she is now pursuing a career. Families caught in this situation struggle a lot with change.

Education of Elderly — Role of Family, Society, and Nation: In his paper 'Multigenerational Relationships: Indian Context,' Dr. R. N. Kapoor, Director General, CCVS, emphasized that even if there was a National Council for Older Persons, the role of family and society could not be taken away. He regretted the fact that India, despite her rich heritage and tradition of care and respect for elders, has done nothing for elder welfare. But the setting up of the National Policy for Older Persons (NPOP) (1999) has in fact mandated the welfare of older people in the Constitution of India (Article 41) and by the Directive Principles of State Policy.

Kapoor then went on to recommend incorporating 'education of the elderly' as a national policy since he felt it imperative to make the steadily increasing elder community skilled and capable of reentering the mainstream workplace. An elder's key problem was inactivity, both physical and mental. Dr. Kapoor was of the opinion that elders should be involved in social services (which Karunakaran had also suggested) so that their learning and experience could be properly utilized in social welfare programs. He also stressed the need for the establishment of geriatric centers in hospitals which would treat the problems pertaining to the physical and mental health of the elderly.

> Old age can be creative or self-destructive, it is your choice to decide. Old age need not be painful and death may not be frightening; it is possible to learn in the days of retirement.
>
> – *Swami Chinmayananda*

Mental Health and Reorientation Programs: Dr. Sajjan Singh, a medical practitioner and a sevak of the pitamaha sadan activities at Rewa, had seen during all his research that the society's perception of elders was negative — an observation he brought out in his paper. This had also been corroborated by the research of Dr. Anupriyo Mallick (see earlier), who had said that the lives of rural elders deteriorated as their young did not live with them anymore.

Echoing Kapoor's idea of elder education, Singh suggested orientation programs in personal economics, psychology, sociology, spiritual philosophy, and yoga, which formed the core areas of influence in the lives of elders. Singh's focus was on mental health, which, he felt, was the key to wellbeing among the elderly.

Age and Wisdom: Dr. R. S. Singh, a Professor of Psychology, Awadhesh Pratap Singh University, Rewa, presented 'Educating the Aged: Conceptual Orientation and Design Fundamentals.' Singh revisited the concept of aging and elaborately redefined that aging was a process that was not degenerative but developmental in nature. He outlined the lifelong developmental perspective and presented the findings of a number of psychological research studies on short-term and long-term memory, intellectual capacity, and creative abilities related to age; he pointed out that the elderly had a number of abilities that were their strengths. In that context, he differentiated between intelligence and wisdom, and said that if someday a wisdom scale was developed, the aged would be found to often score higher than the younger adults.

Blind Faith, Illiteracy, and Correlation to Women's Health: Dr. Neena Kohli of the Department of Psychology, Allahabad University, presented a compelling argument for rural education and the need for an intelligent approach to self-care. Kohli had conducted a study of elderly rural women suffering from cervical cancer. On the basis of causal-attribution analysis of the problem, she had observed that 'faith in God' and 'karma' had led to a certain turning away from robust medical assistance, which had compounded health problems in women. Kohli's findings made a great case for Dr. T. Karunakaran's (see 'Retire, Not Tire') suggestion to pool the intelligence of retired elders and channelize that into rural education and development.

The thinkers and scholars of Allahabad had given the National Seminar of CCVS their best. Their research, conducted as a prelude to the papers they presented at the seminar, had brought into hard focus what would otherwise not be known. Gurudev has kick-started the current generation to stand up and take notice.

Rural Illiterate. Prof. R. M. Tripathi of the Govind Vallabh Pant Institute of Social Sciences, Allahabad, put forth a proposal for a research study with special emphasis on the problems of the rural elderly who often form an illiterate, powerless group. His paper highlighted and tied in with the research findings of both Dr. Neena Kohli and Dr. Sajjan Singh.

The members of the vānaprastha team of Prayāga were not simply presenting papers. They had sought direction from the thinkers of

Allahabad, and their research findings would provide direction for CCVS's future work with elders.

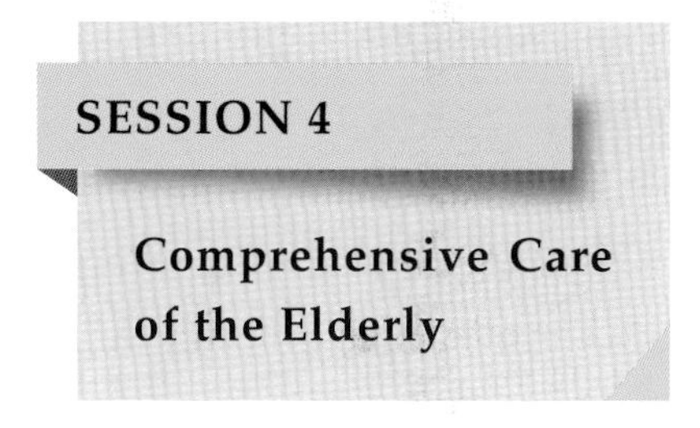

The fourth session discussed the need for early recognition of symptoms of geriatric illnesses as well as the need for preventive care. With advancing age, a person's emotional needs and inner thought patterns influence his wellbeing. Dr. Vinod Kumar underscored the current lack of preventive care and emphasized the need for the elderly to take personal responsibility for such care.

The session reinforced what Karunakaran, Neena Kohli, and Sajjan Singh had said earlier. Every speaker underscored the fact that the elder is capable, is efficient, and as R. S. Singh said, "has a number of abilities that show his or her strength ... that the elder's wisdom alone would guide him onward." All these bring new meaning to Lord Kṛṣṇa's immortal words in the *Gītā:* "Lift yourself by your own Self alone." (*Bhagavad-gītā* 6:5)

Naturally, therefore, an emphasis on diet came next. Speaking on the 'Medical and Health Problems of Elderly,' Dr. D. K. Nigam, Professor of Medicine, Motilal Nehru Medical College, Allahabad, emphasized the need to modify the components of diet as a person ages. He also spoke of group fitness regimens as being valuable for psychological health. Nigam stressed that non-cognizance of the elders' medical needs was responsible for many of their health problems. Hence, timely attention was the means to a healthy immune system.

Dr. R. C. Gupta, another participant, held that aging was not to be merely measured on the basis of physical age, because a lot also depended on mental age. An important parameter of aging is the degree of independence, the sense of an inner free spirit. Gupta's exhortation was especially inspiring: "Be an asset to the family, convert yourself into an asset, have 'healthy' stress instead of 'harmful' stress." Gupta spoke about making careful choices in foods, rather than the mindless and reckless ones.

Adding to that aspect, Dr. J. P. Singh presented the view that spiritual wellbeing was a part of being healthy. Misery, he said, leads to dislikes, which is detrimental to good health. Singh felt that care, respect, and tradition had to be ingrained in childhood. For a healthy tradition to evolve in families — love for children should coexist with respect for elders.

WHY THE PERCENTAGE OF UNMARRIED WIDOWS IS THREE TIMES THAT OF WIDOWERS:

- Statistically, women die later than their husbands, because they often marry men older by several years.
- Widows are restricted from remarrying.
- Women tend to live longer than men.

Dr. Indrani Chakravarty, President, Calcutta Metropolitan Institute of Gerontology, presented a paper on 'Improving the Quality of Life of Elderly Population' in the context of the roles of voluntary organizations in Kolkata. Chakravarty declared that the assumption that the family in developing countries will continue to look after its elders was no more valid. In India, respect, love, and support of the aged were advocated in the scriptures, and demanded by tradition. As a result, there were no formal services outside of a family for eldercare. When the reality of survival demands that both partners work, the gaping hole left by a system without eldercare support is startling. Hence, Chakravarty's paper urged that the role of voluntary organizations should be actively encouraged.

The last paper of the session by Śrī S. K. Mehrotra addressed depression among the aged — its causes and cures. To present this topic cohesively, he described the layers of personality within a human being and showed how each layer had experiences unique to its nature — an idea derived from Vedānta.

SESSION 5

Comprehensive Care

As we leave the physical dimension of aging and look at the mind, we see the issues grow complex and beg for even more attention.

Triple Neglect and the 'Widow' Label. India's traditions, while laudable, have sometimes also become roadblocks as its stakeholders struggle to negotiate them in the face of material progress, which makes its own demands. Dr. T. M. Dak presented, among other things, the vulnerability of old persons in India, with particular reference to aging widows and their needs.

The state of women in India has almost always been subservient and subordinate to the men, especially in the rural areas. Consequently, the plight of a woman, after she loses her husband, is cause for concern. Therefore, Dr. Dak focused on the woes of elderly widows.

The presence of the word 'widow' in our vocabulary, points to the social baggage we continue to carry. 'Widow' does not merely

TRIPLE NEGLECT NUMBERS

An unusual piece of data for 1991 says that there were 14.8 million widowed women compared to 4.5 million widowed men in India. Widowed women + 'never married' and divorced women accounted for 67 percent of all women in the above-sixty age group. Corresponding data for widowed men: 20 percent of men in the above-sixty age group. (Ramana, 1992) cast the woman behind a closed door; it also intellectually handicaps the rest of society from being able to break down the label and reach the woman (behind the label). And this is really at the heart of the suffering of a significant section of society: the elderly woman without a husband.

A core derivative from Dak's research pointed to the triple neglect that women in this category experience (see box 'Triple Neglect Numbers'). Recognizing this, the NPOP urged special attention to elderly 'widowed' women. Dak's research made clear that, in the Indian context, the elderly woman was more handicapped than her male counterpart for another set of three reasons, which the NPOP *did not* list:

- An elderly woman tended to be among the least literate.
- Traditionally, a woman stayed at home, and, as a result, on losing her husband, she was inept in dealing with the world.
- Such a woman was expected to be looked after by her son; women without sons were therefore severely disadvantaged.

Partnering the Elder in Eldercare — Recognizing Social Changes: Dr. Amar Nath Rai, Reader in Psychology, Ghazipur, talked about the psycho-social wellbeing of the elderly; about caregiving through partnership between older people; and about the community service arrangements. He said that the elderly, their families, and the community make a triad in which the family and community should complement each other in care-giving functions.

Rai draws attention to a pertinent question which is startling and disturbing. While aging demanded care similar to the early years of life, why has aging become a thorny issue in modern times? Because of sociological changes in the roles of housewives. Contrasted with earlier times when the housewife doubled as a caregiver, in modern times, she had a career outside the home, and hence was unable to extend herself further.

The questions raised by Kapoor, Karunakaran, Kohli, and Mallick earlier, can be heard in Rai's rhetorics that ask about the role of the government in creating care systems for elders. Rai's suggestion was to encourage the elder to actively participate in some community-level activities, whereby he can be less dependent, and enjoy the benefits of day-care through such participation. Rai's paper also showed a deep sensitivity toward the caregiver and the demands that modern times makes on the caregiver, for he said, "We need a model of day-care services (for the elderly) which gives respite to the family."

Post-Retirement Period and Loss of Power and Authority in the Indian Family: A unique dimension was addressed by Prof. A. L. Srivastava and Dr. U. K. Singh of Varanasi when they directed the spotlight on the changing equations in family relationships in relation to the aged member.

Clearly, owing to the dynamic changes in social norms, in work-life composition, in education, in the response of the individual to the demands of a career, and to lifestyle changes in general, the role of elders has become mostly redundant, so that they find themselves being gradually stripped of their authority and position in decision making. To a large extent, this is a function of rapid technological innovations that have put decisions in the hands of the younger generation. After a lifetime of being consulted on every decision, the new order has made the elder 'unneeded' and hence 'unheeded.'

Singh and Srivastava studied a sample of 300 elderly persons who had retired from their jobs and were living with their families. The results indicated that the aged were consulted mainly during settlement of marriages, and in times of crises and economic setbacks — matters mostly traditional — but not in matters of children's education, career choices, or changes and even choices of residences.

The majority of the interviewed elders reported loss of authority, status, and prestige. Importantly, they experienced a sense of being marginalized.

SESSION 6

National Policies and Societal Support

The national seminar continued to throw the spotlight on the delay and neglect in the formulation of a policy for the elderly. Several speakers highlighted the causes behind the steep rise in some of the numbers — such as a higher number of single women above the age of sixty as a function of resistance to widow remarriage; or the rise of helplessness among the rural elders due to the lack of infrastructure and administration. What was poignant was that a policy on eldercare was drafted in 1986, but formulated only thirteen years later, in 1999!

One speaker, Mr. R. N. Kapoor, observed that the joys of longevity were far outweighed by the problems that the elderly faced — and it was heart-wrenching to see that a longer life may likely be the cause for angst. And in that light, Kapoor placed before the audience the rising quotient of care in Europe, America, Canada, China, and Japan, while India had not even begun to formulate any method of eldercare. [The Policy itself had taken thirteen years to be announced.] Kapoor talked about China as a stunning example of committed eldercare across 40,000 towns and villages. China even had hospital beds solely reserved for elders! Above all, one thousand colleges and a large number of third-age universities in China researched, trained, and educated elders.

Kapoor's suggestion to the University Grants Commission (UGC) was that it should organize workshops as well as centers of gerontology. The work was too enormous for the government to manage alone, he reasoned. CCVS's role in creating a revolution in eldercare would go a long way he felt. In short, policy needed to reflect a responsive attitude to eldercare, and it was a pity that the necessity to care for elders was not naturally felt.

In retrospect, from the research of that National Seminar to the efforts of the present era, it is clear that we need a revolutionary change in perception and attitudes. It is hoped that every Chinmaya Mission member will introduce an attitude change in eldercare in his and her environment. Even more, it is hoped that the CCVS will have the continued support to take eldercare forward across the globe.

WORSHIP THE LORD

Perform your vrata (vows) as worship of the Lord. In the *Gītā* (18.46), Bhagavān says that man can attain perfection simply by worshiping the Lord through his karmas. It is not any specific, or special karma, whatever karma you are capable of, whichever is enjoined to you, whichever is your duty, do it as your worship of the Lord. This is the greatest blessing in gṛhasthāśrama. From here, one slowly proceeds into vānaprasthāśrama.

– Swami Tejomayananda, *Graceful Aging*

X

The Course on the Art of Graceful Aging

One of the reasons that seems to have inspired Shiv Swarup and Sajjan Singh appears to have been their conviction that society, in abandoning its old ways, was verily hacking its own feet; for an unhappy, neglected older community meant that its experience, counsel, and guidance were becoming lost to the younger society, who stood unanchored and risked being misguided.

The thought-provoking papers presented at the National Seminar, Prayāga (Chapter IX), revealed how a neglectful social system had made more complex relationships, living conditions, attitudes, and beliefs surrounding eldercare and support. Even the government had neglected to set up an infrastructure, or care system, for the elders left behind by the youth, who the government had co-opted for the progress of the cities. Many elderly parents had to redefine life — that is, pursue careers well after retirement just in order to find relevance in their seventies and beyond, thus dragging gṛhasthāśrama into later years. Many pointed to the blurring of spirituality in education.

The social structure had changed and it was time to accept that change. It was also time to lead the elders back to school — a school for graceful aging. It was time to bring back spirituality into lifestyles, as without that, people were ill-equipped to face the world. The angst of the elder was essentially his utter spiritual despondency.

Progress had resulted in better lifestyles, but that had come with a price — of some separation, some rearrangement, and a lot of hard work. The migration to cities, continuous transfers both within the country and outside it, drawn-out educational needs, demands on time by job and career, and other stressors tended to keep the younger adults very preoccupied, agitated, and detached from or unmindful of family goals.

Given the rapidity of change, while the young would need the elder's guiding hand, the elder himself needed to find the path not taken — the path toward his or her own Self-realization.

The ideal that elders follow and showcase is what the maturing adults will emulate. They should see their elders as cheerful, happy, satisfied, and nurtured by their spiritual study and orientation. That would sharply emphasize the relevance and value of their spiritual heritage, a heritage that was built to weather every social situation. Importantly, it would urge and encourage those heading into their fifties to plan for the next stage of their lives, as a relevant stage to plan for.

This was the intention behind the vānaprasthāśrama. In the West, the thought is packaged in a developing science called gerontology. In India, the ṛṣis created the āśramas and structured a human's life to fall into a logical system. The ṛṣis tailored the third āśrama, vānaprastha, for those who had accomplished their goals as householders. That stage came with a redefined purpose.

The call to enter vānaprastha was now verily a call to return to discipline and self-inquiry. And the way toward that was through spiritual discipline.

Both at Rewa and Mandhana, the experience had been that many elders arrived at ages between sixty-five and seventy, stripped of their erstwhile labels, positions, and designations. They had no career, no continuing purpose, no health, no wealth, no spirit, and no joy.

Dissipated and unable to hold themselves together, they only wanted a corner where they could end their days peacefully.

Singh and Shiv Swarup held on to Gurudev's guidelines — '[create] the right environment for study and growth and empower them to lift themselves up.' They would create the vehicle to transport such elders into a more wholesome way of life.

Why the Stalk Grew So Tall. Guruji once said at a spiritual camp that a person has a sense of anticipation at every stage of his life. When in school, he looks forward to getting into college; in college, he waits to gain a higher degree; while doing his Master's program, he is enthused about a new job and the growth prospects. Then he plans marriage, then a family, and then ... it is a never-ending flight into the future.

▲ *Swami Prashantananda teaching elders in Rewa*

That flight was never intended to end when a person turned sixty. The flight was meant for exhausting his desires, plans, wants, needs, and dreams. Once worldly responsibilities were fulfilled, it was time to enter a new university, with readiness to commit to self-inquiry and advance on the path toward realization of the pure Self.

And what is the path toward realization of one's pure Self? Exactly all that which his pursuits were *not* until then. After watching a thrilling cricket match from 9 A.M. till 6 P.M., a spectator boards the bus to go home. Though he is unable to disconnect from the excitement and joy of the match, sitting in the stadium is not the way forward. Sitting by the curbside and lamenting his fate is also not the way forward. He needs to move on after the game. Similarly, to hold on to the joy of gṛhasthāśrama is futile; one has to happily board the bus to truly 'go home.'

Those who take to living a spiritual life from a young age come to embrace vānaprastha naturally. Such people see life's struggles as experiences needed to exhaust vāsanās. Once the vāsanās have loosened their grip, such adults welcome subtler and deeper introspection.

However, for those who reach vānaprastha unprepared or less prepared, a course has been designed to help take the first baby steps. It is called the 'Course on the Art of Graceful Aging' (CAGA).[1] How this came about is explained in the following paragraphs.

One of the roles that elders need to play in their third age is that of role models for the young to emulate. Elders therefore need to become exemplary vānaprasthis, by being stalwart students of Advaita Vedānta. Wearing their peace and calm as shining badges of wisdom and masterful acceptance, such elders can become role models for young adults who, at the peak of their struggles, begin to understand why they encounter the experiences they confront and look forward to qualifying for the third age.

Without a robust third-age community, our maturing society has no hope of being continually energized. What our parents were to each of us individually, the vānaprasthis are to society collectively. The CAGA is an effort toward this end.

The Course Architect. Śrī Amitava Banerji had proposed that the CVS should become an institute for the onward education and evolution of people choosing to enter their sixties in a planned, structured manner. Both Banerji and Shiv Swarup Agrawal requested Swami Shankarananda to design such a course.

[1] This has come to be referred to as the CCVS Course, as it is the course offered by CCVS.

Swami Shankarananda used Śrī Ādi Śaṅkarācārya's *Sādhanā-pañcakam* as the fundamental blueprint for vānaprasthāśrama, and he used these lessons to design the curriculum of the Vṛdhāvasthā Samadhan Śibir, a camp that was first held at Rewa in 1985. *Sādhanā Pañcakam* is an essential guide to spiritual unfoldment and mindful living. Thirty-four of those forty steps, in particular, are duties to be performed during the vānaprastha and sannyāsa stages. It must have been well liked by the camp participants, for soon, the course content became the blueprint for the 'Course on the Art of Graceful Aging' (CAGA).

The CAGA was planned by Swami Shankarananda with a view to urge the elders to pick themselves up through sādhanā, to understand Gurudev's vision for them, and then reach a height from where they could be guides and teachers for Bala Vihars, Yuva Kendras, and Study Groups.

▲ *Dr. Sajjan Singh speaking at 'Art of Graceful Aging' Camp at Allahabad*

Swamiji created four different courses — Basic, Preparatory, Advanced, and a fourth unique one, Research. Swamiji was of the view that no elder initiative was sustainable without continuous research. He wanted students to take up research in Indian gerontology based on Vedic scriptures, after factoring in research input from sociology and modern psychology. He wanted to present this back to society as a continuous learning, so that caring for elders would come to be seen as a part of right living.

The Course. Various centers of Chinmaya Mission across the length and breadth of India came to hear of participants' appreciation of the course and wanted to hold CAGA camps. As the Course began to touch lives and leave deep impressions, all 200 centers in India began to establish CVS centers in their towns; their prime desire was to serve and bring together the elders in their towns to adopt the way of life as indicated by the course, hence Gurudev. To facilitate working people, the four-day course was made into a seven-day course with classes conducted after office hours.

Prevailing programs for elders had mostly sought to solve physical and psychological problems, whereas, what was needed was that the elderly recast their attitudes toward themselves, their families, and the society. No doubt the elders did need help and none of the existing infrastructure catered to them. But the elders also needed to bear in mind that looking after personal wellbeing, growth, and spiritual evolution was their unfinished duty in the third age.

Every stage enjoins a duty upon us to accomplish specific objectives. Until the late sixties, the prime aim of many is monetary gain. But once we have reveled in material gains and relationships, we need to step away from the external and examine our inner world to find our real identity. In fact, that is the expectation and purpose of human birth. The scriptures say clearly that having taken a human birth, if man does not realize his inner Self, such a human life is a waste.

Naturally, therefore, the vānaprasthāśrama is the time dedicated to the field of spiritual awakening through an in-depth study and practice of Vedānta. The CAGA, which now came to be called the CCVS course, is structured to bring elders closer to spirituality in the third

▾ *Dr. Sajjan Singh addressing the 'Art of Graceful Aging' Camp Sikkim*

age through study, service, and activities that will help them develop a vision for their new life of detachment. Keeping in mind other age-related needs — such as health, financial planning, psychological, and social problems — other modules are included in the CCVS. Some highlights of the course are:

- **Physical Health:** The value of physical wellbeing and the need to keep fit at all times is emphasized by the curriculum, which includes yoga to enable mind and body wellness. Further, there are talks on wellness by representatives of medical schools, both traditional and contemporary, to enable elders to understand their own role in wellness management, which is a very important part of self-discipline.

  In the context of 'yoga,' it will be appropriate to quote Gurudev from his commentary on the *Kaṭhopaniṣad*: "[T]oday, it [yoga] has a meaning of exertion of disciplined activity of the body; and with reference to the mind, concentration or control through meditation. Śaṅkara therefore ... says, 'Yoga is deep meditation with thoughts withdrawn from external objects.'"

  For vānaprasthis, this definition needs to be the driver, for it implies discipline of the senses to begin with so that the mind itself is reined in.

- **Financial planning for old age:** The purpose here is to guide, or point to the need for, sensible financial discipline, including planning investments, gifts, and donations, and satisfying medical needs.

- **Social relations in old age:** Elders experience social abandonment partly because of a change in their roles and responsibilities, partly owing to a changed self-perception, and partly due to a distorted perception of elders by younger adults. This module helps the elders understand their position in a changing society and see themselves in a new light — as guides and friends, as the custodians of values, and hence as the conveyors of scriptural wealth to the younger generation.

OLD Definition of Health by WHO

Health is a state of complete physical, mental, and social wellbeing and not merely the absence of disease or infirmity.

– World Health Organization

The module addresses the usually experienced loneliness and sense of abandonment felt by elders, while providing tips for feeling useful, assuming duties, sharing roles, and propagating the protection of the ecology and the environment.

NEW Definition of Health

Health is a dynamic state of complete physical, mental, **SPIRITUAL** and social wellbeing and not merely the absence of disease or infirmity.

– World Health Organization

- **Psychology:** This segment lays bare the changes that the mind struggles with in advancing age. Drawing from Advaita, this module discusses the role of the guṇas, the karma theory, and the need to work with the inner personality.
- **Spirituality:** Dr. Bisht, Director General of Health (Health Ministry), Government of India, gently objected to the WHO definition of health, saying, "If health was defined only by satisfaction and happiness at the physical, social, and mental levels, then even a pack of wolves have all three. Then, what differentiated human health and animal health?" Dr. Bisht asserted that human beings have an X factor that motivates the physical, mental, and social dimensions, and that 'X' is the spiritual dimension.

Other dissents, too, poured in. Various regions sent in their papers on the spiritual dimension, whereafter a resolution was tabled in the 37th World Health Assembly, and it was this that brought about an amendment to WHO's definition of health and its Constitution as well.

The spirituality segment of the course covers the entire spectrum of an individual's life, addressing his evolutionary needs and how they manifest at times as problems, which he might mistakenly seek to solve with material means. 'Spiritual means' should not be mistaken for rituals, but as a path using logic and reason born of analysis and thought. Some disciplines are introduced, methods are suggested for group learning, and the group dynamics become a great enabler of learning.

A NOTE ON SPIRITUALITY IN THE CONTEXT OF CCVS COURSE

Different people wear their age differently. Some are usually energetic and enthusiastic, but on the day they retire they tumble into a sense of decline. Some also believe that age results in definite decline in physical and mental wellbeing. Especially in India, age presents itself differently in different socioeconomic classes.

Among the affluent, the advancing years lead more to a decline in physical wellbeing, because their younger days often were not invested in fitness. Hence, this segment is likely to incur illnesses caused by either indulgence or negligence (of fitness). This is aggravated by an emotional void caused by grown-up children leaving home. As Swami Prashantananda of CM Rewa says, "It is a time of dread and angst!"

"Among the middle and lower sections in India," says Swami Prashantananda, "declining physical health leads to reduced earning potential as well as additional medical costs; so, overall, a decline in financial comfort." But emotionally, they are not bereft of family love and care as families in this strata tend to be better bonded. But financial comfort does not restore depleting happiness. "The person comes to realize that money, too, has a limited capacity to give happiness," says Swami Prashantananda.

Also typical of the third age is the pain of losing social relevance and of separation from the very children for whom the elder toiled. Sometimes, the mind deludes and causes the elder to blame their children for their sorry state. Even so, all the money or family attention can bring back neither the past 'joy' nor inner resolution. Swami Prashantananda identifies the precise condition of the prospect: "A person arrives at the vānaprastha stage of life, having lived half a century or more, during which money was made, family was established, and a respectful place was earned in society. But there remains a nagging sense of wanting something more."

What is the inner peace one seeks at that age? One seeks a state of no agitations inside, a state of no regret, no yearning, no pain, no loneliness, and no inner chatter that says, "I worked so hard for a rainy day; here is that rainy day, but my investments cannot remove the agitations!" And this is made worse if physical health is not as robust as it used to be.

The first big difficulty that elders face is managing and dealing with change — change in physical health, mental peace, intellectual drought, and financial strain for those with minimum savings. This is accentuated by a non-understanding of what it is that is changing — not seeing that the One who has been witnessing such change is essentially Changeless. And that is why the CAGA urges and draws the elders to strive toward their changeless Self. While the prescribed format of self-control, prayer, and meditation may be unsavory to begin with, CAGA approaches the spiritual acclimation very gently, yet meaningfully. It is to be reiterated that CAGA helps those who have not engaged in any *spiritual sādhanā* or study.

Targeting the Understanding. Somewhere in all the confusing jargon that we encounter, two words buzz relentlessly — Self and ego. Often, we use the word 'self' when we mean 'ego.'

In their paper 'Improving Mental Health and Quality of Life through the Art of Graceful Aging' (by R. S. Singh, Sajjan Singh, and D. S. Baghel), the authors explain how a person can move away from ego and toward the Self and thus be liberated and attain peace:

> Self is of the nature of freedom, love, and pure Consciousness. All the forces that move us toward the Self are the absolute tendencies of the Self that move in the universe. Ego is the fountain of all the tendencies arising from a sense of separateness and man's indulgence in worldly desires, pain and pleasure, gain or loss. It refers to the preoccupation with 'I' and 'mine.'

And, connecting their research to Vedānta, the authors urge the increase of the role of the Absolute in our lives; to exit the ego in a structured manner and move toward realization of the Self.

Particularly focusing on the vānaprastha stage of man, the authors said that this is mostly the time when a human being moves into self-inquiry — *The objective is acquisition of detachment (vairāgya) from selfish strivings and unconditional attachment with selfless service to the society. Gerontologists may call this the Indian way of differential disengagement.* (Singh, Singh, and Baghel). The elder then begins to detach from the worldly, including the dependence on the ego.

Therefore, the underpinnings of the CAGA course are: Indian spiritual thought, the āśrama system of life management, and related theoretical ideas.

SWAMI SHANKARANANDA

Pratap Chandra Shukla came to the Chinmaya Mission in 1967 when he was forty-one years old. He was from a pious family, given to devotion and worship. An M.A. in Philosophy from D.A.V. College Kanpur, a Gold Medalist as well, Shukla was a professor and taught the *Gītā* at the college. He had a printing press of his own with which he later printed many Hindi books for Chinmaya Mission.

In 1967, when Gurudev came to Kanpur for a *Gītā* Jñāna Yajña, Shukla saw the road taking a turn. Gurudev taught *Gītā* chapter 3 and *Bhaja Govindam*. Shukla experienced a change. After the Jñāna Yajña he was made a Study Group sevak. Thereafter, his life gained acceleration. He had always been spiritually inclined and this was just a returning to his essence, as it were. He began to spend time translating many of the Mission's English texts into Hindi, and even wrote commentaries in Hindi on spiritual texts, like *Pañcadaśi, Maṇiratnamālā,* and so on. For Shukla was a good writer, with fine language skills. Ten years later, in 1977, Shukla's wife Uma passed away. He now turned inward even more, completely surrendered to Gurudev and the Mission.

In 1984, when the Bankhandeshwar Temple Trust property was given to Chinmaya Mission, Shukla looked after the temple and the property. For Shukla, this was opportune, combined with the silence the place proffered and his own reverence and dedication to Gurudev, which he put to the best use for two years, translating and printing Mission books.

On October 26, 1986, Gurudev gave sannyāsa dīkṣā to Shukla at the Jagadeeshwara Temple, Sandeepany Sadhanalaya, Mumbai. He was the first person to be given sannyāsa dīkṣā directly from gṛhasthāśrama. He was now Swami Shankarananda.

In 1991, Swami Shankarananda, his elder sister Smt. Mohini Devi and two others came to live at the Mandhana Bankhandeshwar Temple complex. Gradually, the pitamaha sadan began to evolve at Mandhana. The rest of his work has been mentioned in several places in this book. Swami Shankarananda was the key architect of the vānaprastha camps, including outlining the course, ideating on it, and writing the texts for it.

PROCESS TO PARAMATMA

Graceful aging doesn't happen in a few days, weeks or months. It is a long process, but if followed, its rewards are great indeed. In childhood there is śikṣā learning discipline with values. In youth and adulthood, there is dīkṣā with living with right thinking. And in old age, there is living with dispassion and scriptural study.

Then we come to life's most beautiful stage, its culmination — sannyāsa (renouncing the world and revelling in the Self).

Since early life focuses on studies and adult life on fulfilling various responsibilities, people feel they have less time to practice spiritual disciplines. In vānaprasthāśrama, seventy five percent of one's time is to be devoted to sādhanā and twenty five percent to worldly interactions. But in sannyāsa, hundred percent of one's time should be only for Paramātma smaraṇam.

– Swami Tejomayananda, *Graceful Aging*

XI

So Then, Why Vānaprastha?

The Dis-ease of Dissatisfaction

Gurudev began teaching Vedānta in early 1951. Since then, his following grew to include the very young, the young, the not-so-young, the old, and the very old. For each, all he wanted was the bliss of unbroken happiness. So, he committed himself to bring to everyone the teachings of Vedānta, and as he gathered, groomed, and guided his followers during his incessant tours across the world, many of the elders silently glided into the shade of his august self, basking there in his love and guidance.

But not every elder had the means to reach out to Gurudev, who had begun to see the changes in society, and had recognized that elders everywhere needed to anchor themselves. Many who had not prepared for this stage of life struggled with change. He, therefore, went about creating small centers of care and love, where the extremely old could take shelter and yet stay on the lap of Vedānta.

Those who were growing with the knowledge of Vedānta would find their way, but many elders had not been introduced to Vedānta, and they were restless, unhappy, and dissatisfied.

An Overwhelming Sense of Dis-satisfaction. But even so, why *vānaprastha*? many wondered. Why should there be a change of status on attaining age sixty-five?

A simple, yet revealing, reply came from Swami Prashantananda (Rao Saheb Ran Bahadur Singh), Head of Chinmaya Mission Rewa, when asked what he had seen among the elders as being the problems of old age. "An overwhelming sense of dissatisfaction," he said briefly.

▲ **Sidhbari 1983:** *Gurudev's kuṭiyā. Sw. Prashantananda at the feet of Gurudev. His wife is behind Gurudev*

Dissatisfaction with what?

Said Swami Prashantananda, "Sometimes you do what you think needs to be done. But the next second will demand something more that has to be done. And soon, you are unable to stop! You are forced to come to terms with your intellect's verdict that your life is lacking. And, off you go, doing that, and — bingo! — another lurking lack or deficiency will unravel!"

Very well then, how is this dissatisfaction different from what a thirty-year-old feels? "In the response of the heart," replies Swami Prashantananda. "For a thirty-year-old, the dissatisfaction holds the key to new challenges and improvements. But a seventy-year-old *knows* action is not the answer. The dissatisfaction is now a disease. The attacks come every now and then."

So, if at the vānaprastha stage of life this thought is examined scientifically, then the light shows at the end of the tunnel. *But at seventy or seventy-five, is a person prepared to hear this?* "Not all of them," says Swami Prashantananda.

Then where does the resistance come from?

"That resistance is called the lack of a subtle, discriminating intelligence," Swamiji clarifies. He further explains, "This discriminating quality develops only in a person who has done selfless service for others. Until then, the power of discrimination shall not come, cannot come. And if the intellect is not able to discriminate, then the subtle point of wanting to overcome discontentment can never be grasped. It is possible that deep in their hearts such elders are dissatisfied, but it is equally possible that they do not *know* that they are dissatisfied! And vānaprastha has the capacity to uncover a remedy for that deep-seated, unknown sense of dissatisfaction, which does not leave a person unless he becomes educated in this regard."

And in what words will you explain to this person the nature of this dissatisfaction whereby this person is willing to stop pursuing satisfaction and start thinking about it?

"That is when the role of Vedānta unravels," says Swami Prashantananda. "And Vedānta categorically declares that once you become aware of the futility of this continuous effort at finding satisfaction in the world outside, and you turn your attention to the world inside you, with the proper guidance of the vānaprastha way of life, the error in the idea that 'satisfaction lies in things and beings outside me,' becomes apparent."

Swami Prashantananda continues: "Vedānta tells us that experiences exhaust vāsanās and cauterize desires; so, in youth, we are not stopped from desiring or seeking. But experiences toss us to a high, then a low — then a high again — and thereby we begin to understand the nature of saṁsāra. This is why we do not ask even a forty-five-year-old to stop pursuing desire, because he or she is still on the learning curve." He points out that the āśramas of life are also designed with this in mind.

"Why did the King in the old days leave everything and withdraw to the forest?" he asks. "Because he became aware of the nature of that dissatisfaction!"

Closer to our time, Bill Gates and Warren Buffet became aware of the danger of largesse, a sibling of dissatisfaction. They have long since shifted gears and their wealth has found great occupation in public good. In fact, Bill and Melinda Gates made a breathtaking statement in

April 2014: *Why giving away our wealth has been the most satisfying thing we've done* (TED Talks, March 2014). Simply, the Gates had been looking at poverty even before they married and had asked themselves, "Does it have to be like this?" That is when they agreed that the wealth that had come from Microsoft would be given back to society — through their Global Health and Development Programs and their Global Policy Advocacy Programs. In June 2006, at the age of fifty-two, Bill Gates announced that he would be transitioning from full-time work at Microsoft to work with his Foundation on global issues.

On the other hand, the Hindu scriptures present the woes of the many who succumbed to pleasure, reluctant to exit gṛhasthāśrama, like King Yayati who wanted to remain young and enjoy ever more pleasures of life. The older he grew, the more he wanted, and he finally exchanged his old age with his youngest son Puru. But after a thousand years, he realized the con-game of desire and said:

> Craving for sense-pleasures is not removed but aggravated by indulgence, even as ghee poured into fire increases it. ... One who aspires for peace and happiness should instantly renounce craving and seek that which neither grows old nor ceases even when the body ages.

Yayati then gave back the youth to Puru, and took back his old age. Renouncing the world, he retired into a forest and attained liberation through his spiritual practices. *Śrīmad Bhāgavatam,* Canto 9, Chapter 18.

Śrīmad Bhāgavatam is full of inspiring stories of kings who lived in a value-based manner so that, when the time came, they easily handed over their kingship and moved to study and self-inquiry. But if we study the lives of some of them closely, we see that in each āśrama, they acted according to the prescriptions of that āśrama. As did King Parīkṣit, Arjuna's grandson: When only seven days remained of his life and there was no time to practice vānaprasthāśrama, he chose to listen to the *Bhāgavatam* from Sage Śuka Maharaj and thus attained liberation.

However, our world today is fraught with restlessness and dissatisfaction, and hence a mental state that is not ready for self-inquiry.

Perversity of Illusion. This very sense of dissatisfaction was emphasized by our Parama-Guru Swami Tapovanam when he declared desires to be of the nature of bondage. Swami Tapovanam cautioned that home, family, and wealth are what tie a man to this world. Man thinks he is free, but, in fact, he experiences no freedom.

Is it then wrong to owe allegiance to family, spouse, and offspring? The family is the anchor the gṛhastha builds for his own sake, to enjoy saṁsāra and exhaust vāsanās, and to pay his debt to society. Having done that, he is now expected to cut the cords of attachment and enter vānaprastha, unencumbered.

Of 'attachment,' Swami Tapovanam says:

> All demoniac dispositions stem from this attachment. Leave off attachment, and all such dispositions at once vanish. Desire, anger, covetousness, pride, jealousy, spite, sorrow, fear, and so on, have their origin in attachment. It is the false attribution of beauty to objects that leads to mental attachment. One can get out of this attachment by cultivating discrimination and by practice. So long as the mind remains extrovert, there will be attachment, but spiritual practices will gradually help a person to develop the spirit of all-round detachment.

Recognizing man's slavery to attachment, Swami Tapovanam quotes Śrī Ādi Śaṅkarācārya's *Bhaja Govindam* (verse 15):

> Strength has left the old man's body; his head has become bald, his gums toothless, and he is leaning on crutches. Even then, the attachment is strong and he clings firmly to fruitless hope.

▲ *Swami Tapovanji Maharaj*

So Swami Tapovanam elaborates:

> Even in extreme old age, when the body is in a state of dissolution, man clings to it as if it were still young and healthy and full of vigor; thus aiming at pleasure and eagerly longing for the prolongation of life, man goes on revolving in the endless circle of saṁsāra.
>
> – *Tapovan Prasad*, December 2006

The Inevitability. So, how is vānaprastha the antidote to attachment? Why do we need to consciously adopt (and enter) vānaprastha?

Different masters have said different things on vānaprastha, but each one has homed in on attachment as the main obstacle to liberation, and has identified desire as being the adhesive that strengthens attachment. Since both attachment and desire dominate gṛhasthāśrama, we need to enter the realm of vānaprastha to shed this 'dis-ease.'

In 2011, at the 'Living in Meditation Camp' at CIF in Kerala, Pūjya Guruji said, "We (individuals) have to live with material things, with living beings, with so many experiences, with a lot of inconsistencies and uncertainties, so that there is not a moment when something is not happening."

But the worst, he said, is living with the inevitability of old age. To drive home the point, he gave an infallible explanation: "While infancy comes and goes, youth comes and goes, old age *does not go!* Worse, not only does it stay, but everyone only gets older and older! So we need to know how to deal with this!" Guruji added, "Truth is also that, as we grow older, we will have fewer people willing to be patient with us. But if we have met our true Self, we will be well anchored."

So, pinpointing the cause of elders' disillusionment, Swami Prashantananda exposed the overwhelming sense of dissatisfaction unleashed by dormant desire. Swami Tapovanam warned about desires stemming from the 'perversity of illusion,' and Guruji underscored the inevitability of old age.

The Birth of Faith — Swami Abhedananda, Ācārya, CM South Africa. Swami Abhedananda says:

> Vānaprastha is not merely 'going to the forest,' but it is the graduation in the conviction of the intellect, which echoes the principle of discrimination that has often been said to elude man. In gṛhasthāśrama, a person has the conviction that a life of enjoyments, living with family, or performing duties for the near and dear can give us joy and fulfillment. However, with the various experiences in life, this conviction crumbles. Then faith enters the mind, so that a person starts seeking detachment, freedom from sensual joy, and the company of saints. Most importantly, the intellect feels the importance of duty toward God alone.
>
> This conviction or faith is the birth of vānaprastha vṛtti (the thought or thought pattern conducive to vānaprastha). Yes, an external āśrama setting and the quietude of forest life could facilitate this vṛtti. This state of mind could come at an earlier age as well, and that is why the scriptures say, *yadahareva virajet tadahareva pravrajet.* (the day one experiences dispassion, the same day one should leave all worldly duties).

▶ *Swami Abhedananda*

The Decision to Detach — Pūjya Guruji Swami Tejomayananda. In some cases, the desire to detach is experienced on arriving at vānaprastha. Hence, the entry into vānaprastha should be a deliberate action, because it is here that the 'art of leaving' is learned.

Knowing this to be the purpose of vānaprastha, Guruji instructs, "Do not come armed with plans and portfolios. Allow vānaprastha to teach you." And teach it does, the art of letting go, the art of leaving all that we hold onto.

And Guruji includes the obsession with body, health, and restoration. To those who complain of aches and pains, he asks, "What else did you expect at seventy-five?" Guruji says this is to be expected in the third quarter of life, hence subsistence-level care is logical, but care that is obsessive, he says, "let go."

Vānaprastha is where we commit ourselves to serve for the greater good, service that is selfless. And it is service that purifies the mind, and a purified mind is all that we can take with us. To illustrate this, Guruji tells the story of Duni Chand, who was very wealthy and also miserly. Giving him a needle, Sikh Guru, Nanakji said, "You please take care of this, and when we meet in heaven, I will take it from you." Duni Chand was surprised, "I can't take this needle with me, can I?" Nanakji replied, "Ah, so then, when you can't take along a simple needle, how do you expect to take your money and wealth? Everything is going to be left here. Neither would you have enjoyed it, nor are you letting others enjoy it!"

What we do take away with us is our mind, says Guruji, and selfless work purifies the mind.

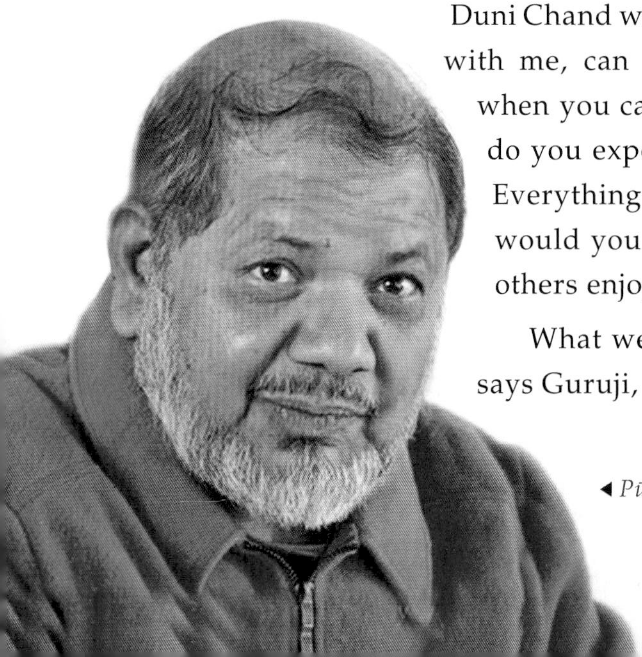

◂ *Pūjya Guruji Swami Tejomayananda*

O*r, What Modernity Calls Third Age.* As Guruji had once said, from childhood we can graduate to youth, from youth to adulthood, and from adulthood to maturity, to being an elder. From there, no more doors lead out. There are no more categories left. We only get older and older.

And, as we get older, it does become imperative to find answers to questions such as, "Who am I? Where did I come from? What is my relationship with this world? What is this world?"

REDEFINING HDL AND LDL

In a talk he gave at a camp, Guruji in his characteristic style asked seekers to increase the readings on these: Highly Divine Life and Living a Divine Life!

And this is the new university we enter at sixty or sixty-five, joyfully, leaving behind all that we did the first six decades of life, now seriously committing ourselves to the yoga (union) of ourselves with the Yogīśa, Śrī Nārāyaṇa Himself.

Different regions of the world handle or approach this third age from different standpoints, depending on their cultural leanings. For example, in the U.K., owing mainly to poor employment conditions, availability of jobs reduces as a person grows older, so that people above age forty are considered disadvantaged.

Depending on cultural SWOTs (strengths, weaknesses, opportunities, and threats), a country or a region will seek to build strengths that are commensurate with its own need gaps. So, where age is a discriminator or limiting factor, the region will work toward setting that right. Other cultures see the end of working life as a phase where the individual is no more bound by social expectations or duties. And then there is the Vedānta culture that continuously reminds us of who we are while also rejecting as false ('neti, neti!') our identity as this or that.

The Chinmaya Mission, as one such spiritual community to whose Guru-paramparā we owe allegiance, has thus been shepherding us on the path of Vedānta. Hence, at age sixty, we arrive — not depleted or disadvantaged or devalued, but victorious, valorous, and valuable as resources who will on the wings of Vedānta step onto the next course of action — rebuilding our identity with our Creator. We then realize that "I am not this husband or wife, son or daughter, father or mother, worker or breadwinner anymore." And when these labels are peeled off, "I am .... Who am I?"

Again and again, authors and commentators direct older people to "find meaningful activity after retirement." But when we arrive into our sixties, after six decades during which attachment is glorified, permanency is lauded, accumulating is the way of living, love is defined and conditional, what do we do with this baggage? Finding 'meaningful activity' can only be more of the same, as this is the only meaning we have known.

> We come fresh to the different stages of life, and in each of them we are quite inexperienced, no matter how old we are.
>
> – Francois de la Rochefoucauld (1613–1680)

For different cultures, the definition of age is aligned with their viewpoint and experience. While third age sounds nice and covers what is called 'post-retirement years up to eighty,' it has also been credited with "positive aspects of aging," to quote Stephen Barnes, a professor at San Diego University, "including relative good health and social engagement, functional reserve capacity, knowledge and expertise, and considerable adaptive flexibility in daily living." Vedānta would say that is fine as far as the BMI (body, mind, intellect) goes; but those are your tools, your equipment for experiencing the world; those are not you! And given that they are matter, they will decline. But you are Brahman, and you need to attain your legacy before your equipment declines. Hence, vānaprastha.

And vānaprastha sets us on the path of Self-realization, and enables the journey beyond the BMI, beyond our instruments, to know our real Nature — the reason for our human birth.

Thus Declares Vedānta. The Vedas term the third age as vānaprastha and assert that elders enter that doorway to know their real identity. That was what Guruji meant when he said that elders don't want just caring and concern. They want empowerment to move on toward the Goal. And that was what Gurudev meant when he asked the Chinmaya Seva Trust Rewa to apply itself to the moral and spiritual resurrection of society.

How glorious is Vedānta! Whereas the fourth age in other cultures is described as the period of acute decline, including 'cognitive decline,' Vedānta's fourth age, which comes after the spiritual momentum gained in vānaprastha, is the period of intense ascent on the ladder of internal growth. Called 'sannyāsa,' it is the age of continuous cognition of the supreme Reality consequent to an intense inner letting go of the identification with the BMI and a total surrender to the Supreme. It is a state where the individual, as trustee of the Lord, serves humankind, serves the society, and serves the needy — including the spiritually needy. And such a status is what an elder can grow into, thanks to vānaprastha, during which phase elders train

REMOVING REBIRTH

ā-brahma-bhuvanāl lokāh
punar āvartino 'rjuna
mām upetya tu kaunteya
punar janma na vidyate

Worlds up to the 'World-of-Brahmaji' are subject to rebirth, O Arjuna; but he who reaches Me, O Kaunteya, has no rebirth.

– *Bhagavad-gītā* 8.15

toward a life of service and surrender to the Higher. Vedānta lauds the sannyāsī elder and needs him for the spiritual resurrection (and renaissance) of society, as Gurudev had envisioned.

VĀNAPRASTHA — FOR PREPARING THE MIND

What is the purpose of human life? We know that human life is not meant only for sense pleasure; for, if that was the case, we would not be blessed with an intellect. Man's life is not meant only for living at sense level. The purpose of man's life is to discover and realize the highest Truth, the supreme absolute Truth which is one's own Self. That Truth, if it is to be realized, can be attained only through Knowledge. And for that Knowledge to be attained, the mind should be pure and single-pointed. If the mind is impure and distracted, there is no question, Knowledge will not take place.

– Swami Tejomayananda in his talks on *Rāmacharitmānas*

XII

The Way They Lived

We are scaffolded by a long history of great lives that seamlessly moved into vānaprastha. The *Śrīmad Bhāgavatam,* the *Rāmāyaṇa,* and the *Mahābhārata* are replete with examples of gṛhasthās — kings, ministers, and even laity — who approached vānaprastha naturally, without the tug of gṛhasthāśrama.

Here is how they lived.

The Message of the Gray Hair. Kalidasa, the historic Indian poet and dramatist, in his *Raghuvaṁśam,* a Sanskrit masterpiece about the Raghu dynasty in which Śrī Rāma was born, alludes to a poignant moment in the life of King Daśaratha (father of Rāma) of Ayodhyā. One day the King, while grooming, spotted what seemingly was his first gray hair, which whispered into his ear, "Let Rāma be crowned!" (12:2) Kalidasa says that was old age under the guise of gray hair that whispered to King Daśaratha.

In the old days, human beings used simple indicators to make their next move, such as the flight of birds at dusk pointing to the sunset.

So, too, King Daśaratha, on seeing the gray hair, was alerted to his advancing age, which he had not noticed amid his work. Thereafter, King Daśaratha lost no time in planning his succession.

In presenting this very episode in the Ayodhyākāṇḍa of his *Tulsi Rāmāyaṇa,* Goswami Tulsidas talks about the glory and greatness of King Daśaratha of Ayodhyā: "Every monarch sought his favor, even the guardians of the world cultivated his friendship and respected his wishes." Sant Tulsidas adds, "In all the three spheres of the universe, and in all time, none could be found so abundantly blessed as Daśaratha."

At the height of such a glorious career, and then with Lord Rāma Himself as his firstborn, we see how the King treated the advent of his third stage of life. There he was, looking into a mirror and adjusting the crown on his head, when the great King noticed the gray strand of hair. Sant Tulsidas personifies the gray hair as being old age whispering to the King: *"Make Rāma your regent and thereby realize the goal of your birth and life in this world."*

In that portrayal of the King's encounter with a strand of his gray hair, Sant Tulsidas reminds us of the purpose of our birth and the objective of our lives. The King did not tuck the errant hair behind his ear and carry on with business as usual. He went to his Guru Vāsiṣṭha, and with great happiness — not with regret or a sense of doom — he said that everything had gone smoothly until then by Lord Śiva's blessings, and that the only longing of his heart was crowning Rāma as King. "Then I will not mind if my body survives or not, *so that I may not have to repent (my inaction) afterward."*

King Daśaratha had voluntarily announced his vānaprastha. This came from the recognition of his varṇa-based dharma, from the recognition of his duty to the kingdom, to society, to his gṛhasthāśrama. And when his ministers echoed his sentiments and praised his plan to coronate Rāma, Daśaratha did not feel devalued. He was doing what was expected. To make way for the next generation, too, was his duty; and his progeny and people would watch and learn, as he had watched and learned from his predecessors in the Raghu dynasty.

That day, in the royal court, King Daśaratha announced his wish to anoint Śrī Rāma as King.

Manu and Śatarūpa. The life of Swayambhu Manu and his wife Śatarūpa offers another example of graceful entry into old age. They were considered peerless in God's creation. Manu and Śatarūpa had three children — the famous King Uttanapada, father of the even more famed Dhruva; Priyavrata, much praised in the Vedas; and daughter Devahūti, who married Kardama Muni and to whom the Lord Himself was born as Sage Kapila.

Manu ruled for a long period and followed the Lord's scriptural commandments with perfect commitment. Yet, one day, he brooded over his continued relish for pleasures and thought, "I have reached the fourth stage of my life [reference is to his old age] while I am still living as a householder; but I have not yet lost my relish for the pleasures of the senses." And Manu felt very sad that his life had been wasted without devotion to Śrīhari.

With his children grown up and settled, and after he himself had ruled for so many years, Manu willingly assigned the throne to his son and departed for the forest of Naimiṣāraṇya with Śatarūpa.

Manu, Maslow, and Modernity — Understanding the Elderly. Many thousand years later came a man named Abraham Maslow (1908–1970), who gave economists the famed pyramid of human needs. The first, or basic four, are physiological needs, need for safety, need for acceptance, and need for self-esteem. If those four are not met, human beings feel uncomfortable and will remain driven to fulfill them. But of the last four needs — the need for knowledge, beauty, self-actualization, and transcendence — human beings never get enough, and their quest for more of these will keep motivating them. Maslow also said that a need motivates only when the earlier needs (called 'lower-level needs') have been met. This unique principle is found in the prescriptions for vānaprastha, which says that an inefficient gṛhasthāśrama becomes a hurdle to success in vānaprastha.

The higher four needs in Maslow's view were not based on the lack of something but on a need to grow, evolve, and reach one's potential. Maslow said human beings have the need to increase knowledge and intelligence — to probe, explore, discover, know, and understand the world better. The aesthetic need assumes that human beings have an inherent need for beauty and aesthetics, for closeness to nature. That need then drives them toward self-actualization.

According to Maslow, self-actualization corresponds to ultimate psychological health.[1] But other expansions and explanations are found, which suggest 'fulfillment of the highest needs; those for meaning in life, in particular.' In one place it is also described as: 'It refers to the person's desire for self-fulfillment, namely, to the tendency for him to become actualized in what he is potentially.'

Clearly, Maslow was grappling with defining self-actualization. Thus, he came to refer to another stage that he called 'transcendence.' Likely, he divided self-actualization into the attainment of one's potential and the fulfillment of spiritual needs. Whereas it has been seen how professional successes and the gratifications they bring are viewed by many as the ultimate satisfaction to be attained — and may remain so as part of the human quest, Maslow must have felt that the realization of one's potential was not enough for reaching self-actualization.

This is where Vedānta steps in to tell the seeker (of self-actualization): stop the excessive pursuit (of self-actualization), as such a process is endless. It will create desires which trap a person in a vicious circle. Because desires come supported by vāsanās and

---

[1] 'A Cognitive-Systemic Reconstruction of Maslow's Theory of Self-Actualization' by *Francis Heylighen*

action, this triad is a roller coaster that does not stop. Such pursuit will, as Swami Prashantananda says, lead to an overwhelming sense of dissatisfaction and a frustrating hopelessness, which cause one to pursue desire without end. The content of desire may change, but desire as a disease would remain.

Maslow's work has been underestimated and even oversimplified to explain only man's lower needs as these connect with economic theory. However, four decades of his writings on the concept of self-actualization points to his deeper probing into the needs of man.

> So many left their royal comforts to search for the Lord. For each of them, this was a continuum of life, the road to be taken.

When self-actualization as proposed by Maslow remains as an objective, desires will remain, just as India's ṛṣis and Masters have said. It is clearly the state of being unfulfilled that motivates man to seek fulfillment. While pure economists direct this desire for fulfillment toward career growth, material gratification (hence, growth of economy), and secular excellence, Maslow, had he lived longer, may have explored his idea of transcendence further.

Maslow grappled with one question: "Why don't more people self-actualize if their basic needs are met?" Vedānta would have told him that where there is desire there is greed and a burst of additional desires. That is why Pūjya Guruji advises, "Once you are done with gṛhasthāśrama, develop the 'Art of Leaving' — letting go."

Vedānta works at a causative level and asks us, instead, to work at nipping the roots of desire. And so one can return to trusting Vedānta and the reasons for the āśramas, in which prevention is favored over cure. All the cognitive decline and physical deterioration in the elderly is preempted when vānaprastha is adopted as a discipline.

And that is how they lived in the old days ....

THE POSTER-PASTER OF MADRAS

YASHWANT T. TARKAS

Śrī Yashwant T. Tarkas was a founding member of CM Chennai and worked relentlessly for Gurudev's vision and mission. Gurudev called him his 'silent worker.' In his younger days, he was known to have accompanied Gurudev on his bicycle, pasting posters for yajñas. At age seventy-one, Śrī Yashwant wished to enroll at Sandeepany Mumbai to study Vedānta. But his wife was not wholly comfortable with the idea. Oftentimes, gṛhasthāśrama poses this challenge, and the ability to carry family along with grace is itself titikṣā that Vedānta teaches the gṛhastha. This letter from Gurudev is in reply to that situation:

Chennai, Oct 1987
Śrī Y. T. Tarkas/169, Vellala street/Madras 600007

Hariom! Hariom! Hariom! Salutations!

Spend much more time in study, reflection, japa, and meditation — both of you!! All other responsibilities Lord has shifted from your shoulders. Spend time in satsangs to take in fresh ideas, and to give out what you know. ...

The session was great this time and the teamwork of your Sevaks was such a beautiful thing to watch.

The temple in Thamaraipakam will come up in a year's time. All His Grace alone.

Love – Chinmayananda

▾ *Yashwant T. Tarkas, a commitment too deep, too sweet*

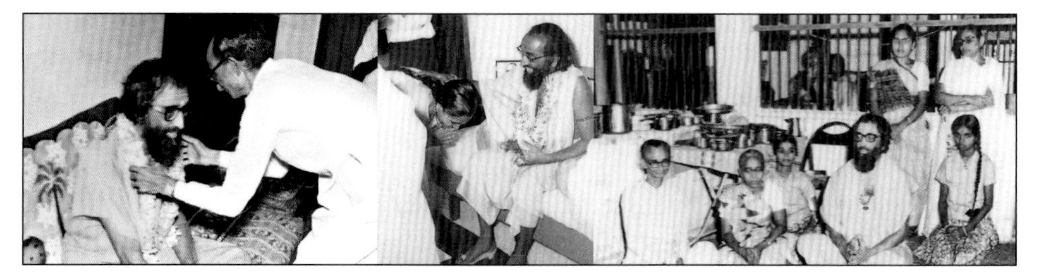

And he did just that and so diligently. Yashwant dedicated his vānaprastha years to sādhanā, swādhyāy and sevā — including sevā at home. During the day he would visit some Gujarati medium schools and teach Gīta chanting. He would also conduct some study classes in the evenings. He spent a lot of time helping with organizing yajñas for Ācaryas like Swamini Vimalananda, Swamini Premananda (she attained samadhi) as well as in raising funds for Mission work.

Śrī Yashwant was the grandfather of our Swami Swatmananda, Ācarya CM Mumbai.

Lessons from Elders in the Śrīmad Bhāgavatam. The stories of the lives of great vānaprasthis are as varied as there are types of human beings. We can draw from each story unique lessons for our own lives.

In narrating excerpts from these stories, the intention is to show the natural human disposition in the more evolved yugas. In modern times, it is not even gṛhasthāśrama that binds us; it is the peripheral pastimes that society has created to entertain the jīva. In stark contrast, in the stories of the *Bhāgavatam*, we read about great kings and small kings alike seamlessly exiting gṛhasthāśrama, relinquishing kingship, and entering vānaprastha with the anticipation and joy of accepting a new mission. Many of these kings were guided by the teachings of their gurus. So many left their royal comforts to search for the Lord. *For each of them, this was a continuum of life, the road to be taken.*

Those kings were all in the prime of their success and glory, some far younger than sixty years of age. How did they do it? And almost none of them were wasted, decrepit, invalid, incapable, ailing, or abandoned when they stepped down. Pūjya Guruji describes their status thus: *"These kings and monarchs gave up the world, as prescribed, before the world gave them up."* This is why none of them reached the stage of being physically and mentally wasted.

Dhṛtarāṣṭra's Dilemma. The epic *Mahābhārata* describes a poignant situation in which Vidura, the youngest brother, advises his older brother King Dhṛtarāṣṭra, the blind King of the Kuru dynasty, on vānaprastha. Two brothers torn apart by war and family circumstances!

When the war between the Pāṇḍavas and Kauravas had become inevitable, Vidura had left the Kuru palace and gone away on a pilgrimage to restore his pained mind. During that time, he had met the sage Maitreya, who conferred on him the supreme Truth. Vidura, fulfilled and enlightened, returned home to Hastinapur. The Kurus were very happy to have the wise Vidura back.

While Vidura shared anecdotes from his pilgrimage with the clan, he devoted all his attention to the spiritual instruction of his oldest brother, Dhṛtarāṣṭra — blind at birth, lost in life, and defeated in war.

The Pāṇḍava brothers, who had been mistreated by Dhṛtarāṣṭra, had won back their lawful kingdom; happiness returned, and there was all-round prosperity. The *Bhāgavatam* says: "Many years thus passed unnoticed, as it happens with people attached to home and family and grown heedless because of engrossment in their worldly affairs. None indeed can overcome the sway of time."

Vidura had been observing Dhṛtarāṣṭra and his condition ever since the war ended. The blind king had been given respectful refuge in the palace by the very Pāṇḍavas whom he had wronged. Addressing his brother, Vidura said one day (1:13:18–29):

> O King! Bad times are ahead! Leave home and possessions, and come away to the forest. Death approaches all of us finally. If men have to abandon their very life-breath, so dear to them, at a

> moment's notice, then what to speak of other coveted things like wealth and possessions? Look at yourself. Father, brothers, sons, and their friends have all been killed. You are far advanced in age, and even the hair on your body has grayed. You are living now in another man's house supported by him.
>
> How much you cling to life .... Today, you live at the mercy of the same nephews whom you once connived to kill, set fire to their house, poisoned them, humiliated their wives, your own daughters-in-law, usurped their kingdom, wealth, and self-respect!
>
> Now you are pitiably clinging to your body, with intense desire to keep it alive, but it is getting worn by Nature's process of aging!

Thereafter, Vidura showed his older brother what path he really needed to be on. Having quoted the scriptures on that, he said, "Instill the Lord in your heart, leave home armed with renunciation and self-control born of discrimination. This is wisdom."

Great must have been Vidura's entreaty, for Dhṛtarāṣṭra understood his younger brother's counsel and broke the strong cords of attachment and entered vānaprastha with his wife Gāndhāri.

Kardama Muni Exemplifies Vānaprastha. Kardama Muni had decided, long before his marriage to Devahūti, when he would exit gṛhasthāśrama and enter vānaprastha! Knowing the nature of worldly pleasures and their convincing ensnarement, he told his bride's father Manu, before the wedding, that he would stay in gṛhasthāśrama only until a son was born to them. After that, he would head for the forest.

Kardama Muni and Devahūti thus remained in gṛhasthāśrama for many thousands of years. He partook of the joys but all along knew those were false. Then a son was born to Devahūti. It was Lord Viṣṇu

Himself who had promised to be born to the couple. Kardama knew that the birth of the son meant his departure to the forest, as that was what he had asked for. And he kept his end of the promise. Supported by Devahūti, he left for the forest without any attachment to wife or child — a child who was the Lord incarnate! Having resigned gṛhasthāśrama, Kardama Muni spent his time in contemplation and meditation. (*Śrīmad Bhāgavatam* 3.22.19)

Kardama Muni's story demonstrates how even marriage and progeny were received with a view to fulfill one's debt to life, a life to be lived without forming deep attachments, so that when the next stage of life arrived, one moved into it seamlessly.

Yet another Puranic role model, **King Uttānapāda,** the son of Manu and Śatarūpa, had a very prosperous kingdom and ruled over the entire earth. He lived in grandeur, amid luxuriant comforts. Yet none of those bound him. He (like most people of the time) knew the next stage was vānaprastha — the age when he would dedicate himself to study and worship. When his son Dhruva came of age, Uttānapāda consulted his ministers, ensured that his son was liked by the ministers and the subjects, and anointed him Lord of the earth. King Uttānapāda then considered his work done. His duty had been toward his subjects and his son. Having accomplished both, he then entered vānaprastha. (*Śrīmad Bhāgavatam* 4.9.66–67)

Then there was **King Pṛthu,** a very successful ruler who had conquered the whole earth and beautified it. He ruled according to the śāstras. Pṛthu, an ardent lover of the Lord, wanted to teach his beloved subjects when they should end the pursuit of the worldly and commence work on inner growth. So, when he realized that he had entered old age and had completed all his responsibilities toward society and family, Pṛthu entered vānaprastha. He left the palace, gave up all comforts, and began to practice austerities, study, and intensify his sādhanā — as had been taught to him by the Sanatkumāras. Having gradually dropped his physical and mental attachments, liberation followed. (*Śrīmad Bhāgavatam* 4.23.1–10)

Another exemplary story about detachment centers on **King Priyavrata,** another descendant of Manu. Priyavrata was a disciple of Nārada and an ardent devotee of Lord Kṛṣṇa. He had attained the knowledge of Ātman and had resolved to stay in continuous meditation on the Lord. But his father asked him to assume the responsibilities of kingship!

Priyavrata was caught between obedience to his father, his wish to stay on the spiritual path, and an overriding fear that the secular life would distract him. Lord Brahma counseled him, and soon Priyavrata, a complete renunciate at heart, was crowned king of the whole earth. He married and had ten sons, three of whom sought to become sages. To the rest of his children, he gave an island each.

Early in his life, Priyavrata had understood that worldly pleasures were the gateway to hell. After coronation, he saw how state administration, even though it kept worldly pleasures at bay, still kept him occupied and distracted.

Giving up his many queens, children, kingdom, wealth, and power, Priyavrata took refuge in the forest. There he spent his time following the teachings of his Guru until he realized the Truth. (*Śrīmad Bhāgavatam* 5.1.38) The story of Priyavrata illustrates that the vānaprastha vṛtti is a mind-set and not a function of age.

King Priyavrata had a great grandson, **King Nābhi,** who, taking after his grandfather, was an austere and righteous king. He protected the brahmins and served their cause. Pleased with this, the brahmins performed a sacrificial yajña. They were taken aback when the Lord Himself appeared and asked King Nābhi to ask for a boon. The childless King Nābhi expressed his desire for a child who would be like the Lord Himself. The Lord was touched by the request and agreed to take birth in the womb of Meru Devī, Nābhi's wife.

Thus was born to King Nābhi a son whom he named Ṛṣabha Deva. King Nābhi obeyed the prescriptions of the scriptures as the brahmin priests had taught him. Meanwhile, Ṛṣabha Deva grew up into a fine young man much loved by the people. So, when he came of age, and it seemed to everyone that he was now fully capable of handling the administrative affairs, his parents decided to leave for Badarikāśrama. Having completed his duties, King Nābhi took to a life of study and penance (vānaprastha), thus following the scriptural prescription for the third phase of life (vānaprasthāśrama). Even the fact that his son was the Lord incarnate did not stop him from following the injunction of āśrama dharma. (*Śrīmad Bhāgavatam* 5.4.5)

In all cases, we see that these kings detach from worldly life quite easily, are prepared for the third phase, and do not wait to grow old. Instead, they wait for their child — once accepted by the subjects — to take over the kingdom. So, too, King Nābhi. Easily separating from his son and kingdom, he entered vānaprastha.

With so great a father, could the son Ṛṣabha Deva, the incarnation of Lord Viṣṇu, be far behind?

Ṛṣabha Dev studied under a master in a gurukula, then entered gṛhasthāśrama and begot one hundred sons, who were worthy and efficient. He performed one hundred yajñas according to the rules set by the scriptures. During his rule, all the residents of his country were fully contented, healthy, and happy. Having led a dharmic life, he wanted to teach the world about renunciation of actions, devotion, knowledge, and dispassion. Toward that end, he installed his son Bharata as ruler, after which he left his kingdom. He had attained so much vairāgya, that he entered sannyāsāśrama directly. Eventually, Ṛṣabha Deva also attained mokṣa. (*Śrīmad Bhāgavatam* 5.5.28–35)

THE FEARLESS VĀNAPRASTHI

VERONICA HAUSMAN

▲ *Veronica Hausman*

Veronica was born into a family of seekers, and was captivated with the possibilities of Vedānta from a young age. She was among the first members of CM Washington D.C. At Gurudev's instruction, she moved with her family to California to study under Swami Tejomayananda while he was the resident Ācārya at San Jose. Veronica became a much admired Bala Vihar teacher popular with the youth. She kindled many with her loving and vivacious spirit, and inspired many by the fearlessness with which she endured cancer treatment. She accepted the condition of her health as His will, her moonlike eyes gleaming in peaceful, devoted surrender.

How did she live her vānaprastha years between hospital visits? Her family says she drew inspiration from Gurudev's lectures and reading his numerous writings. In her words:

> Gurudev said, if you watch a caterpillar, it attaches itself to the higher, and then it lets go of the lower. And then it comes up, attaches to the higher, and then it lets go of the lower. But if you don't attach yourself somewhere, you're out in space. And that's the warning. So that's why one has to be attached... It's actually medicine to contemplate upon the Truth. And many people find it very difficult to do, me also, but I did it because I had faith in the Guru. But now it makes perfect sense. But one has to just do it, I think, initially out of faith. And then you declutch. What happens is you declutch, like that caterpillar.

Continuing his father's legacy, **King Bharata,** the son of Ṛṣabha Deva, led a holy and pious life. Bharata was the ruler of the whole of Bhāratakhaṇḍa (India, including the neighboring countries). He performed many yajñas and offered all the merits gained back to the Lord, thus purifying his mind.

King Bharata ruled for ten million years, but he did not get attached to his kingship or the accompanying comforts. At the appropriate time, he distributed the kingdom among his sons and headed for the Himalayas. Leading the life of a vānaprasthi, he prepared for continued spiritual ascent. But unfortunately, a spark of attachment to an infant deer made him take two more lives, first as a deer, which life it gave up and was reborn as the son of a pious brahmin. In this third birth, he remained unattached to family and uninvolved in anything. Thus he came to be called Jaḍabharata, teaching us that attachment is lethal and can happen at any stage. (*Śrīmad Bhāgavatam* 5.7.8)

NĀRADA'S INSTRUCTIONS FOR SUCCESSFUL GṚHASTHĀŚRAMA (FOR LIBERATION)

Successful vānaprastha is a function of the previous āśramas having been lived correctly and fully. Hence, Sage Nārada's instructions to gṛhasthas are also a prelude to successful vānaprastha.

Sage Nārada explains the path of liberation for householders. (Skandha 7, Chapter 12, *Śrīmad Bhāgavatam*). The householder should perform his duties in line with his āśrama. Those householders who seek the path of righteousness should never hurt any being by way of body, mind, or speech. Following the duties of the relevant āśrama will ensure the peace of perfect completion.

All the rules for householders are to direct the mind toward the Lord after conquering the six latent enemies of the mind — desire, anger, greed, delusion, pride, and jealousy. Inability to do so is considered failure in gṛhasthāśrama.

During life as a householder, a person should watch the mind's capacities and prepare for the next stage — either vānaprastha or sannyāsa. If the mind is completely free of all desires, lusts, and emotions, the individual should take permission of the Guru and enter directly into sannyāsa life. Thereon, life should be led as directed by the scriptures: by meditation and reflection on the Self. If the individual is not yet ready, then after the completion of householder duties, he or she should enter vānaprastha and prepare for sannyāsa life. The individual should serve a Saint or Master and live according to the prescribed disciplines.

VALUE OF GṚHASTHĀŚRAMA

The āśrama of householders is to train the mind to conquer desires by renouncing thoughts, to conquer anger by renouncing desires, and to conquer greed and fear by thinking of the Self. A seeker can cross all the limitations of his mind by surrendering to his Guru, who is the Lord Himself in another form.

– Skandha 7, Chapter 12, *Śrīmad Bhāgavatam*

The Lord is very pleased when one serves a Saint. The householder who follows the rules given by the scriptures easily crosses the ocean of transmigration.

Vānaprasthi's Duties Toward Young People in His Care. Being an elder, a vānaprasthi, comes with duties to society, and that was one of the indications that Pūjya Gurudev gave to Rewa when he underscored in their Trust Deed that the pitamaha sadan should be applied toward the spiritual resurrection of society. When elders show the way, the young learn and follow, as shown by the royal dynasty of Manu and

BESTOWING VALUES

▲ *Gurudev with a young Jujhar Singh, 1989, Las Palmas*

A vānaprasthi should work toward bestowing values as the most enduring inheritance to his progeny. 'Thus, Gurudev's statement about 'spiritual resurrection of society'.

Śatarūpa, who set the pace since the beginning of creation. Their exemplary living was followed by son Priyavrata, then his son King Nābhi, his son Ṛṣabha Deva, and his son Bharata. The way of life was accepted and adopted as a matter of course.

The role of elders in upholding dharma is clearly told through the story of one of Manu's descendants, Nabhaga, who taught his son by conduct. **King Nabhaga** had many sons. When the youngest — Naabhaaga — was away in a gurukula, the other brothers shared the family wealth and excluded Naabhaaga. When he returned and claimed his share, they gave him the father as his share!

King Nabhaga was upset and found a way to compensate young Naabhaaga. At an elaborate yajña in the neighborhood the hosts did not know a certain mantra that needed to be chanted every six days. The King asked son Naabhaaga to go help the yajña hosts, saying that at the end of the yajña, the hosts would give to Naabhaaga whatever wealth was left at the site. But just when Naabhaga was taking the leftovers, Rudra (Lord Śiva) claimed the leftover wealth as his and asked the father, King Nabhaga, to validate his knowledge (about this rule). Nabhaga agreed and said, "Everything that remains from the sacrifice is by the sages considered a share for Lord Śiva, so they have once decided [during the sacrifice of Dakṣa]. He is the demigod who deserves it all."

Naabhaaga promptly prostrated at Rudra's feet and said, "As my father said: 'Everything from the sacrificial arena belongs to you, oh, Lord!'" and begged His forgiveness. Rudra was pleased that the King wished to stick to ethics, even though his son stood to lose — a son who had already been cheated and deprived. Rudra therefore gifted away the leftover wealth to Naabhaaga *as well as* instructed him in the knowledge of Brahman!

The *Bhāgavatam* thus shows that a vānaprasthi should apply the knowledge he has gained to ensure and protect dharma. Where adharma has occurred, he should work toward restoring dharma. Thus, he should work toward *bestowing values as the most enduring inheritance to his progeny.* This ties in with Gurudev's wish to spiritually resurrect society.

The conduct of young Naabhaaga also teaches that a young person has to ensure dignified behavior toward elders, even in the face of a seeming error or negligence on the elder's part. This is a sādhanā for younger people. Naabhaaga got a chance to serve his father, heed his words of advice, and excuse an error that an elder had made (as the King erred in forgetting the law regarding the right of Rudra). As a result, the young Naabhaaga received a great blessing: spiritual largesse from Rudra, that is, Lord Śiva Himself! (*Śrīmad Bhāgavatam* 9.4.1–12)

ALERT LIVING

Let there be no inadvertence or negligence in self study. In order to know satyam and dharma, do your self-study of scriptures. [...] study the Vedas daily, because these profound teachings are so subtle that we sometimes cannot clearly see what is satyam, dharma, or hitam. That is why [...] one must remain steadfast in scriptural studies.

– Swami Tejomayananda, *Graceful Aging*

XIII

Pitamaha Sadans and Day-Care Centers

Gurudev had set a vision for elders which comprised care, self-effort, study, and empowered living as core components.

The CCVS course designed by Swami Shankarananda was gaining subscription at some CM centers in India. However, the course, by itself, cannot guarantee changing one's life vision. Those who were attuned to vānaprastha enrolled in these courses. But there remained a vast segment of elders who quietly wasted away, unable to find direction. Eldercare, therefore, has expanded into elder support, elder counseling, or even elder protection in some cases. The fact that the elderly were not respected in many cultures explained their neglect.

An earlier chapter explained what gerontologists from different parts of India had to say about the plight of elders and the need to attend to their life stage. In many ways, the repeated workshops, gatherings, and meetings only reinforced the fact that there was a huge gap in what was needed to be done for elders.

Full of Grace. Despite the societal lag in awareness, the movement had spread to CM centers all over India. Repeated requests for the Vṛddhāvasthā Samādhan Śibirs (comfort with old age) came from

▲ *Pathway leading up to the pitamaha sadan kutiyas at Laxmanpur, Rewa.*

different towns in India. Already, nine vānaprastha camps of varying durations had been held in 1998–99. Dr. Sajjan Singh had initiated many elder programs in Rewa, and that initiative was to become an eye opener.

Amid the progress, a very sensitive learning moment had to be resolved. It turned out that the elders were unhappy with the name 'Vṛddhāvasthā,' for it also labeled them as 'vṛddhaḥ,' a word which carried a negative connotation of senility in their society, a colloquial used casually, often summarily. And the elder community indicated that they did not want to be so tagged. Singh had seen that in the villages the elder was colloquially referred to or called *budhau,* meaning anything from old man — to its appurtenant adjectives such as waste, useless, worthless, old (as the opposite of new), and so on. Such terminology was a complete antithesis of what CCVS stood for.

The CCVS camps were then renamed 'Art of Graceful Aging.'

Home Alone. The camps covered social health, spiritual health, emotional health, and the study of texts, such as *Sādhanā-pañcakam* — all assuming that every elder was capable of making a choice with regard to attending a camp and elevating his or her spiritual status.

Gradually some tough truths were realized:

- Not all elders were mobile.
- Not all elders, even if physically mobile, had the capability or wherewithal to travel to a camp or lecture.
- Not all elders had succeeded in staying coordinated with their body and mind. Physical and mental infirmity — and in some cases cognitive impairment — demanded the elder be kept at home.

Now, such handicaps do cause difficulty for both the elder who is confined and the caregiver who is at a loss to know what to do for the elder. In the case of elders who were physically disabled due to age and consequent illnesses, the mind continued to want the company of others, some recreation, some cheer, some satsaṅga, in short, some change. Some families did not have the means to provide any of this. Or, as was often the case, the families did not have the time to take the elder to such forums, suitably chaperoned.

There were cases where younger families had to relocate in response to their career demands; either the elderly did not want to be relocated, or in cases where the relocation was to a foreign land, the elder could not obtain the visa. Instances were coming to light of elders wanting to leave their homes out of sheer desperation for 'freedom.' Some claimed neglect, abandonment, and ill-treatment. Or there were those who felt lost and lonely after losing their partner, especially when younger family members were unable to empathize with their agony.

Such reasons begged the formation of homes for the elderly, where elders would find context and purpose, which would naturally result in their wellbeing. Over the years, it became noticeable that more and more elders began to consider life at 'elder homes' as an option preferable to a life spent alone with memories and worries.

Pulling the Door Shut Behind You — Willing to Step into a Discomfort Zone. The first pitamaha sadan originated as a whisper from Gurudev, when, as early as 1982, Bhagvati Singh from Rewa offered to Gurudev a tract of land and Gurudev had said, "Yes, we will take the offer of land and use it for a pitamaha sadan."

Gurudev was ready with a plan and a blueprint: "Elders will come and stay here with us and do their spiritual practices; we will look after them, assist them, attend to their health; we will cook for everyone; they will all study and grow." Then, within a year, Gurudev had inked over his original words with a fine-tuned agenda for Chinmaya

Mission pitamaha sadans: "Create an environment for the moral and spiritual resurrection of society."

The plan was bigger, wider, deeper, and richer. Verily, it was to be a socio-spiritual renaissance.

Gurudev's first step was to very gently call the elders of the 1980s to his fold, to return to Vedānta, a call similar to Vidura's appeal to Dhṛtarāṣṭra to let go of the comfort zone — both physical and mental (see Chapter XII). The sentimental bondage was a bigger challenge where elders staunchly held on to 'family home,' '*pushtaini* property.' The first thing to give up, said Gurudev, was the familiarity of home, and only when elders pulled the door shut behind them did they truly enter the doors of vānaprastha mentally, shackle-free.

Of course, what happened was that many elders, depleted by age, confused in their perception of care, of aging, of respect, and the accompanying expectations from others, thought of the pitamaha sadan concept as akin to a storeroom where the old were cast away or parked. That doubled their agony.

Gurudev had great respect for tradition and encouraged it, but he also had a keen sense of when tradition became a strangulating, regressive noose. And when he encountered these, he single-handedly plucked out the constrictive tradition and threw it away. In constructing pitamaha sadans, Gurudev had made a delicate move to negotiate tradition.

Yes, it had been traditional in the India of the '40s to the '70s, for children to take care of elders. But industrialization, and then technology, called youngsters to spread out, to grow India. The elder therefore needed to allow this and not suffer this as an insult. In 1983, in a message to members of Chinmaya Mission Kanpur, Gurudev said:

> Friends, old age can be creative, or self-destructive. It is your choice to decide. We are opening up a shelter for elder citizens,

planned to help them live a healthy, peaceful, forward-looking life of ease and inner beauty.

Old age need not be painful. Death need not be a frightening mystery. To learn to live in devotion and surrender to Him is possible (and is easy) in the days of retirement.

Come! Join this relaxed crown of elderly citizens! You will be looked after in an atmosphere of home amidst parivāra (family).

This was Gurudev's message to members of Chinmaya Mission Kanpur, when its pitamah sadan followed that of Rewa's, in 1983. By then pitamah sadans had begun to come up in Cochin and Chennai, too. Gradually many began to join the pitamaha sadans.

A roundup of the various pitamaha sadans under Chinmaya Mission follows:

Pitamaha Sadan Rewa, Madhya Pradesh, was the first pitamaha sadan to come up. It was established in April 1983 with the blessing of Vanvāsi Rāma, the idol sanctified in the Śrī Raghunāthji temple.

First, the annakṣetra complex and water supply systems were built, followed by residential cottages/rooms, a dormitory office, and a dispensary run by a charity. Quite a few of the residences were sponsored by the senior citizens themselves. A well-equipped library of spiritual literature, daily satsaṅga by the resident Ācārya, and study groups keep the āśrama atmosphere spiritually vibrant and uplifting.

Built on a plot of four acres, the āśrama is located amid mango orchards and well laid-out parks running alongside the residences. The serene roads around the āśrama are tempting paths for strolls in the mornings and evenings.

Pitamaha Sadan Mandhana has thirty functional residences in the āśrama. There is a well-equipped kitchen and dining hall capable of serving 200 persons, a satsaṅga bhavana (hall for congregating for study or lectures), and a dispensary run by a charity, which also looks after patients from the surrounding villages. At Mandhana's pitamaha is the Hindi Publication Division of CCMT. Erudite elders help with translation and proofreading of texts.

Pitamaha Sadan Allahabad is situated on a three-acre plot in a prime locality of the holy city of Prayāga. It has twenty-five self-contained single-room and double-room residences built to suit modern tastes. Almost half of these kuṭiyās, as they are known, are sponsored and occupied. The rest are available for periodic sādhanā camps and for the stay of pilgrims and visitors. Like the other pitamaha sadans, it has a dispensary served by qualified doctors, a full-service kitchen, a serene Śrī Akhileshwar Mahadev temple, and a commodious 400-seat-capacity Satsanga Bhavan. Resident Ācāryas conduct study classes and satsaṇga regularly.

The property is a visual beauty with its rose gardens and fruit orchards, not to mention a gośālā (cowshed). The location of a Chinmaya Vidyalaya on the premises adds the right touch of cheer and laughter. Blessed and enriched are the students to be amid vānaprasthis.

Pitamaha Sadan Vijayawada, Andhra Pradesh, was set up by devotees who studied under Gurudev. They came together to continue their

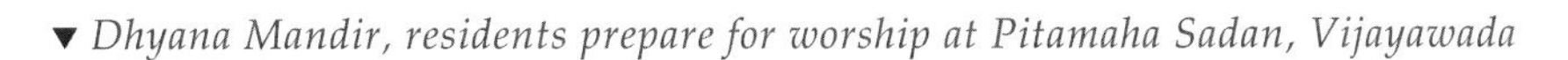

▾ *Dhyana Mandir, residents prepare for worship at Pitamaha Sadan, Vijayawada*

yajña through their vānaprastha years, the fire of bhakti, jñāna, and karma burning bright. Given its genesis, this pitamaha sadan has stoked the spirit of vānaprastha in such a way that Mission members are requesting it be further expanded to accommodate more elders. They say it is the ideal place for vānaprasthāśrama!

▲ *Swamini Sharadapriyananda*

Established in 1999 by Swamini Sharadapriyananda, the then regional head of CM centers in Andhra Pradesh and Tamil Nadu States, this pitamaha sadan is built on 900 square yards on the outskirts of Vijayawada, the abode of Goddess Kanaka Durgā. Nearby flows the river Krishna in a gentle hum of obeisance to Gurudev. A part of the 900 square-yard property was donated by Ms. P. Rajakumari, a senior devotee-worker of the Mission, and the rest was purchased with Mission funds. Soon, generous donations poured in from many Mission members, many of whom quietly enrolled as vānaprasthis. At this writing, the ten vānaprasthis living here share the cost of living expenses. This pitamaha sadan is very active with satsaṅga, chanting, and Study Group classes.

Chinmayasarada Tapovan, Kothapatnam, Andhra Pradesh. The āśrama is located on a seven-acre plot at walking distance from the seashore in Kothapatnam, a town in Andhra Pradesh. Rows of beautiful trees and flower gardens surround the cottages of the residents, while cool breezes and rhythmic music from the oceanic waves make the place an enjoyable treat for the senior citizens staying there.

This pitamaha sadan, blessed by Lord Dvārakādhīśa (Kṛṣṇa) holding a cinmudrā, has superior modern residences. A high level of spiritual atmosphere prevails in the āśrama. Resident Ācāryas regularly hold classes on the *Gītā* and the Upaniṣads. Several sādhanā camps are organized every year for the benefit of the residents.

Chinmaya Gītāśrama in Renigunta, Andhra Pradesh, as the pitamaha sadan is called, is situated close to the railway station. It is built on 2.5 acres of land. Satsaṅgas, celebrations, and study abound. Uniquely, a large number of people from the neighborhood attend as day students, partaking in Vedānta studies via Study Groups.

Pitamaha Sadan Coimbatore, Tamil Nadu, is a division of Chinmaya Garden Trust located in Coimbatore. It started functioning in 1986 with the construction of the first four residences. Pūjya Gurudev himself had performed the bhūmi pūjā, which makes this pitamaha sadan especially blessed.

▲ *Pūjya Gurudev inaugurating Pitamaha Sadan, Coimbatore*

Entering Vanaprastha — A State of Mind? Pitamaha sadans have their place in the scheme of vānaprastha. There are regions and geographies where an elder home is the only way forward. But Gurudev himself had once said there is no need for a distinct exit or a separate entry to mark the vānaprastha stage of life. When asked about modern forests for the vānaprasthis, Gurudev said:

> Decide firmly that you want to lead the life of a vānaprasthi, vacate the master bedroom for your eldest son, and shift to the

> You need not go to the forests to become a vānaprasthi. You can start the life of a vānaprastha immediately, while living in your own house.
>
> – *Swami Chinmayananda*

outer room of your house. Separate the bed [if it is twin beds for you and your spouse]; get your food in your newly occupied room, start spiritual studies and satsaṅga, try to complete your cherished hobby, discharge the remaining responsibilities toward your family, and finally take to selfless social work in association with other elderly people around. After living this way for some years, you will be inclined toward peaceful āśrama life and develop spiritual yearnings. You will then be fit to shift to an āśrama, along with your wife or without her — and that āśrama need not be in the forest.

In the story of Śabarī in the *Rāmacaritamānasa,* Lord Rāma explains the nine kinds of bhakti to Śabarī. When Śabarī came face to face with Lord Rāma, she was stupefied. Unable to either glorify Him or worship Him, she said, "I am the lowest of the low and also dull-headed; how can I extol you?" The Lord then replied (Araṇya Kāṇda 34.2), "I recognize no other kinship except that of Devotion.

"Despite caste, kinship, lineage, piety, reputation, wealth, physical strength, numerical strength of his family, accomplishments and ability, a man lacking in devotion is of no more worth than a cloud without water. Now I tell you the nine forms of Devotion; please listen attentively and cherish them in your mind."

And Lord Rāma explained the nine forms to her in detail (refer – Araṇya Kānda 34, 35) — Pūjya Guruji Swami Tejomayananda says that the sixth kind of Devotion should be the guiding line for vānaprasthis:

Chaṭha dama sīla birati bahu karmā
Nirata nirantara sajjanadharma

> Practicing control over the senses, developing dispassion, withdrawing from too many worldly activities, and devoting more and more time to the ways of saints and sages.[1]

Guruji adds, "In our śāstras, it is said that, as soon as one sees the grandchild's face, one should move out of the house." And as for where to begin developing control over the senses, Guruji's advice is: "Give up attachment to eating and control your eating habits."

But leaving home for vānaprastha does not mean that one should surrender to an inactive life in a home for the aged. In fact, Guruji discourages that approach. Pitamaha sadans should be vibrant places with nāma-smaraṇa and work that restores society.

Day-Care Centers — Learning from the Experience of CM Bhubaneshwar. It is one thing to choose to give up comforts or luxuries and opt for a minimalistic life. It is yet another when, having chosen to live as a dependent in one's home, one is denied essential care and the means for decent living. Do family members choose to treat the elder poorly, or do things just happen that way in the course of a hectic life?

Swami Sadananda, Ācārya of Chinmaya Mission Bhubhaneshwar, encountered similar confusion. Swamiji often makes voluntary calls on the homes of elderly devotees of Gurudev. Once he visited Mr. and Mrs. Bezbaruah (name changed to protect the identities of devotees);

[1] 'The Secret of a Wonderful Old Age,' *Tapovan Prasad*, December 2006, Swami Tejomayananda, pg. 16.

they were maintaining the home for their married son and daughter-in-law who had been posted overseas. Like a bolt from the blue, Mr. Bezbaruah suffered a fatal cardiac stroke. Mrs. Bezbaruah did what she knew to help, but she lost her husband to the stroke. The children came from overseas and attended to the rites and ceremonies, but, as their careers demanded, they had to return to their home overseas. The brave Mrs. Bezbaruah thought she could manage successfully alone. But it was not to be.

In the very large house, Mrs. Bezbaruah began to grow increasingly lonely, lost, and even frightened on some days. Memories of her happier days with her husband haunted her nonstop; memories of the joy of bringing up her little children in a haven of laughter rang incessantly in her ears. All around her now was a deafening silence and memories that teased her faith and belief in her children. The city spread all around their vast home, preoccupied with its numerous trivia. Large as it was, the city held no relief for her, nor did its multitude have time for Mrs. Bezbaruah.

Mrs. Bezbaruah realized that time, after all, was not a healer. Time hung heavy, taunting. It was on one such day of agony that Swami Sadananda came by her home to see how she was doing. Eyes swollen with incessant crying, she bent her head low and requested to be relieved of such pain and misery.

▾ *Inauguration of the Bhubhaneshwar Day-Care Center in December 2013*

"I have no one to share my problems with," she said. "If there is a place I can go to for a few hours a day, away from these four walls, where the memories of my husband will not haunt me ...." That was when Swamiji realized that some preliminary redress for elders' problems was needed before talking to them about vānaprastha.

Swamiji promised to think about a solution for her. A few days later, Swamiji dropped in on the Sahoo sisters (name changed). Both were unmarried and now both had also retired from their jobs. The two sisters, who were in their mid-sixties, were a study in contrast. While one remained immersed in reading the whole day, the other was unable to suffer the silence and inactivity. The moment Swamiji entered their home, the second sister became exuberant. As she spoke, Swamiji realized that loneliness was destroying her peace. No neighbor visited them, a rare relative called once a month. "Even the household help come, do their work, and leave in a hurry, as they too have things to do, except me!" she cried.

When Life Changes for the Active. Swamiji realized that old age need not be a curse. Several elders were people without aim and purpose and they needed both.

▾ *This page and next, scenes from the inauguration of the Day-Care Center, Bhubaneshwar (seen in the background).*
Left*: L to R: Er. Vishwananth Panda, Er. Antaryanai Panda (President CM Bhubaneswar), Swami Sadananda, Br. Piyush (at the back), and on extreme right Sw. Shivaswarupananda from Divine Life Society*

Then, one day, something else happened. An elderly devotee, who was an active member at the Mission and on whom the Mission had come to depend very much, was hit by paralysis after a bad stroke. Mr. Raut became bedridden and sad. When Swamiji visited him, he was alarmed to see how a perfectly energetic, happy man was wasting away, unable to get up and go out. Mr. Raut lay alone in a dark corner of a room, the sounds of the world around causing him more pain and torture. No one at home had time for him, as they were all very busy holding their lives together. Nor did they have the means to take Mr. Raut for an outing or to the Mission Center. Life was tough for one and all.

Mr. Raut was different from the Sahoo sisters, yet his life was no different. The former knew what he wanted to do but had no means to accomplish it. The latter had the means but did not know what they should be doing with their lives. As for Mrs. Bezbaruah, she knew what she wanted; she had the means, but she lacked the spirit to do it. As Mr. Raut said to Swamiji, "If I can go to the Mission somehow, and be with everyone there, I will be able to contribute to the work just by looking at the people, that is all!"

The obstacles the elders faced were not just physical. Mentally, too, they felt the need for a break, a small break from a day that stretched emptily before them, as another elderly couple, the Patnaiks shared with Swamiji. If only they could get away for three to four

▾ ***Left:*** *L to R: Swami Sarvapriyananda C. M. Dhenkanal, Br. Piyush Chaitanya CM Bhubaneswar, Br. Garga Chaitanya CM Jagatpur, Br. Janardan Chaitanya CM Balangir; Swami Sadananda (with black bag) CM Bhubaneswar*
Right: *Er. Antaryanai Panda received Pujya Guruji. Extreme right is Brni. Richa Chaitanya, CM Bhubaneswar*

hours a day, when they could spend time doing something enjoyable, enriching, and inspiring. "Just consider my wife's condition if I were to die," said Mr. Patnaik. "I like to know she has a place to go to, where she will be in the company of good people, who will share mind with her, where she will sing or study with them, where there will be some well-meaning people to talk with, to be consoled by."

Thus Was Born the Idea of a Day-Care Center. Swamiji knew that getting elders to enter vānaprastha was a challenge, as they all saw it as an āśrama that compelled them to leave home; and many had not ever directed their minds toward such a change. Most saw themselves aging, getting their children married, watching grandchildren dotting the landscape, and themselves tending to the little ones while their married children pursued their careers. That all this should *also* include vānaprastha was startling to most.

One day, Mr. Raut managed to go to the Mission. He was so happy being there, seeing faces, and exchanging the familiar greeting 'Hari Om.' Swamiji could see he needed to come more often. So he requested Mr. Raut's son to bring him once a week to the Mission center; however, that was neither feasible nor affordable. The culprit is India's public transport system, which is not yet elder-friendly. All these thoughts culminated in Swami Sadananda thinking actively of a day-care center where elders could gather and spend time.

Swamiji had considered a pitamaha sadan at one point in time. He had visited a few pitamaha sadans in Bhubhaneshwar and had seen that they did not suit the cultural leanings of the typical Odisha elder.

While the day-care center idea grew in his mind, Swamiji began to request the elders to come to the Mission center during the day. And they did come to enjoy spiritual discourses. Sometimes they attended his camps for senior citizens, while some also came for personal discussions with Swamiji. Swamiji began to organize special health camps for them, which included bone density checkups, an ortho and physiotherapy camp; blood-pressure monitoring and heart check-up camp; prostate gland check-up camp; eye and dental check-up camp; and so on. Such preventive checkups were direly needed — many elders had not undergone a medical checkup, needed help, and, in many cases, did not know how to ask for it. Talking to the doctors, hearing them talk, getting health issues clarified, helped those elders very much.

Holding On to Gurudev's Vision. Swami Sadananda himself had tried visiting the homes of devotees, sitting with the extended families, and hearing their woes. After he heard them speak at the annual camp for senior citizens, Swamiji understood that the singular problem elders faced at home was LONELINESS. Pondering longer on that, Swami Sadananda concluded that a day-care center (DCC) would serve their needs very well: a place they could come to for a few hours or longer, be in each others' company, eat abundantly, and be with those who could give them their time joyfully.

A Center to Add Life to Years. Swami Sadananda derived the vision for a DCC from what Gurudev himself had once said about elders: *We cannot add years to their lives, but we can definitely add life to their years.* That statement then became his driving force.

The Bhubhaneshwar DCC was inaugurated in December 2013 by Pūjya Guruji. Swamiji had bought land from the government, making a personal appeal for a day-care center for the sizable elder population of Odisha.

The day-care center was designed to be useful for:

- Senior citizens who would like to spend a significant part of their day in a spiritually conducive environment.
- Senior citizens who wished to interact with like-minded people of their age group.

- Retired people who were grappling with their retirement and the sudden vacuum caused by not having a regular job anymore.
- Senior citizens who needed care during the day and had no one at home to attend to them.
- Conscientious children of elderly parents who wanted a temporary place (for one or two weeks) for their parents to stay when they had to go out of town.

Swamiji wanted Mission families to have the care and comfort of their own; the DCC at the Mission could be equipped to step in during their times of need. "Eventually, non-Mission members, too, will grow to trust us to take care of them," says Swamiji.

As mentioned in an earlier chapter, Gurudev planted the seed of vānaprastha but did not tell how the fruit should look; that he left to his devotees. He knew they would imbibe his vision. Gurudev's vision is clearly evolving into new forms to suit a variety of needs!

FREEDOM!

We must make an effort not to be reborn. No birth, no saṁsāra. No punar janma. No disgraceful aging, no graceless aging, no graceful aging. No problem at all. Complete freedom. This is what our śāstras lead us to — complete spiritual enlightenment.

– Swami Tejomayananda, *Graceful Aging*

XIV

Global Vānaprastha Initiatives

The third age, as the age span after the seventies is called in the Western world, has its definitions surrounding finance, health, and companionship in most countries. The members of Chinmaya Mission Centers in the West have been alert to continuing study and sādhanā into their post-retirement lives. In some ways, this may be attributed to the manner in which the reverence for the Mission evolves in foreign lands, where it becomes the node which members — both Indian and non-Indian — remain affiliated to, and anchored in, as a larger extended family. This, in itself, has provided for the members the direction as they age.

With time, the accent on a structured spiritual life in the third age is gaining expression in countries besides India, alongside a need for a quieter, assisted life. The experience and learnings of the U.K. and the U.S. are worth studying.

VĀNAPRASTHA UNITED KINGDOM

It was like any other day at the Chinmaya Kirti in Egerton Gardens. The Ācārya-in-charge was scheduling the study classes for the next year. After Bala Vihar came CHYK, then Junior CHYK, then adult classes, and, finally, he said very nonchalantly, "Now the vānaprasthis."

His announcement did startle the elders, for until then, they had been quite happy being called 'adult members.' However, this 'vānaprasthis' did have a sweet ring to it, and so the fifteen 'unclassified so far' elders looked toward the Ācārya. And even as they did, they realized that vānaprasthāśrama was where their Ācārya was directing them.

When Pūjya Guruji visited London for a yajña, the newly named vānaprasthis asked him, "What should we do at this vānaprastha stage of life?"

Guruji explained that this stage was for gradually withdrawing from the usual concerns of life, spending the morning meditating, reading the scriptures in the afternoon, and singing bhajans and kīrtanas in the evening — thus keeping their minds absorbed in the Lord, gently eradicating thoughts of any other kind that sought to engage the mind. It was the time to start enjoying solitude, Guruji elaborated, a time to de-fatten the mind, empty the cupboard of vāsanās, and gently engineer a state of inner environment where the agitations of worldly life were toned down significantly.

The fifteen elders then sought Guruji's blessings to start a vānaprastha wing in the U.K. But, even so, they remained unsure what they needed to do.

In an unusual twist to their own decision, they teamed up with the Junior CHYKs to stage a play at their center at Chinmaya Kirti in Hendon, on the occasion of Janmāṣṭamī. The play was a success of an unusual kind with all the seniors forgetting their lines and bringing the house down with laughter.

Soon, another play was staged by the vānaprasthis with *Bhaja Govindam* as the theme, on the occasion of Guru-pūrṇimā. Scripted by a senior CHYK and directed by their Ācārya, the vānaprasthis were now edging closer to the topics for which they were gently developing a flavor.

Even then, they were not getting a hold of what vānaprastha activity should entail. That was when two of them, accompanied by their wives, decided to pay a visit to a camp for vānaprasthis at Sandeepany, Mumbai. They watched the CCVS in action, attended a few classes themselves, and with due guidance from Swami Prashantananda and Swami Yogasthananda, along with Dr. Sajjan Singh, they found the right path to enter aging gracefully.

The vānaprastha movement was not 'one more event' for the London group. Their desire to form a vānaprastha presence had been triggered — as always — by the vagaries of life that post-retirement had thrown at them. Elders in the U.K. were facing severe self-doubts. After years of trying to establish themselves as first-generation or second-generation Indians in a foreign land and succeeding at it, retirement left them with doubts.

Life was one thing as working citizens. But now, post-retirement, and relabeled as 'pensioners,' the elders found that with their children now out making a living, they, the elders, would have to find their way around their homes. That included cooking, cleaning, gardening, repairing, and, in the process, discovering their own shortcomings. Many of them who had taken great pride in establishing themselves in their careers now struggled to find a new identity after retirement. Indeed, that became a great 'Oh, no!' moment in the lives of many people, since they believed that life without a career was, in fact, a useless life. Explaining this, Mr. Mannu Bhalla of the U.K. vānaprastha team says, "We see quite a few older people of Indian origin sitting in the parks drinking their life away."

The first thing the retired Indian elders did was to set up a satsaṅga class at the Mission Center. They naturally chose a book on old age, but their Ācārya suggested that they study *Sādhanā Pañcakam,* which enabled the shift from gṛhastha to vānaprastha in an effortless and seamless manner, without grappling with labels like 'old.' Thus, they began to understand the end of gṛhasthāśrama as their stage of life and, hence, a prelude to vānaprastha.

Soon a new opportunity presented itself to the London chapter of CVS: to interact with 'Age Concern,' an organization in one of the suburbs of London, Kingston, set up by the local Christian community to make life for elders cheerful and productive. Age Concern was a day-care center for able and not-so-able elders, mostly of English origin. CVS held for them a weekly satsaṅga, where an English senior would encourage interactions on the platform of Vedānta, yoga, and meditation. Gradually, Ayurveda was introduced, and the program gained popularity.

That was when the Ācārya, who had been guiding them all along, was transferred to India, and now the group had to fend for itself. But it actually turned out to be a turning point, for they were forced to give their satsaṅga more meaning, more structure, and more content. The group came by a teacher, Mr. Kanoo Patel, who was proficient in a system known as 3SRB (Three Step Rhythmic Breathing) — a combination of

▼ *U.K. vānaprastha group with Swamini Umananda, CM France*

gentle exercises with prāṇāyāma. The weekly classes continued with prāṇāyāma, guided meditation, a talk by a guest speaker on health, wealth, and similar matters of interest to retired people, followed by the study of a Vedānta text with commentary written by Gurudev.

The London vānaprastha group with the help of the new teacher, Patel, has begun to expand with memberships across Indian and some non-Indian communities also, but mostly inviting people hungry for knowledge. Encouraged by the class at Kingston, they have begun to expand activities to other towns like Leicester and Birmingham. A trustee of Chinmaya Mission U.K., Śrī Ramesh Pattni has taken CVS U.K. under his wing and guided them to put more and more of the study into practice. Toward this, CVS U.K. is toying with the idea of a residential course that will provide the setting for practical experience of vānaprastha.

VĀNAPRASTHA IN THE UNITED STATES

Cultural Influences: East versus West. The spiritual need of a human being remains the same everywhere in the world. Strong identification with the body creates an array of emotions as one begins to age. However, the expression of a spiritual need may vary with culture. India's ṛṣi culture has already defined this need and placed it before the people as a milestone to achieve around age sixty, maybe saving them from needless wandering and hopeless wondering.

The ways of the people in the East vary from the ways of people in the West, where the focus on right living, right diet, fitness, and annual medical checkups is significant. On a related front, it is common to find people battling age with cosmetic treatments, pills, and surgeries, as these options are culturally widely accepted.

One notable area of difference in the living style of the West is that living with children is not an available 'retirement plan,' whether one is a native or an immigrant. Children leave home when they grow up. That is when one starts thinking about possible 'affordable' places to retire in — closer to medical facilities, around areas with warm weather, and places that promise recreation activities. There is a clear understanding that life thereafter needs to be differently structured, differently planned, because the rules will change. Even so, the basis of this difference remains linked to the gross body. So it is not unusual, for example, for a person living in the Western world to seek a companion in the evening of his or her life for emotional support. In the East, it would typically be an occasion to advise the spouse left behind to turn to the scriptures, at first for emotional stability, and then for spiritual evolution.

But cultures are defined by their perceptions and their beliefs, their customs, and their comfort zones. The Western approach aims at retiring with comfort; long-term nursing care and even funeral plans

▼ *Devotees at the residence of Gulu and Indra Advani in 1975*
Back Row Standing: (L to R) *Nalini Browning, Dorothy Brooks, unidentified male, Alan Charles, Bill Sheldon, Gulu Advani, Pūjya Gurudev, J. Luis Jauregui, Imelda Rosenthal, Praveen Prasad, Byron Hayes, Malti Prasad, Robert Berg, and Meena Advani in sari.*
Sitting/Kneeling: (L to R) *Vijay Kapoor, Uma Jeyarasasingam, Anita Jauregui, Rudite Emir, Raj Prasad. Right in front: Pranjiwan Lodhia*

are approached clinically, whereas, the Eastern approach aims to educate elders about detachment and divinity before death. However, the current consumerist trends in India have threatened the wisdom of aging gracefully, and question the happiness for the aging elder who continues to choose dependence on progeny.

Again, in the predominant culture of the West, there is no overt call in the twilight years to tend to spirituality — such as vānaprastha. Those who can afford often focus on external fulfillment through travel or leisurely hobbies. In the East, either there is no money left or there is no safe, comfortable and affordable transport, enthusiasm, or security for the majority of elders to travel and pursue other interests.

So, what stands out differently? Chinmaya Mission centers in the West say that the biggest visible difference is the attitude. Most elders in the West, they say, are energetic and tend to have a positive attitude toward retirement. They are independent and most live well. And among them are those who have been involved with the Mission for a long time. They have matured into their elder years, considering other Mission members as their extended family, generously availing themselves of guidance from Ācāryas, and using their post-retirement time for their uninterrupted pursuit of their spiritual goal.

Challenges Faced by Aging Indians Overseas. And what about aging Indians who have made the U.S. or the U.K. their home? The Indian community in the U.S. is composed of two major categories — those who migrated in the 1970s and 1980s and those who came in the beginning of the twenty-first century. The first group came to study and then made the U.S. their home. The second wave came as programmers and IT workers. This group is the larger, much younger group.

The first group is retired or approaching retirement between 2010 and 2020. and this group includes Mission members who were closely associated with Gurudev. These members, continue to live in their homes and are able to function with adequate independence. In a bid to create an enduring community for the elderly devotees, in 1990, Gurudev had invited a group of members of the CMW (Chinmaya Mission West) Board to visit Florida to view a community for seniors, with an idea to develop residences for CMW members. The plan was to encourage vānaprastha via svādhyāya, sādhanā, and sevā. Given the shared Mission values, it was felt the community would thrive.

The plan itself was grand. There was to be a temple and a resident Ācārya who would conduct Vedānta classes and celebrate Hindu festivals and holidays. There would be rental units so that children and grandchildren who visited could be comfortable in their own suites. The concept to this day makes a great deal of sense — a community of like-minded people aging in a wholesome environment with support for virtually all their needs. Sadly, that plan did not take off.

Different Woes, Different Strokes. The Indians who emigrated to the U.S. in the 1960s and 1970s have recently begun to evaluate their retirement options in the U.S. What faces them is no different from what elders face the world over in developed economies:

- Diminished quality time with children/grandchildren due to their job mobility and working hours.
- Diminished income from fixed retirement savings because of low interest rates — a global financial trend.
- Reduced level of physical care at home and increasing caretaker costs (currently USD 30.00 per hour). Home retirees facing extreme loneliness due to physical disabilities or loss of spouse.
- Increasing retirement community housing 'buy-in' and maintenance costs.
- U.S. retirement communities not catering to Indian elders' social or dietary needs.
- Uncertainty of Social Security benefits and increasing medical insurance and drug costs.

Given these and other related issues, the *Chinmaya NRI Vānaprastha Community (CNVC)* pondered on coming together and developing a retirement community in India. The plan was to create a world-class luxury retirement community, in a serene, pastoral, spiritual environment near Chinmaya Vibhooti, which would provide continuing care (independent living, assisted living, nursing home, and hospice) services for members.

A reputed builder was identified, the plan was shared, and costs were evaluated. Land was also identified adjacent to Chinmaya Vibhooti in Kolwan, on the east side, and earnest monies were also paid to the responsible authority toward the purchase price. But sadly, the legal issues pertaining to purchase of land and ownership of land by NRIs fell into debate, and the earnest money deposit was returned.

In the second phase of this idea, other locations were examined that were more desirable and closer to larger cities. The main challenge was to have a core group commit to moving into such a community away from where they had lived during their active careers and away from where their children grew up. That idea created reluctance. Despite all desire to reduce attachments, the anxiety of moving away from familiar surroundings was a hindrance. So the idea of creating a large elder community has not worked, so far.

According to Pranjiwan (Pranji) Lodhia, Treasurer of CMW (Chinmaya Mission West), currently many centers are considering facilities on a smaller scale close to existing Mission centers. Some have acquired land and made plans; however, at this writing nothing has been built yet.

In general, Mission members and others in or approaching retirement have the same view about how they want to spend their twilight years. Mission members do have the advantage of a spiritual edge, thanks to years of Mission influence; but, even so, Mission members still prefer to be close to their children and grandchildren and choose not to move away from them. Issues remain the same, be it in India or overseas — elders desire to stay close to family, and children have a hard time balancing their careers and caring for their elders.

D*ouble Income Techies.* A different, but allied, problem faces the Indians in the U.S. who immigrated after 2000 to join the IT industry in the U.S. Many of these immigrants have brought their parents to the U.S. and depend on them for childcare while both spouses work. Such a situation has created a different challenge. The parents, in their fifties and sixties, are often unable to meld with U.S. life, thanks largely to their inability to drive a car as well as limitations of language to facilitate social interaction. Sadly, they become 'trapped' at home. This community is growing quite rapidly. A few of the elders, who are physically able, walk to local community centers and find some activities that interest them.

Pranjiwan Lodhia feels — as do many others who have lived for many years in the U.S. — that the new aging community has a need to be accepted and feel comfortable in a foreign land, before disengaging to follow vānaprastha. It almost seems that the choice of living abroad brings challenges that one may not find in India. The support system of family, friends, community, and paid helpers is very difficult to duplicate in the U.S. As a result, Indians overseas devote a lot more time to everyday survival, thus being robbed of the time for self-inquiry.

The 1990 Florida initiative to start a retirement community of Mission elders had faded away. The plan, which had envisaged setting up a settlement in a different place than the one where members had been living the last two decades, was not preferred. The conclusion was that most individuals would prefer retiring in a place where they have lived all their working lives, especially so since many become fearful when they think of the body becoming infirm. Even so, Gulu Advani, one of the Directors of the CMW Board, feels that the time is right to reactivate the CM Retirement Community project. He says, "I believe that CMW is ready for a Chinmaya vānaprastha community in the U.S. Some Chinmaya Mission grandparents may, in their twilight years, like to live a contemplative life in an āśrama-like environment, free of the responsibilities of parenting and grandparenting."

VĀNAPRASTHA — DEDICATED REFLECTION!

▲ *David and Margaret Dukes*

At eighty-two and seventy-four, respectively, David and Margaret Dukes look back at how their vānaprastha was crafted by Gurudev way back in 1989 in Washington, D.C., after meeting briefly at one of Gurudev's yajñas. Unbeknownst to them, Gurudev's divine design led them to practice karma yoga in their vānaprastha years together. Today, Margaret manages the editorial work for the Mananam series, while David crafts the layout with utmost precision while assisting with editorial work. Their lives are fully dedicated to honoring Gurudev and his teachings — through the weekly study groups they attend diligently and through the inspiring Mananam Celebration Series that they are working on in every which way. Their energy, the discipline with which they work, and their quiet commitment are remarkable and exemplary.

CHALLENGES FACING THE INDIAN IMMIGRANT

During the 2000 U.S. census, Asian Indians ranked the fourth highest with regard to the number of immigrants over the age of fifty-five. That factoid calls into question the attitude and accommodation toward aging required within the maturing Indian community in the U.S. (and Canada). Indians aging in North America are not immune to the challenges of growing old. For the generation of Indians who immigrated in the early 1960s to learn and earn in foreign lands, a lifetime of the 'do-it-yourself' attitude translates into 'trying to be independent for as long as feasible.' However, this does not come handy when the body becomes less able. At that juncture, they are at a loss to know the turn they need to take. After years of independent living, and acculturation in North America , they can neither move in with their children nor return to India.

Continuing Care Retirement Communities (CCRCs) — housing designed for self-sufficient older adults — are still unattractive options due to high entrance fees and monthly fees, as well as food-related preferences, especially for Indians. There are some government-subsidized homes, with huge waiting lists, but the majority of those residences are not desirable.

When age-related problems intensify, homecare is available only on a short-term basis and the costs are very high. Healthcare turns into a nightmare, especially in the U.S., where the debate on medical insurance promises to outlive the aging adults. It is ironic that in a land of far-reaching medical breakthroughs, elders are far from being assured of decent medical care.

In reality, while it may be said that the Western approach aims at dying with dignity, very few *in fact* do.

– A summary of the feelings expressed by Indian
and American devotees in the U.S.

XV

Gems from the Crown Jewels

Gurudev's Vānaprasthis

Gurudev began his divine mission way back in 1951. Ever since, he has been impacting many lives, many minds. Some seekers (devotees) watched from a distance — wary, unsure, yet enjoying him; some came very close and hugged him; some read his books, some heard him; some thought about him deeply; some questioned him, some challenged him; some laughed at his jokes and thought he was a good speaker because he was humorous. And there were those special ones who heard him loud and clear even if they did not understand his language! To those who wrote to him, he gave guidance. But many simply stood in his presence and went away inspired for the rest of their lives. To some he slipped in a few words — words that germinated and became veritable gospels that, over time, worked their wonder.

Indeed, it is amazing to retrace the manner in which his few words could and did build venerable role-models out of simple humans.

Vānaprastha is a state of mind that one adopts, gingerly at first, wary and unsure, but with the blessing of the Guru. And Gurudev always encouraged devotees to let the scriptures take charge. Often, when the road forked, he guided the minds and lives of people and showed them the way.

To some, he spoke through letters, with some, in person. Some, he merely held by the hand and led in the direction of where they had to go, and some others he simply watched them slip effortlessly onto the path of vānaprastha. But each one got exactly what he needed, wherever on that road they stood. For, they were all his.

Following are a few samples of the guidance that Gurudev endlessly provided:

Do It Right Now! Rudite Emir is a devotee who learned to see the world through Gurudev's lenses early in her life and was edging close to the vānaprastha stage at the time of his Mahāsamādhi. Did Gurudev lead her to vānaprastha? Rudite does not recall such demarcation but says she tried her best to follow Gurudev's directives, but in the following case admits that she did not realize the full import of his words until later:

▲ *Rudite Emir serving Gurudev at Krishnalaya, Piercy, 1991*

> Gurudev's words always have far-reaching value. He would often tell us during our younger days that we better start meditating seriously while we are young, because, as we grow old, even sitting cross-legged, he said, would require a major effort. He urged us often to "do it right now!" Today, with joints creaking and muscles pulling, I'm often reminded of what he said then, even if I didn't fully absorb it then!

Many devotees received precious advice about the vānaprastha stage of life through Gurudev's letters:

Tirelessly for the Community. To Śrī Venkatesh Deshpande, Gurudev wrote in March 1993:

> Congratulations, young man! You are only just 72 on March 4th and don't tell me that you are tired and exhausted because you are talking to one who is 76 and going strong. Till death, work tirelessly for the benefit of the community.

Filled with Ram. To Mr. T. N. Parathasarathy in Chennai, Gurudev wrote in July 1992:

> Congratulations on your 60th. Be happy; serve your loving, grateful children. You deserve this joyous stage of your old age retirement.
>
> Don't get involved with the children or their ups and downs. Surrender them and their future to the Great Protector, the Lord. You remain as a 'Cracked pot.' Receive everything, reject nothing, but soon be empty of everything. Let your mind be quiet and pure, filled with your Ram.

Be Satisfied. To Mr. S. S. Gutgutia, Jamshedpur, in March 1988:

> Your duties toward children have all been fulfilled. All Lord's Grace. The work is going on. More work can surely come. But that means more money, less spirituality, more anxiety. Let us be satisfied with what Lord gives us.

Gurudev's words can be a sharp pointer for those who wish to extend their working life further and further, unable to end it.

Two Lives, Two Styles, One Master. Roads fork in every life. Often, the path of the good (śreyas) and the path of the pleasant (preyas) beckon equally. As we mature in our spiritual study, the path of the pleasant also matures in character — so that those activities that we enjoy but fear giving up, like working, socializing, either wither away or get transformed to acquire a spiritual character. It is in the ability to make the right choice that Gurudev's guidance is always felt.

In the accounts related below, we will see the hand of the Guru at play, the lessons of the Guru, and the efforts of the Guru to inspire us to detach us from 'all this,' to attach us to 'That.' The following two examples illustrate a study of apparent opposites — one about a person already deeply drawn to the spiritual life, the other about a person who was rooted in a life of material success and enjoyment. In the lives of both, we see the subtle effort of the Guru to shepherd the individual onto the right path, an effort only the Guru can exert.

Swamini Supreetananda, head of Chinmaya Mission Mangalore, entered vānaprastha at a very young age, at a time when she had not yet met Gurudev. She did not tell him anything, but she says, "He knew when he saw me." To no one in particular and yet for Swamini amma's ears, he said, "A Guru finds his disciple, no matter how far the distance is in time or place," similar to how he had found Supreeta-amma, his gold mine from Kolar.

Then there is Ranganathan Krishnamoorthy, a very loved and respected devotee of Gurudev, who was not, at first, a devotee, though his wife Lalita was. Krishnamoorthy, or Krishna, as Gurudev addressed him, was a high-flying businessman who merely presented himself at some Mission activities and allowed the Mission the use of his resources — until, one day, Gurudev put his arm around his shoulder and said, "Enough Krishna! ..." and took him along to build temples.

▲ *Śrī R. Krishnamoorthy (Thatha)*

The stories of Swamini Supreetananda and Krishnamoorthy may seem like regular stories, but on a closer look, they reveal how the saṅkalpa to give up the gṛhastha life, after the duties are fulfilled, leads to rapid growth in spirituality. Mr. Krishnamoorthy's life will inspire everyone who feels he or she is not worthy of being 'found' by the Guru. Or that he or she is not 'ready.'

Swamini Supreetananda — Chinmaya Mission Mangalore. At fourteen, Daakshaayani (as she was known then) was already married and the marital home had many people. Besides that, the family was very poor. Food, water, health — everything was a challenge. Daakshaayani and her husband, who was older than she by sixteen years, did whatever jobs came their way to earn money. Then life smiled at her, a wan smile. At seventeen, she found a temporary job as a primary school teacher. Then in 1951 at the age of eighteen she was confirmed by the government as a teacher in Kolar, Karnataka. The salary was too low, Rs. Forty-Two (less than a dollar), but it was real money to supplement her husband's earnings as a policeman.

Life was very hard. The day began even before the previous one had ended; and there was little or no money. But hard work was bearable, largely because Daakshaayani was of devout disposition. She had heard stories of devoted loyal wives and lived according to the tenets of pativratā dharma (the code of a devoted wife). Then, she gave birth to a child, who did not live long. Later, another child was born, but did not live either. Some years later when her

▲ *Swamini Supreetananda*

body was healed, she delivered two more children. But life was bleak. She looked at her whole life and marveled at the sorry state it was in.

Her husband was forty-one years old and she was twenty-five when they decided to take gurudīkṣā from their family preceptor, Śrī Śrī Śrī Jagadguru Channa Basavadeshi Kendra, Nidumamidi (Ja. Cha. Ni). Thereafter, Daakshaayani's spiritual focus grew stronger. Following her Guru's advice, she committed her life to serving the Guru and observing fasts along with her husband. "I wanted to know the Truth. I was not worried about the world but was more inclined toward God. What is God? I wanted to see Him. I wanted salvation. I had no interest in other things," she said. Her husband, too, was spiritually inclined and wished to free himself from saṁsāra.

At thirty-two, Daakshaayani and her husband decided to enter vānaprastha. Her children were grown up by then. She had persuaded her Guru to give her permission to enter vānaprastha. He had, at first, resisted and said that it would not be possible. Then, divine Grace came to her aid, and she was able to settle both of her children in marriage and careers. With all duties completed, her desire for the Lord was so fervent that the Guru could not decline Daakshaayani's request any longer. She and her husband began to follow vānaprasthāśrama. They lived in the same house, but in separate rooms, with no attachment to things or preferences for food or comfort.

The amazing couple lived thus for twelve long years. Their lives also included social service, and Daakshaayani continued teaching in their home.

In the course of time, Daakshaayani and her husband — along with a lawyer, a doctor, a scholar, and a banker — decided to propagate Hindu philosophy. The six of them heard about the Chinmaya Mission in Mysore. That was in 1976.

When the 6th National Yagna was announced in Chennai (January 1978), Daakshaayani decided to attend. It was her first ever meeting of Gurudev, Swami Chinmayananda. Almost immediately after introducing herself, she asked Gurudev if he would come to Kolar. Gurudev agreed instantly, "Yes, I will come!" he said. Everyone around was surprised, because it was rare for Gurudev to consent so readily, let alone for someone to invite Gurudev even during her introduction!

That same day, Daakshaayani also met Br. Brahma Chaitanya (later Swami Brahmananda) for the first time. He had heard that she had invited Gurudev to Kolar. With care, he guided her on the decorum to be adopted in interacting with great Gurus. That led to a close association and learning under Swami Brahmananda.

The innocent entreaty of Daakshaayani to Gurudev, asking him to come to Kolar, echoes Sabari's story in the *Rāmāyaṇa.* Sabari, with the purity of a sincere devotee, had invited Śrī Rāma to her humble abode. However, devotees say that the Lord does not come on calling. That the call has to also come from a pure heart, a heart made pure by years of tapaṣyā (penance).

Recalling that first meeting, Swamini Supreetananda says that if the Guru is in the disciple's heart, he comes. And Gurudev had hinted at this during a yajña in Cochin, when he had said, "From where Ramakrishna Paramahamsa and from where Swami Vivekananda! From where Swami Chinmayananda and from where 'Kolar'!" Swamini amma treasures those words as a timeless reference of the Guru-śiṣya relationship. No matter the distance, the Guru always finds his disciple.

▲ *Sw. Brahmananda at an event to honor Swamini Supreetananda for her work at Kolar*

Daakshaayani had found new direction on her path. She now began to monitor the schedule of the national yajñas and took to attending every national yajña of Gurudev's.

Life was now drenched with śravaṇam, svādhyāya, and contemplation on what she learned. Thus, she attended the 7th, 8th, 9th, and 10th national yajñas. When the next yajña was announced in Delhi, with a caveat that Gurudev's cardiac health was deteriorating and may restrict the conducting of more yajñas, Daakshaayani ran to Delhi to Gurudev. It could not have been any different, she says.

Daakshaayani had committed herself to vānaprastha when her śraddhā and bhakti had become overwhelming, and when the thought arose every day, "There must be an end to saṁsāra." Once her children were settled in marriage and jobs, the couple granted each other the permission to enter vānaprastha and ended their relationship as husband and wife. This was at Daakshaayani's age of thirty-two. Her pursuit of sāttvika sādhanā was relentless and steady in her seeking out Gurudev, in attending his yajñas, and in her studies and works of service.

For a person living in Kolar in the South of India, to follow her heart to the North was remarkable. Her perseverance must have been apparent to Gurudev. When the person who led the opening prayers in the morning session did not arrive, Gurudev asked Daakshaayani to chant instead. Soon, it became the tradition for Daakshaayani to sing or chant a stotram standing next to Gurudev at meal times. In this manner, her life drew closer and closer to the Guru, and further and further away from the world. It is the nature of vānaprastha — if one accepts it, vānaprastha leads onward.

Around 1980, a Mission āśrama was established in Chokahalli, sixty kilometers from Kolar, where Daakshaayani brought together the village women and taught them tailoring to provide them livelihood.

▲ *Swamini Supreetananda with students of a tailoring class, Chokahalli*

Thus, sevā was subtly added to her menu. When Gurudev made three or four visits to the Chokahalli āśrama, it was apparent that he was pleased with her work.

Study, service, listening to the Guru's teachings; serving the Guru, contemplation, protecting the needs of society — these were the content of her work and Daakshaayani's life was fully dedicated to uplifting the society. Her life was melding beautifully into vānaprastha.

In 1990, the Chokahalli āśrama had grown significantly and was in need of full-time care and attention. Gurudev asked Daakshaayani to take charge and receive sannyāsa. Her husband, delighted with her progress, allowed her to do her Guru's bidding and enter the life of a renunciate. After all, this was the future they both had looked forward to. Daakshaayani moved out of her home and into the Chokahalli āśrama full time.

In February 1990, on Mahāśivarātrī, Gurudev initiated Daakshaayani into sannyāsa. The fifty-seven-year-old Daakshaayani was now Swamini Supreetananda. Her family, to this day, is in Kolar, while her life has been devoted to the women of Chokahalli, Chinmaya Mission, Bala Vihar, and service of the Guru.

In December 2004, Swami Brahmananda requested Swamini Supreetananda to move to Mangalore and take charge of the Mission Center there. In Mangalore, not just individuals but entire families have become members of the Chinmaya Mission. They ask to be guided so that they all make the right decisions in their lives. Indeed, they look up to Swamini Supreetananda as one who took a strong decision to enter vānaprastha, and seeing her as a sannyāsinī, they know her experience will hold them all in good stead.

At this writing, Swamini Supreetananda is eighty-one years old! When she looks back, Amma feels that had she remained in gṛhasthāśrama, she would have still continued her svādhyāya, her sevā, her guru-pūjā anyway. But the decision to enter vānaprastha helped her serve more and more people, while also committing herself wholly to the Guru.

Swaminiji says that Gurudev knew, just on seeing her, that she was in vānaprastha. Later, when she went to Sidhbari to attend the installation ceremony of Lord Hanumān's idol, Gurudev told her not to take the temporary orange clothes that were given to campers: "You are already in kāvi (saffron)," he said. "You must take the permanent colors of a renunciate." This was in October 1982. Clearly, Gurudev had seen that she was fully headed for renunciation. But it was only much later that he would grant her sannyāsa dīkṣā. In the meanwhile, she followed Gurudev faithfully.

Today, the concept of 'time' has long left her vocabulary. For her, every breath is an offering at the feet of her great Master.

▾ ***Below Left:*** *Swamini amma with Pūjya Guruji at CM-Mangalore*
Below Right: *Swamini amma teaching Veda-pīṭha students*

Enough Krishna! The Temple Builder of New Delhi. This is a story as much about the vānaprasthi as it is about the unfolding of vānaprastha, when one wills to walk with the Guru, even if faith is faltering.

Krishnamoorthy's story begins like any other, and then suddenly changes course and takes you by surprise.

Krishna married young, had a good job and salary, then set up business which grew extremely well, minted his millions and went on to make more millions. His home was lovely, too: loving, devout wife, good children, obedient staff, everything in place. What is more, Krishnamoorthy was successful in whatever he was doing. This is how we think of success.

Close on the heels of business success came a luxurious life — and then an excess of everything. "All the bad habits that go with a successful man, I had — drinking and smoking and so on," says Krishnamoorthy candidly. It was this way of life he nurtured.

Then in 1962, Krishnamoorthy was briefly introduced to Gurudev in Kolkata. By 1968, he had become more actively associated with Gurudev but continued to pursue his business interests with a passion. Some more years passed and Krishnamoorthy moved to Delhi, to live in a well-appointed house in Maharani Bagh (an affluent neighborhood). That was 1974, when Br. Radhakrishnan (later to be ordained as Swami Jyotirmayananda) was looking after the Mission activities in Delhi. He was a regular visitor at Krishnamoorthy's home, and gradually he began to draw Krishnamoorthy more and more into Mission work. Krishnamoorthy owned several cars, had drivers to chauffeur him, and ran his own factory; being the boss and the master of his schedule, he could give time to the Mission when needed. By 1978, Krishnamoorthy was organizing Gurudev's Delhi yajñas.

One day, in 1983–84, Gurudev came to his home for bhikṣā. When the rush of visitors had abated, Krishnamoorthy and his wife sat with Gurudev in silence. At that time, Gurudev said, "Look,

Krishnamoorthy, don't become a slave to these luxuries. You have made enough money. Now leave everything and do some work for society, and I will give you a field to work in."

Krishnamoorthy felt a sweep of something he could not describe. He had built that business over ten years of very hard work. There were 800 people working under him; as far as they were concerned, Krishnamoorthy was their union and union leader! His wife, Lalita, a devoted housewife with no interest outside the home, personally looked after the workers' medical and welfare needs.

As Krishnamoorthy wondered how to make any sense of what Gurudev suggested, he heard his wife say, "Yes, Swamiji, yes, of course. I want him to work with you." Krishnamoorthy was shocked. *Whose side was she on?!* His wife and Gurudev were exchanging words while he stood there, numbed by the suddenness and finality of the suggestion. "I did not think that I could leave all those luxuries, the chauffeur-driven car, the air-conditioned house," he says.

Of course, it was not easy. He was just fifty-six. He was quite happy working with Gurudev, but to also give up secular work? That rankled. His mind flashed back to snippets of his relationship with Gurudev until then — a relationship that had begun eight years ago. Gurudev who had the knack for locating people for areas where they had proven strengths, called on him for a lot of organizational work. And Gurudev found that Krishnamoorthy, with his knowledge and skills in structural, mechanical, and chemical engineering was an asset for some of the Mission projects.

Krishnamoorthy's father was very spiritual and a Brahmin scholar. Gurudev had once visited their Chennai home and met the father, whom he addressed as pitamaha! Ironically, that father's eighth-born child, who was lovingly named Krishna, was a rebel of sorts, a nonconformist.

That Krishna now stood spellbound, having heard the one man whom he never thought he would have to dissent with, pronounce a harsh verdict: at fifty-six, enter vānaprastha! Frankly, it did not make sense to him at all!

The children were grown up — one had graduated, and the other was still studying. His wife gently prodded his conscience and said, "How often you are made to do what you don't like to do? You have often admitted that your conscience does not permit you to do what business makes you do." Krishnamoorthy knew only too well. Business and politics have a unique interdependency, often demanding a negotiation of values. So 'donations' happened, albeit reluctantly. Of course, Krishnamoorthy did not like doing all that, but at the same time, "I was making such a lot of money!" he said.

Finally he gave in. He decided that he would first need to steer the business into a position where it could run without him. So he asked his son, who was working in Sweden at that time, to come and take over; as luck went, the son refused to do so. Krishnamoorthy had to reluctantly leave the entire business in the care of professional managers.

Then Gurudev asked him, "Where would you like to work from?" Krishnamoorthy said, "I have a wonderful house in Chennai, which is very beautiful and faces the sea. There are only two kinds of places I would ever like to live in — by the sea or facing the mountains."

Gurudev agreed, "Good. In that case you can go to Sidhbari and take over the management there!" Krishnamoorthy declined. He said he preferred to stay where he already had a house, and the house in Adyar (a suburb of Chennai) was perfect.

Gurudev agreed again, "There are seven acres of land in Tamaraipakkam which is a gift from someone; it has been lying vacant for the last four to five years. Go and build a temple there." But Krishnamoorthy's Adyar house was in the south of Chennai! And the project site was far north of Chennai with the roads in between the two locations in a bad state. The idea was turning sour.

Fortunately, he had his cars and his engineering skills. And Gurudev gave expression to Krishnamoorthy's abilities and let him design the temple. Architect Mythili's design for the Sarveshwara Temple was approved by Gurudev and Krishnamoorthy was asked to execute it. On the day of the foundation/brick-laying ceremony, Krishnamoorthy tied Gurudev's headgear and Gurudev carried the first brick on his head to lay it at the construction site, and he asked Mr. and Mrs. Krishnamoorthy to lay the second and the third bricks. Pratiṣṭhā of the now famous sphāṭika liṅga was performed by Gurudev.

Soon after came the construction of Chinmaya Vidyalaya at Anna Nagar with the late Śrī Vasudevan, then managing it, followed by assistance to Chinmaya Mission South, and the construction of the Ganesha Temple at Chinmaya Vidyalaya in Virugambakkam.

History repeated itself in 1979–80. The Himachal government had donated land to the Chinmaya Mission. The team from Delhi, together with Gurudev and Krishnamoorthy, arrived at the village of Sidhbari, only to see a wide stretch of land on a hillock and a small hut in the middle of nowhere!

▼ *The land that would be home to Gurudev eternally — Sidhbari, 1979, just barren land then*

The villagers prostrated eagerly before Gurudev, but declared, "Nothing will grow here because of the very heavy rains and fierce winds from the Dhauladhar Mountains." Gurudev, however, in his characteristic style, put his stick on a particular spot and tapping there, he said, "Krishnamoorthy, here we will build a Hanumān statue, open to the sky. And you will organize the whole thing."

Krishnamoorthy looked around him. From the abundance of Maharani Bagh to the wilderness of Sidhbari — the contrast was devastating. *"Good Lord! Where have I come!"* he thought. But the doubt did not linger. Presently Gurudev, who was already miles ahead, said, "I am coming again after two months; by then you please get the śilpī Kashi from Bangalore to design the idol that we will establish here."

Krishnamoorthy, the mechanical engineer, put his entire weight behind this assignment while wondering all along about the route his life had taken. Soon, he got the sample prototype made, which was approved by Gurudev. And preparations for the now-iconic, 32-feet tall Sidhbari Hanumān was underway. The Grace of the Guru is unimaginable. The first abhiṣekam of this glorious Hanumān was performed by Gurudev with Krishnamoorthy and his wife Lalita as mukhya yajamānas (primary hosts) on October 10, 1982.

▲ *Installation of the 32-feet Hanumān – Gurudev leads with the holy waters for the abhiṣekam*

Later, Gurudev wanted a huge ramp built to access the idol at its height, and Krishnamoorthy enlisted the services of the Chennai Chyks. They were led by a young lad who would one day lead other

Chyks in service of Gurudev, much like Hanumān led the vānaras to serve Śrī Rāma. He would be named Swami Mitrananda. Thence commenced the tradition of mastakābhiṣekam every five years.

Twenty-five years later, in 2006, on the eve of the silver jubilee abhiṣekam in 2007, Lalita passed away. A grieving Krishnamoorthy told Guruji, "Lalita and I always performed this abhiṣekam as a couple. Now, you please give this opportunity to another couple."

Guruji looked at him and said, "Who says that she is not going to be there? Of course she is going to be there!" And Guruji placed a kalaśa on the topmost rung of the pyramidical structure of kalaśas and himself named it 'Lalita.' "There she is," he then said. Krishnamoorthy recalls, "I tell you, I cried and cried."

▲ *Guruji carrying Lalita Kalaśa*

If vānaprastha is difficult, as it was for Krishnamoorthy after Lalita's departure, the Guru is near at hand to ease the pain.

Between 1993 and 1994, Krishnamoorthy had moved to Hyderabad. Gurudev had attained Mahāsamādhi by then, and Guruji had taken over. The responsibility of grooming vānaprasthi Krishnamoorthy had moved over seamlessly to Guruji.

There was a small school in Kundanbagh with two-and-one-half acres of land. Guruji asked Krishnamoorthy to build a temple there. Designed by architect (the late) Raghu, Krishnamoorthy built the Parameshwara Temple on the site and managed the construction right up to the temple's consecration. He had done likewise in 1986 when Gurudev had sent him to Assam to build a temple of Śiva at Gyabaree Tea Estate.

Krishnamoorthy had glided into vānaprastha not knowing that was where he was going! Krishnamoorthy, who had worried and wondered how he would ever survive without his business and cars, even if he had been sincerely committed to Gurudev, had reluctantly turned his back on a materially luxurious life and gone in the direction where Gurudev first (and later Guruji) pointed. In willingly accepting the Guru's request to give up the secular pursuits, his lessons in renunciation began. But he didn't know that.

Krishnamoorthy had watched Gurudev and imbibed what he needed. For example, what he has been doing since Gurudev's Mahāsamādhi seems almost scripted by Gurudev. He runs the dispensary at Chinmaya Vibhooti, entirely funded by his savings, and even pays for his stay. That aspect of service, too, came out of an experience that he considers was a blessing from Gurudev. Long before, in 1989, when the temple at Tamaraipakkam was being inaugurated, Krishnamoorthy had a close-up view of what is true compassion. On the day of inauguration, thousands of villagers were thronging to see Gurudev and touch his feet. So did one lady with a tiny infant in her arms. The protective Krishnamoorthy, tall and stately as he was then too, who stood like a wall between Gurudev and the crowd, stopped her. But over his head Gurudev was already asking her what the matter was with the baby. "Unwell!" she cried.

▲ *'Sadhu sant ke tum rahware — You are the protector of sadhus and saints!' Hanumanji comes to Sidhbari — 1979*

Gurudev looked at Krishnamoorthy and said, "After the inauguration and pūjā, you will ensure that she is taken in and vibhūti is applied to the forehead of the child!" Then Gurudev told the lady,

"The child will be ok, don't worry."

Later, on his way out, pointing to the left of the place where he had met that lady, Gurudev said, "Krishnamoorthy, here we will build a free dispensary for the public." The rest of the story must be told in Krishnamoorthy's words:

▲ *Sidhbari Hanumān 2012 — at mastakabhishekam: Showered with the love of his devotees!*

> As usual, I said, Swamiji, we have only 25,000 rupees in the bank account. He said, "Don't worry about the money, it will come. You take the saṅkalpa to complete the dispensary. And tell me that you are taking a saṅkalpa." I took the saṅkalpa honestly. Two days later, one Mrs. Saraswati Anant came to meet Gurudev and said that her husband — a dear devotee of Gurudev — had passed away. His insurance policy was maturing and there were 300,000 rupees coming to her. "I want to give it to you, Swamiji!" she said. Gurudev looked at both of us in turn and, pointing to me, he said, "Give that money to this fellow who is standing here."
>
> I shyly thanked Gurudev, who said, "That shows your saṅkalpa was genuine. See! The money has come!"

Krishnamoorthy learned by simply being with Gurudev. A vānaprasthi learns to be pure in intent, leave his or her negativity, and remain detached from the outcome of a request made in prayer. This is one of the significant lessons that Gurudev taught Krishnamoorthy. In slow stages, Gurudev was scraping off his world of strategy and showing him the art of surrender. Krishnamoorthy was being initiated into karma yoga and selfless service — the hallmark of vānaprastha — and even he did not see it coming. He was choicelessly doing whatever Gurudev told him to do.

After the passing of his wife Lalita, Krishnamoorthy, now fondly called Thatha (grandfather) by everyone, decided to take shelter in Gurudev's home — in one of the Chinmaya Mission āśramas. Guruji, Swami Tejomayananda, had a plan and asked him to stay at Vibhooti. Amazingly, it was as if the Pranava Ganesh Mandir was waiting for Thatha. "You go take charge and complete it!" said Guruji. Temples always waited for *Thatha*!

Looking back, when Krishnamoorthy/Thatha was asked to give up everything by Gurudev, did he? Was there a conflict within? Was it simple to disregard the conflict and move along with Gurudev's suggestion?

Thatha says there was a bit of a conflict. It was a shift from a totally luxurious life to one that promised another kind of luxury about which he had heard a lot, but could not fathom at all. When he had spoken to his wife, she had admonished him, "How much money do we want? We don't need more. Let's go and do as Gurudev is saying. There is some meaning in what he has said."

Krishnamoorthy had contemplated for a few days. The truth was his business and its related life had a thrill, but not peace or happiness. It was the same old routine every day, unchanging. But he had trained himself to balance himself on that thrill and enjoy it. He did not think there could be more to thrill! "I feel sorry that I didn't get in touch with him

[Gurudev] earlier than when I did. I envy some of the youngsters who are now with Chinmaya Mission. They are exposed to this [Chinmaya] way of thinking so early in life!" he says.

Krishnamoorthy had placed all his trust in Gurudev; he could not think of any other course of action. Still, was it difficult to give up one kind of life to adopt another kind of life? In hindsight, it seems that the Guru had a structure and a plan. Gurudev knew that Krishnamoorthy would have to fly regularly into Delhi as his business demanded. Gurudev said, "Spend five percent of time in the first year, ten percent of the time in the second year, ..." recommending a slow increase in Krishnamoorthy's participation in Mission work. As fate would have it, in the second year, his son returned from Sweden and voluntarily took over the business!

THE BHARAT RATNA THAT *THATHA* CHERISHES

You have exemplified in your life the combination of material prosperity and spiritual divinity most beautifully, through your service to Pūjya Gurudev like that of Śrī Hanumān to Lord Śrī Rāma. On this auspicious occasion of your 80th birthday, I pray to them all to bless you with a total fulfillment in life.

With utmost love
& regards,
Tejomayananda

To listen to the Guru one must; but fickleness is the nature of the mind. Was Krishnamoorthy constantly calling up to find out how the business was doing, calling up to find out how the children were doing, and fretting over this and that? Krishnamoorthy admits that such exchanges happened for the first two years. During that period, he trained his son to take charge as chairman of the business. "After that, I never bothered to find out what was happening. He used to show me the quarterly results, but I had lost interest."

Once Gurudev had tethered him to work, Krishnamoorthy did not see how more than twenty-five years had passed. Ever since the beginning, he has been working, building temples everywhere, getting into all types of construction projects — that was how vānaprastha was laid out for him. Maybe the kind of work was nearly the same as his earlier career, but the people he dealt with while working on Mission projects were very different. Earlier, he might have lost his temper; now he explains patiently: "I am not a jñāna yogī. I can work — from morning to night — and that is my strength. But the only change is that earlier I used to work for my own benefit, for accumulating more wealth. Now I work, but the result is not for me. It is for the Mission!

▲ *The best certificate! A hug from Guruji acknowledging Thatha's work*

But Thatha was also quietly working at his own inner wealth when he took up and completed the 'Gītā Home Study Course' in 2012, at the amazing age of eighty-two. In an amusing moment at CIF's Adi Sankara Nilayam, when Guruji had awarded Thatha with a certificate, he said, "Now here is something I have for you!" and a beaming Thatha put out both hands in the manner of a bhikṣu (one who seeks alms). And Guruji placed in those hands the first lesson of the Advanced Vedānta Course!

And Thatha acknowledges, "Let us just say, that a shadow of Knowledge, or the Truth, is slowly but surely coming into the karma yoga that I am doing!"

WHEN AMERICAN SCIENTISTS CAME A-CALLING

A LIGHT MOMENT AT TAMARAIPAKKAM

The temple at Tamaraipakkam was unusual in structure. The outer shell resembled a Śivaliṅgam. Once, some American scientists accompanied by officials from the Indian Embassy visited the site and asked to see the property. The reason — a U.S. satellite had found that there was construction going on which looked like an atomic reactor; hence, this brouhaha. "What are you building?" they asked Krishnamoorthy. And he answered, "A temple." They wanted to go in, but he refused to let them in. "I don't know you or your purpose," he declared to them. He said later, "I thought it was not proper for me to let them in."

Then they asked, "Who are the builders?" Krishnamoorthy, eager to see them go, said, "L&T" (the company contracted for the construction), and, for good measure, added the name of the responsible official at L&T. Thatha recounts how Gurudev laughed heartily when he heard about this: "Mahā mūḍha![1] "he thundered," You should have told them that there is something more powerful than an atomic bomb inside, which they can see when the temple is completed!"

▾ *Sarveshwara Dhyana Nilayam at Tamaraipakkam*

[1] O great fool!

XVI

The Changing Structure of World Population

A report on world demographics says, "The rate of growth of the elderly is increasing at an alarming pace." 'Alarming' more because the available or visible infrastructure and intent to support this growth is not commensurate with the numbers.

As we delve deeper into the statistics and projections supporting this statement, we need to keep in mind the ever-increasing role that a spiritual approach to aging may need to play in the years ahead.

The following table gives some perspective on the growth of the aged population, comparing three points of time:[1]

	1950	2000	2050
World population	2,526 m.	6,128 m.	9,551 m.
Age 60 or over	1 in 12	1 in 10	2 in 10
Percentage of 60 or over	8%	10%	21%

The last number, 21 percent, has a lot to say as the ensuing pages will narrate. The five countries with the greatest projected population, including their percentages of age sixty or over, are shown in the following table. As projected, in 2050, these countries will make up 42 percent of the world's population.

[1] Population Pyramids of the World from 1950 to 2100.

	1950		2000		2050	
	Total Pop.	% of 60 or Over	Total Pop.	% of 60 or Over	Total Pop.	% of 60 or Over
India	376 m.	4.2	1,047 m.	7.0	1,620 m.	18.0
China	544 m.	7.6	1,280 m.	10.0	1,385 m.	34.0
U.S.A.	158 m.	12.6	285 m.	16.2	401 m.	28.0
Indonesia	72 m.	6.2	209 m.	7.2	321 m.	16.6
Pakistan	38 m.	7.8	144 m.	6.2	271 m.	15.0

When we see that the world's population is expected to grow by a little over 50 percent between 2000 and 2050, while the sixty or over population is expected to double, that is, grow by over 100 percent, this is where we become truly alarmed.

We need to be justifiably alarmed for another reason — the UN report on aging says blandly, "At that point [2050], older persons will outnumber the population of children (0–14 years) for the first time in human history."

Without too much number crunching, here are some facts:

- There will be far fewer people under age fourteen in the world because the community in the middle, between twenty and forty, are going to be having fewer children. The reasons for that are myriad.
- The older segment of the population is growing at a rate faster than the total population.

So, a glance at the global numbers is important to understanding why this book is relevant for each of us — vānaprastha is not just a scriptural call; the state of the population which we see unfolding around us, is the statistical consequence of continuing to live our lives without spiritual discipline and forethought to potential future outcomes.

This is a warning bell for us. It is a warning because, if a greater part of the world is going to be populated by older people, the total health of the world will depend on the health of these elders who — from what we have seen so far based on the experiences of so many Mission Centers — have shown a propensity for unhappiness, failing health, and pessimism, thanks entirely to the absence of a society that is friendly to all ages. *Do we have a plan for this?*

The Oldest Old. It will be good to bear in mind throughout this chapter that 'older population' refers to the '60 or over.' However, within that demographic there is an all-new category — the '80 or over,' or the oldest old. The global estimate for people 80 or over by 2020 was placed, in 1989, at 100 million. Recent reviews of that estimate by the UN reveal startling variations. Quoting from the review: "By 2050, 20 percent of the older population will be aged 80 or over. The number of centenarians (aged 100 or over) is growing even faster, and is projected to increase tenfold, from approximately 343,000 in 2012 to 3.2 million by 2050." Which segment of population is going to provide or have the medical resources?

To get a perspective:
WORLD Population

World 2000	6.13 billion
Est. 2050	9.56 billion
India 2000	1.00 billion
Est. 2050	1.60 billion

From 2000 to 2050, the Indian population is expected to grow 60% compared to the rest of the world's population growth of 55%.

Velocity of Aging. How fast are the changes in the population demographics? When we look at projections for 2050, with 2012 as the base year, we must understand that the doubling of numbers is happening in less than forty years, even during the lifetimes of the present generations. The gravity of this pace of change is felt even more when we read this sentence from the World Health Organization (WHO):

> By 2020, more than 1 billion people aged sixty years and older will be living in the world, more than 700 million of them in developing countries.

Here are some more key number shockers from WHO:

- *The number of older persons has tripled over the last fifty years; it will more than triple again over the next fifty years.*
- *The older population is growing faster than the total population in practically all regions of the world — and the difference in growth rates is increasing.*
- *The proportion of older persons is projected to more than double worldwide over the next half century.* At the global level, in 2012, one in every ten was aged sixty years or older, and one in every fourteen was aged sixty-five or older. By the year 2050, more than one in every five persons throughout the world is projected to be aged sixty or over.
- *More developed regions have relatively high proportions of older persons.* By 2050, one in every three persons living in the more developed regions is likely to be sixty or older, and about one in every four is projected to be sixty-five or older.
- *High proportions of older persons in Europe; low proportions in Africa.* Europe is projected to remain stable in this demographic category for at least the next fifty years. In contrast, only 10 percent of the population of Africa is projected to be over sixty in 2050.
- *The older population will be increasingly concentrated in the less developed regions.* Over the next half century, this trend will intensify. In the more developed regions, the number of persons aged sixty or over will increase, while in the less developed regions, the older population (aged sixty or over) will more than quadruple during this same period. It is estimated that *by 2050, nearly four-fifths of the world's older population will be living in the less developed regions.*

It must be understood that societies take a long time to adjust to rapid changes in age structure. And a time span of forty years (2012 to 2050) is not a long time. Why, even for organizations to revamp their superannuation schemes, to restructure pension plans, will not be easy. Such financial packages have far-reaching impact on not just fund flow but also on employee morale and understanding — both in the private and public sectors.

What is thought-provoking is that while average life expectancy is increasing in nearly all developed countries, the birth rates are registering sharp declines. When increasing life expectancy combines with declining birth rates, then we have a phenomenon called 'Population Aging.' The numbers analyzed in the earlier segment will be useful here. In developing countries, population aging coexists with poverty. Hence, a lot more old age related diseases — including mental health — may remain untreated.

Most developing countries are typified by: inadequate funds for health care; lack of social security; and the prevalence of double-income families, implying that women are not available as traditional caregivers. We need to be alert to this anticipated change in society and start building alternatives for eldercare.

What Does All of This Mean to Me and to the World? All of this means that the structure of the population has changed and will continue to change. When the structure changes, it implies that our forecasts can no longer be based on the past population structure; therefore, we must zero-base our approach and be more dynamic about changing what needs to be changed. Hence, the call is for preparedness.

Are we prepared? We should have started long, long ago. But late is better than never; so, in the following paragraphs, let us first look at some of the rapidly changing dimensions.

The year 2050 will be the first time that the share of children (from birth to age fourteen) and the share of persons who are sixty and over will be the same. Both categories will clock in at about two billion each. This means that 22 percent of the population, typically, will be also nonearning, nonworking, and high on health/development needs.

Are we mentally prepared to give them the love and care (read: time and patience) that will be needed? Better still, *that* 22 percent is made up of many of us who are reading this book, people in the age groups of 'thirty or over' today. This is a wake-up call for this group! You have to make a comfortable bed today so you can lie in it thirty years from now.

Close to 53 percent of the world's older population is in Asia, while 24 percent is in Europe. By 2050, Asia's share will go up to 63 percent while Europe's share will decline to 11 percent. This means that China and India — two very large countries in Asia — need to be prepared. As for India, given the current state of its elderly population, the preparedness demanded is on a war footing. India is not a poor country but a country with many poor people who are coexisting with many rich people. The need is for physical infrastructure, for sure, but also for spiritual infrastructure for the poor and the rich.

Now, to look at the 'oldest old' (or 'eighty and over') — currently (year 2000 data), 37 million in this age group live in the more developed regions, and 33 million live in less developed regions. This is stated to be the fastest-growing segment of the older population, so that by 2050, this segment is projected to be five times as large, accounting for 4 percent of the world population. Every society needs its elders, its grandparents, because the elder is the nourisher, the compassion-giver, the one who blesses.

Demographics includes gender distribution. Is population aging gender sensitive? Very simply, with the male gender having a higher mortality rate, an aging population will be made up of more women.

(But time will tell, as with all change, even the norms stand to change. As more and more women enter the workforce, their dual role playing as workers and mothers can have an impact on feminine mortality rates. Then again, if child-care infrastructure is not dependable, the dual role itself will beg a trade-off.)

According to the UN's Population Aging Chart: 'In 2012, at the world level, there are 84 men for every 100 women age sixty and over, and only 61 men for every 100 women age eighty and above.'

Other findings point to the following:

a. Dependency of the nonworking population on the working population. With the fertility rates declining, the potential number of entrants into the workforce is clearly declining, too. The number of people dependent on a thinning workforce is a major cause for concern.
b. Also consequent to the above, the dependency will now shift to the elders, who may need to return to the workforce.
c. Clearly, therefore, business and government plans will need to be sensitive to demographic changes. Can businesses afford to stay with their current competitive approach, or will the workforce shortage be an equalizer? These are not choices but demands for action.

With Vedānta as our guiding force, every Mission Center must ponder and discuss how its local society, and society at large, may be prepared for living with and empowering the aging many. The importance of such foresight and planning cannot be overemphasized.

The next chapter highlights Pūjya Guruji Swami Tejomayananda's suggestions to everyone on managing vānaprastha — whether as an elder or as a future elder.

IN PURSUIT OF EDUCATION

When Dr. P. Geervani met Gurudev in 1979, she felt she had met God. Not wishing to disturb him, she decided to get closer to his thought through study and by attending his every lecture in Hyderabad. But in 1986, she had to leave a spiritual camp midway because of her work. Gingerly, she went up to Gurudev to explain why she had to leave. Gurudev held her by her shoulders and said, "Do not worry. You will come back after retirement."

▲ *Dr. P. Geervani*

When she retired twelve years later, this Vice Chancellor of a University, gave up several international consulting offers, reflecting: "Gurudev gave me the strength of purpose during my career, I must give this time to him." And her vānaprastha years began with helping the administration of the Vidyalaya in Hyderabad. Before long she was writing for children, she translated the *Valmiki Rāmāyaṇa,* and her work with education grew in leaps and bounds.

Dr. Geervani's work truly exemplifies service for the betterment of society as prescribed by Gurudev for vānaprasthis. She has contributed immensely to CM's academic effort — as the Academic Advisor to CIF (across its Home Study Courses), its Shodha Sansthan, getting it recognized as a Doctoral Research Center, advising on the Anusāraka project, and much more. Hers has been the cause of knowledge creation or dissemination. She recognized the potential of CIF and wanted to bring it closer to universities.

Today, in her eighth decade, she is a force to be reckoned with in CCMT's Education Cell, establishing many Chinmaya Vidyalayas in India. Why? In her words, "I feel Gurudev's institutions should be of a high standard and not compromise with quality. He himself was meticulous."

Uncanny, but the name 'Geervani' is one of the rare names of Goddess Saraswati.

THE WORLD IS WHAT YOU MAKE IT

Never insult or ciriticze the world. In the larger vision, the whole world is created by the Lord. If you insult the world, you are insulting the Lord. If your mother or wife has cooked your food and you throw it out, you are not only insulting the food, but also the one who made it. Therefore, do not criticize food. Scriptures teach us the importance of developing vairāgya or 'dispassion' upon learning which we must criticize our excessive attachments, not the objects. With food, objects, and the whole of creation, every youth must learn and fulfill this vow reverentially.

– Swami Tejomayananda, *Graceful Aging*

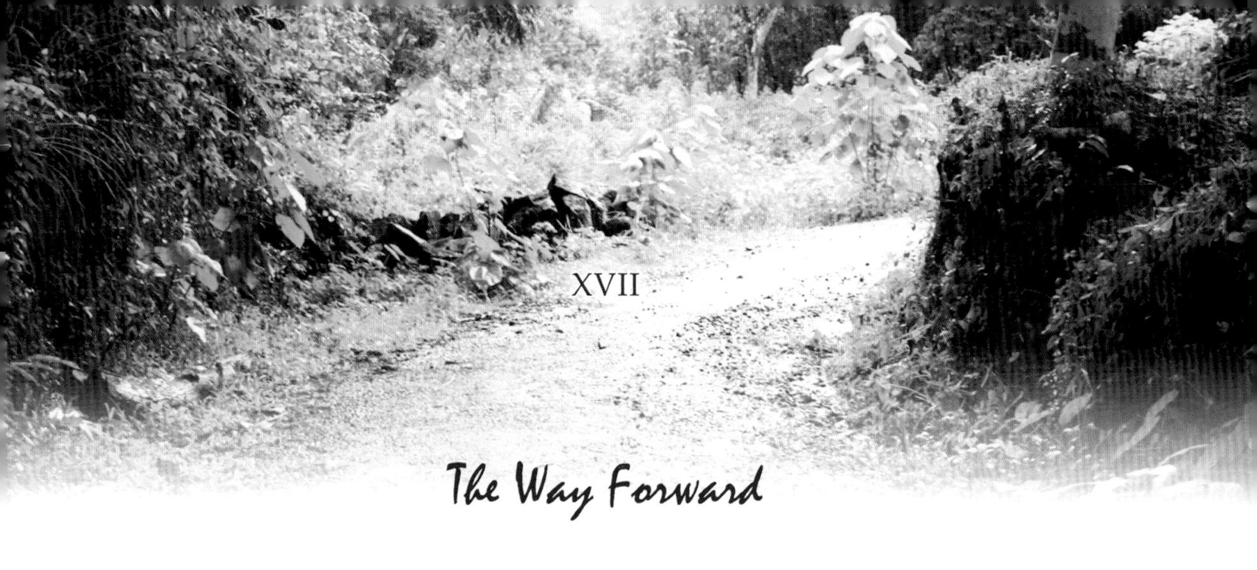

XVII

The Way Forward

When we come to the end of the book, we look for a recap, for clear answers to questions such as: What is the best way to move into the vānaprastha stage? How would that directive apply to everyone — both the young and the not so young? What do we need to do to remain prepared for the later stages of life? What are we missing? What are we failing to do? This entire chapter highlights thoughts as given by Pūjya Guruji Swami Tejomayananda.

From Larva to Sannyāsa. In zoology, there is a biological process called overwintering, during which insects and some plants wait out the winter season when temperatures are very low, food is limited, weather is dry, and normal activity is impossible. Some organisms hibernate, some migrate. In the case of overwintering plants, activities around reproduction and growth of vegetative tissues stops.

All organisms have coping strategies conducive to evolution, strategies for dealing with change. Plants, insects, and animals are programmed to follow their built-in instinct. They simply do what they are supposed to do when the climate or environment changes.

▲ **Photo:** *The path leading to Śrī Ādi Śaṅkara Nilayam, Kerala*

On the other hand, the human being has an intellect which he uses to make choices — sometimes, sadly, suboptimal choices.

If we look at the essential stages in the evolution of a butterfly's life, we see some startling lessons for human beings, lessons we have ignored, albeit lessons that are needed.

In the first stage, the egg is placed in an environment safely away from predators, where it can get the food it needs while it awaits its purpose: to become a caterpillar. Hence, the egg is attached to leaves and stems. This can be likened to man's brahmacarya stage.

The larva then grows into a caterpillar — a voracious feeder so like man's young adult stage. These two stages roughly compare to infancy, childhood, youth and adult stages in a human's life, when the focus is on physical safety, physiological growth, and goal attainment.

When a caterpillar has attained the right size, the larval growth is said to be done. It now prepares for pupating. First, it stops eating; then it empties its digestive system; then it looks for a sheltered spot where it will encase itself in a chrysalis.

Compare this to man's vānaprastha stage. *There is no food intake while it allows the change to take place — change that will bring to it the purpose of its birth: the transformation into a butterfly.* A physical change occurs first — the caterpillar tissues are broken down and the structures of the adult insect are formed! This may last many days or even months, depending on the kind of butterfly; this compares to the period of sādhanā of a person whose intensity and focus determine the attaining of mokṣa. Many similarities are seen here with the vānaprastha stage, the age of maturity, where aging at a physical level takes place, and with it the inability of the digestive system to digest many kinds of foods.

The pupating caterpillar that encases itself into a chrysalis does so to be able to emerge as a free soaring butterfly.

PARROTS, DEAR

During his last lecture at the Washington, D.C., Camp in 1993, Gurudev concluded with a poignant story. In this story there is a compassionate man who tries to teach a flock of parrots how to avoid being trapped in the net of the hunter. Gurudev would slowly repeat these sentences over and over during the telling of the story with great emphasis, which is one reason it stuck so deeply in my memory.

"Parrots, parrots, parrots dear. The hunter will come, he will scatter the seed and spread his net; you will peck at the seed and be trapped in his net. Beware, the hunter! Beware, the hunter."

Sadly, the parrots are caught by the hunter anyway because they had only learned to "parrot" back the warning to each other without ever understanding the real meaning of his words.

Gurudev was giving us a serious message. He was warning us not to merely come to camps year after year and "parrot" back the words of Vedānta, without making a sincere effort to assimilate the real meaning of the words and liberate ourselves from the world of delusion.

I see it now as Gurudev' parting message to us: to not take this blessed opportunity for granted. He was about to leave us and was telling us that he had given all the Knowledge we needed in order to free ourselves from the suffering of spiritual ignorance. It would now be up to us to sincerely and deeply contemplate on the words of Vedānta and to realize that Truth for ourselves, not merely parrot back the words. Or else we would end up in the net of the hunter, saṁsāra.

– Swamini Radhikananda (formerly Brni. Arpita) is the Ācārya of Chinmaya Govardhan, the picturesque āśrama near St. Augustine, Florida, U.S.A.

▶ *Swamini Radhikananda*

And, finally in the spring, the matured butterfly emerges, freeing itself of the shackles of the pupa, free of its growth stages, to now soar high as a butterfly. This is springtime in the life of a human when having successfully pupated, he or she emerges ready for sannyāsa!

Building Our Chrysalis — Choosing Growth. It is in recognition of our need to mature spiritually (pupate) that Gurudev established pitamaha centers for those who do not have a quiet place. The effort that the Mission has invested in unfolding the potential of vānaprasthāśrama, and then harnessing its power to gather us toward it, is tremendous. The people who came together — at Rewa's National Workshop (Chapter VIII) and Prayaga's National Seminar (Chapter IX) — to awaken interest in a structured third age, included many who were not initially part of the Mission but who desired to utilize the platform of the Mission to share their insights. What they brought to center stage was the significant research and academic findings which fine-tuned the direction of the vānaprastha initiative. And, of course, many of them were elders themselves — professors, doctors, researchers, sociologists, anthropologists, and gerontologists. What makes this even more poignant is that *they were people who were also experiencing neglect and indifference as aging citizens,* people who wished to make a difference. That made their efforts both subjective and laudable.

Fueled by Gurudev's vision and the research of experts, this book on vānaprastha intends to sow into all minds the need to bring into hard focus the much-neglected and unused, or even misused, third stage of life — not just among those who are in their third age, but also among those who stand on the threshold in denial, as well as those younger adults who sidestep the elder — be it failing to recognize their potential or respect them or include them or help them.

True, the duties of a householder life wane around sixty, but Gurudev wants us to pay attention to a harder truth: growth begins with introspection; and sixty may be the right time.

G*oing Beyond CVS.* It is one thing to study Vedānta, the scriptures, the texts — it is another to live as directed by the texts. To those who have enrolled for the CVS course and tested the waters, Guruji says that the sanctum sanctorum of the vānaprastha *forest* is still far away. But even entering the precincts of the forest is laudable. Of those who have entered that far, he asks, "Thus far and no further?"

The CVS course is a precursor that mildly hints at the lessons for the third age, but the real work lies ahead. Even so, CVS has done a tremendous job of shepherding the many elders who lacked a definition, and has provided them with a map to the stage of Realization. At the time of this writing, over fifty CVS centers engage with roughly five thousand elders all across India. Clearly, that many elders have now begun to think about vānaprastha, whereas earlier they had not.

But what next? The next step is to know one's responsibility, and before that, recognizing that there is a responsibility. This life is entrusted to us — it is our responsibility to ensure that we grow in the right direction. As an example, Guruji says, "I am a trustee of the Chinmaya Mission. A trustee is one to whom something is entrusted. He has to work; he does not get paid, but he must make sure that the assets and earnings of the organization are applied for the purposes of the Mission. Nothing in the Trust belongs to him. Yet he has to ensure that the Trust is growing and growing well." Using that same logic, the question arises, "Are we trustworthy? Are we using our lives in the right manner?"

Such introspection would then need a plan. Just as we would plan our day or week, we must have a plan for the entire life, spreading across the four broad stages of life. Vānaprastha, the third age, is part of that plan and must be an integral part of our plan for growth.

D*econstructing Gṛhasthāśrama or Householder-ship.* Vānaprastha is the unlearning, the unwinding process, of all that we have acquired as habits (read, attachments). Vānaprastha starts the

A SAṄKALPA AND A SOLUTION
SHANTI AND RAM MOHAN

Shanti and Ram Mohan exemplify Guruji's idea as elaborated in this chapter. As soon as their second daughter got married (which in the Indian context is 'settled'), they decided to make a clean break and enter vānaprastha. Ram Mohan was a vice president with Computer Sciences Corporation in Atlanta, Georgia, U.S.A. A chain of several unplanned occurrences found him first attending camps and lectures and then, after a transfer out of the San Francisco Bay Area, becoming a part of the CM Alpharetta, Georgia. As he coordinated satsaṅgas for Bala Vihar, Yuva Kendra, and the older adults, he found his Vedānta was inadequate. When he heard of the Sandeepany Course, he resigned from his job and, along with Shanti, enrolled for the two-year course and moved to India.

After their graduation from Sandeepany, they accepted an offer from Chinmaya International Foundation in Veliyanad, Kerala, India. Shanti will eventually serve as Ācārya and administrator of the Home Study Courses; Ram Mohan will unleash his IT skills to enhance CIF's study course offerings, in addition to serving as course Ācārya.

▲ *Shanti and Ram Mohan in their room at Ādi Śaṅkara Nilayam*

Today they both live at CIF, serving it and leading a minimalistic life.

Their entry into vānaprastha is an extension of their philosophy — the moment one's duties to children and parents are accomplished, one must plunge into vānaprastha.

breaking down of the structure and bondage. Because we are human and endowed with intellect, the deconstruction needs to be conscious, planned, and voluntary — unlike the caterpillar, whose metamorphosis is physical and instinctive. Therefore, our renouncing must include the material, the emotional, and the intellectual. Gurudev would have liked to add here, "Think!"

Vānaprastha is a period of letting go. That is why it is a struggle, but such a struggle is nothing to fret over. It is the only way that change can come about, and such change is what vānaprastha instills in order to qualify us for sannyāsa, the stage at which we can be the guide for others following on the path.

So, what is the journey onward all about? Guruji says, "Real vānaprastha is only about preparing for higher and higher spiritual evolution." Spiritual evolution will come out of discarding, like the caterpillar, the skin of the BMI. Currently, the CVS course is introductory in nature. Thereafter, stepping fully into the waters of higher wisdom and enjoying the flow is up to each individual. But Guruji has an advice: "Those who wish to study further and take their sādhanā to a higher level may join the two-year Vedānta course or the six-week Dharma Sevak Course (DSC) and move forward on the path of growth toward Self-realization."

From Minimum to Maximum. One step in the direction of deconstructing gṛhasthāśrama is to explore and then experience a minimalist life, a life of limited choices alongside a life of study and sādhanā. For it does take time. The intention is not to oppress oneself. Many elders will have experienced that the mind, in its own way, begins to prepare for simplification; this is seen in the need for less noise, for simpler food, for better literature, for softer music, for smaller gatherings — in short, for most things subtle. Uniquely, the brief spells of āśrama life are not resisted by the mind.

The two-year Vedānta course may seem like too much, too soon, for some. They can opt for the six-week Dharma Sevak Course (DSC), as it offers a great preview of āśrama life for a short duration. (By āśrama life is meant an inward-looking life with minimum needs and maximum study and contemplation. Gurudev himself has said that such a life can be led in one's own home.) Many people worldwide have been inspired simply by reading about the course online. They have come from places as far away as Romania to attend a DSC, and having attended, they have been filled with the spirit that they needed to shift their life from this to That. As a result, they have thereafter devoted their lives to serving the Mission, the society, the community, and, through all this, have unwittingly contributed to lifting their own minds higher than they ever imagined. Indeed, the DSC can be one of the finest enablers of the vānaprasthāśrama. There are many in the Mission today who attend even two DSCs a year, every year, so that the āśrama life becomes an integral part of their life.

The Vedānta Course that the Mission conducts at Sandeepany is technically created for those who have decided to dedicate themselves to study and service or teaching Vedānta. But it is as much open to anyone who wishes to study deeply, as have so many of our Mission workers. They are today teaching full-time in our Mission Centers in many parts of the world. So those who really want to immerse themselves deeply into Vedānta can pursue the Vedānta Course, as some gṛhasthas do every year.

Next Is What? Next is a menu of options! As stated earlier, the CVS course helps make that beginning for those who have never engaged with Vedānta. However, for those who have studied the Foundation and Advanced Vedānta Courses or the *Gītā* Course offered by Chinmaya International Foundation (www.chinfo.org), or engaged steadily with Vedānta, the call is to step up their involvement in their

THE DHARMA SEVAK COURSE — A LIFESTYLE

The name of this course does not reveal everything it holds within itself as gifts. Hence, a decoding is necessary to appreciate its offerings.

The Dharma Sevak Course (DSC) equips one with the knowledge needed to serve the cause of dharma. It is a perfect experience for those wary of committing to twenty-four months of Vedānta study. In as little as six weeks, the spiritual discipline, in fact, grows on the camper.

Swamini Vimalananda, the architect of the DSC, describes the DSC as a condensed form of the two-year Sandeepany Vedānta Course. Therefore, all the elements of the Sandeepany Course are available in it. Specifically, the DSC is meant for gṛhasthas and vānaprasthis who can, after the DSC, become dharma sevaks.

For those six weeks, the DSC defines boundaries — physically, mentally, intellectually, and spiritually. From morning meditation to dinner, the time slots are sharply defined and followed. Study times are carved out, and what is planned is studied. But important in this course is the design — all four āśramas are embedded in the DSC. The gurukula style of living and studying embraces brahmacarya; that different kinds of people of all ages come together creates the extended family with built-in diversity. The very fact that one has left home to enroll for a residential camp exemplifies vānaprastha in a manner in which the pursuit is only of dharma and mokṣa (not ārtha or kāma, that is, no earning, no pleasures, including television). As for sannyāsa, it is the core aim of all the study; even the dress code is mandatory: saffron (in particular, at DCSs held in India) for all campers during the six weeks. In an instant, this releases the mind from the burden of, "What shall I wear today?" The camper is expected to wash his or her own clothes, and since the eyes are seeing only saffron all around, and the same sari or dhoti, there is no envy, no pride, no pull of external distractions.

◀ ***Left:*** *One of the core elements of a DSC is fine-tuning the link between thought, word, and deed. Thus, prayer finds expression in idol decoration and service to creation. Seen here, sevaks participating in 5.30 A.M. Gaṇeśa abhiṣekam, beginning with learning to decorate the idol.*

Below Left: *Sevaks feed cows.*

Below Right: *In the classroom*

▲ ***Left:*** *10th DSC students with 2nd purohit course students carrying the utsava mūrty.*
Right: *DSC 11, Raksha Bandhan ceremony with Guruji.*

The DSC makes the individual firm and grounded in every way. Following are other lessons taught in a DSC:

- The entire background of Chinmaya Mission is presented.
- How to run each of CM's grassroots activities is taught.
- Pūjās and other methods of sādhanās are demonstrated and learned.
- Early morning is devoted to dhyāna, and evening is dedicated to study of the *Gītā*.
- Learning Sanskrit is compulsory.
- One hour is allotted for walking in solitude.
- The day includes ārtī, bhajans, and chanting.
- Bhakti texts are studied in the evening.
- A post-dinner video lesson of Gurudev's teachings connects the participants with the Founder of Chinmaya Mission.
- Lastly, there is family time when all campers pray together. They also play together — team building and team spirit are enforced. A complete lifestyle is forged.

The camp is designed to leave a lasting taste for a different way of living — a living that celebrates the Path of Good, a path that shows no fear about detaching. Campers are known to sense a great change in their view of life when they return from the camp to their secular life.

Indiscipline is a major cause of problems in the third age, and developing discipline is difficult at this late age. But the DSC encourages the participants to reorient themselves, and following a discipline becomes a joyful experience. Giving up attachments happens gradually and joyfully. And then one comes to understand how easy it is to be happy without the many things which we usually hold onto, and which we feel are indispensable for living.

That is when we see clearly how we fill our lives with objects and relationships only in anticipation of joy. And the six weeks at a DSC camp bring the realization that those six weeks went by with barely any material things — and joy was experienced anyway.

third age. To them, too, Guruji's advice is to enroll for a few DSCs so that the mind stays tuned to the new life that awaits them. Likewise, those who have completed the CVS course should begin to enroll for DSCs if they are really serious about making their vānaprastha meaningful toward self-inquiry.

Study Together, Grow Together. Guruji goes one step further. He has offered to create a team that will design courses for those interested — for example, enhancing the CVS with an advanced course for those who are serious about their vānaprastha stage. That

▼ *DSC students pray and worship together.*

WHEN PRACTICE CONTINUES TO BE DAUNTING...

Often, no matter how much we read about a topic, a doubt remains: I have read all that the Ācāryas and Guru say. I even understand it at an intellectual level. But it is very difficult to put this into practice! What should one do?

To a similar question Pūjya Guruji replied: "Understanding can be only intellectual. There seems to be a big gulf between what we understand and what we practice. The only solution is to 'do it.' If someone asks — how to get up early in the morning — the only answer is, 'Get up!' One may set an alarm or arrange for a wake-up call from the telephone exchange, but even after one is woken up, one can just turn around and go back to sleep. One has to make up one's mind to get up and then, do it.

"Further, real understanding takes place when it becomes a way of life. If someone is sitting before a beautifully decorated plate of delicacies and is then told that one of the food items, only one of them , is poisoned, what will happen? Will the person try even one of them? Will he say, 'Intellectually I know it is poison, but the food is quite tempting. Let me taste it and see for myself. After all, only one of the items is poisoned.' Do you rationalize like this? Even if there is only a suspicion that there might be poison in it, we will reject all of it outright. Why? Our understanding of the consequences of poisoning is very clear. Giving in to temptation means death.

"Our attachment to the physical body is such that only physical death scares us. We do not take mental torture seriously. If we can see the hidden consequences, we will never be tempted.

"Our śāntipatha says, 'tejasvinavadhitam astu. May our life be brilliant, may our life be in accordance with our knowledge.' Only then is it real understanding. Our values must reflect in our actions."

– Swami Tejomayananda, *You Ask, HE Answers*

option is enriching from several perspectives. A group of friends, let us say, may wish to lend purpose to their third age by integrating spiritual practices into their lives. This can be a great way to pursue vānaprastha by creating a group where close friends come together and commit to a study plan. A structure and a syllabus can be designed for them.

Such a group can even ask for a fixed-period course of one or two months to be structured for them. The group can attend the course together, and grow. Chinmaya Mission will also help find and appoint an Ācārya who will facilitate and teach. Thereafter, the group can evaluate their needs with the Ācārya and determine the texts needed for introspection and application of the teaching, followed by commitment to that sādhanā. For those who are really interested, says Guruji, the sky is the limit.

For the Mission Centers and Ācāryas. Rapid change is foreseen in the years to come, as the chapter on demographics reveals. The difficulties in aging that have been discussed in this book will become increasingly severe and will occur at an accelerated pace. An aging world needs compassionate management, more patience, and a greater surrender as life unfolds.

For vānaprastha to be seamless (when the time comes), Ācāryas and sevaks can encourage members of their Mission centers to adopt a structured plan of study while they are still young. Let the youth of today factor into their work the needs of the elderly and construct careers that are enabling and accepting of elder persons. In whatever work we do, let us ask if we have included our elders or alienated them even more.

And to those who are going on sixty, the earlier that spiritual living is factored into living, the greater will be the ability to deal with change.

From a Seed Sown So Many Years Ago. It is intriguing how Gurudev gently initiated the vānaprastha movement, without intending it to be just a wing of Chinmaya Mission but as an anchor for his aging devotees. As the global head of Chinmaya Mission, Pūjya Guruji continues to carry that same enthusiasm that Gurudev felt for the elders.

The question is: Do we really want this road map? There are possibilities for those who do the DSC, and who thus become more inspired; they can persuade Chinmaya Mission to construct the road to a spiritually enlightening and inspiring vānaprastha for its members.

Some of us may flex a few limbs and think that is yoga, some may do a few strings of japa and call it uplifting, and some others may chant some stotras and imagine that to be a hotline to Bhagavān. What vānaprastha entails is much, much more. Vānaprastha demands of us a daring, a courage, a will, a commitment. Vānaprastha is, as its name suggests, the entry into rough terrain, a terrain that is out of the ordinary, a terrain that is fraught with discomfort, which comes with its different rules and regulations.

The choice rests with each one — to prepare for vānaprastha, or enter it clueless and rudderless.

Pūjya Gurudev's words, "Wisdom is the antidote for all confusions, the solace for all fears," hold the key to vānaprastha. When we learn to live through each stage of life with alertness, the transitions from youth into adulthood, and then into the age of inquiry, can be faced with firm yet gentle strength. And that strength can only be born of knowledge — the bedrock of every endeavor of Chinmaya Mission.

The Vedānta Course that the Mission conducts at Sandeepany is created for those who have decided to dedicate themselves to discovering, then living for that higher purpose. But it is as much open to anyone who wishes to take to deeper study; many people have done that and committed their lives to serving Gurudev's vision. These include gṛhasthas as well.

For those who might find that too much too soon can begin a structured self-study program or in a group. Chinmaya Mission offers other options as well: Study Groups, sustained sādhanā, and selfless service, as well as thought-provoking camps and yajñas.

Many are the possibilities for aging gracefully. Gurudev came down in 1951 from the hills to forge for us a *Joyous Journey to Liberation.* Come, let us walk this road ... with the good shepherd, following him sometimes, walking with him sometimes, but being with him all the time, allowing him to lead us to freedom.

OM SRI CHINMAYA SATGURAVE NAMAḤ!

Glossary

A

ānnakṣetra	literally, food zone; common cafeteria
artha	objects of the senses; wealth
āśrama	the residence and teaching center of a spiritual teacher and his students. Also, Indian philosophical thought, which divides man's life into four distinct stages: brahmacaryāśrama, gṛhasthāśrama, vānaprasth-āśrama, and sannyāsāśrama. The goal of each stage is the development and fulfillment of the individual.
Ayodhyākānda	the section in the *Rāmāyaṇa* about the life of Rāma after His return to Ayodhyā after His marriage to Sītā

B

Bhagvat Saptah	a *Śrīmad Bhāgavata Mahā Purāṇa, Śrīmad Bhāgavatam* (or *Bhāgavata*), refers to the same text that details stories of the Lord and His various incarnations. Saptah means one week. Tradition has it that Parikshit, son of Arjuna, on realizing his death was seven days away, approached Suka Maharaj and asked to be told the story of the Lord, and then attained mokṣa. Although an extremely vast text, practice of narrating the *Bhāgavatam* in seven days is an accepted aspect of tradition.
Bhaja Govindam	'Seek the Lord,' also known as Moha Mudgara, the hammer that smashes delusion; a composition of Śrī Ādi Śaṅkara written in the eighth century
bhikṣā	alms of food offered to monks and sādhus (mendicants)
bhikṣu	a renunciate, one living on bhikṣā, alms

bhūmi pūjā	a ceremony performed to inaugurate a new construction site, performed according to the tenets of *Vāstu Śastra*, the ancient Indian science of structures and architecture
brahmacārī	an adopted lifestyle of a monk in spiritual practice for the attainment of Brahman
Brahmananda	the joy experienced in the Brahman-state; Bliss

D

dakṣiṇā	offerings made by devotees to a priest, teacher, Master or Guru out of gratitude for their teachings.
Devi Group	an exclusive all-women group formed in all Mission Centers to provide a platform for their study, discussion, and devotional singing/chanting

dharma, ārtha, kāma, and mokṣa — the four goals or aspirations of human life: duties, riches, desires, and liberation

dhyāna yoga	the yoga of meditation
Dwarkadisa	Śrī Kṛṣṇa, King of Dwarka, the city He built

F

Friedrich Engels	German author, political theorist, and philosopher, most known for his monumental work with Karl Marx, *The Communist Manifesto* and *Das Kapital*

G

gośālā	shelter for cows, where they are raised and nourished.
gṛhastha	householder; gṛhasthāśrama, the second stage of the āśrama system. Here the individual is vested with the responsibilities of running a household, starting a family, educating his children, and serving society with a part of his earnings.
Guru pāda-pūjā	offering worship to the feet of one's Guru. In doing so, the worshiper is invoking the Lord and his teacher through the feet of the teacher. Likewise, the Guru, too, turns his mind to his teacher.

Guru-pūrṇimā paramparā — festival or celebration of the teacher who is the remover of the darkness of ignorance; falls on a full moon day in June-July of every year

Guru-śiṣya — the lineage of the teacher and student in the Indian tradition, through which knowledge passes and is protected and preserved. Lord Śiva is the first teacher who then taught Śrī Ādi Śaṅkarācārya.

gurukula — ancient schooling system where students lived with the teacher, often in his home, serving him, performing chores, while also learning

H

havan — ritual where offerings are made to the Lord via a consecrated fire

hitam — benefit, welfare

J

Janmāṣṭamī — birthday of Lord Kṛṣṇa

japa yoga — yoga, the union with the higher Self; hence, using japa intensively as a means in yoga

jñāna yajña — 'sacrifice of knowledge,' by which man renounces all his ignorance into the fire-of-knowledge kindled BY Him and IN Him (*Bhagavad-gītā* 4:28)

K

kāma — desire

kalaśa — a metal pot filled with holy water or grains upon which a coconut is placed on a bed of mango leaves. Now called pūrṇa kalaśa, it symbolizes abundance, longevity, prosperity, and auspiciousness and is a traditional part of ceremonies.

Kaṭhopaniṣad — a key Upaniṣad that examines the mystery of death

kula-guru — family preceptor

kuṭiyā/kuṭīra — a tiny hut or a small compact residence

M

mahāsamādhi	final samādhi, where a Self-realized Master consciously wills to drop his body
mahātmā	'Great Soul'; a veneration used to address someone revered for his great wisdom and, often, selflessness
mastakābhiṣekam	the pouring of holy water on an idol so as to drench it from the top of the head, thus energizing it. The water is collected from India's holy rivers, and energized with mantras. Symbolically, it represents our mind's thought-flow (water) embracing the deity in meditation.
māyā	the concept of illusion in Vedānta, connoting that what we see is not what is, leading to a deeper exploration of Reality
mudrās/chinmudrā	symbolic gestures adopted during prāṇāyāma (see under 'P') where the fingers are poised in specific ways to enable the flow of specific energy. In chinmudrā, the index finger (ego) meets the middle of the thumb (cosmic Consciousness), while the other three fingers — standing for the three guṇas of personality — stand apart. This merging of the ego with the cosmic Consciousness, not identifying with the guṇas, is used in meditation.

N

naivedyam	an offering to the Lord before partaking of it, typically in the form of food; it is then received back from the Lord as prasāda, His grace-filled gift.
nāma-smaran	constantly remembering the Lord's name
niṣkāma karma	action performed without desire or expected result

P

pādukās	olden-time Indian footwear consisting of a sole and a knob that is gripped by the big and second toes; used even today by great sādhus
paramparā	a lineage of (usually) teachers and disciples in succession, whereby knowledge passes from one to the next, uninterrupted, without any dilution

pitamah — grandfather, elder

prāṇapratiṣṭhā — the ceremony by which the consciousness of the deity is called to inhabit the idol

prāṇāyāma — a set of breathing exercises that result in the control of the body's vital energies through the breath. Blockages preventing the free flow of the prāṇa, or vital energies, cause physical health to fail.

preyas — the sensually pleasant, hence of emotion and ego, as opposed to the morally good (see śreyas)

provident fund — social safety pool to which workers contribute out of their salaries; paid out at retirement or is available for emergencies, such as healthcare.

punar janma — rebirth

puṣtaini — a Hindi word meaning ancestral

R

Rāmāyaṇa/*Rāmacharitamānasa*/*Valmiki Rāmāyaṇa* — The *Rāmāyaṇa* is the story of the Lord in His incarnation as Śrī Rāma and how He lived that life. The story was originally written by Sage Valmiki in sanskrit, hence the name *Valmiki Rāmāyaṇa*. Thereafter, retold by Goswami Tulsidas, in the common man's language, Awadhi. Hence, one name — *Tulsi Rāmāyaṇa*. Also known as *Rāmacharitamānasa*, or the story of Rāma as stored in the mind (mānasa) of Śiva and which He narrated to his wife Parvati.

S

sādhanā — any practice toward attaining a higher spiritual goal

sādhanā camps — conducted by Mission centers as residential camps around a single text, often two, led by an Ācārya, combined with japa or meditation practices

sambar — a lentil and tamarind-based broth that is eaten on a mound of rice; a staple in Tamil Nadu, with variations found in Andhra and Karnataka

saṁsāra — cycle of birth-life-death and the related experiences

Sanat Kumaras	four mind-born sons of Lord Brahma and reputed to be eternally young and purposed only to teach
saṅkalpa	an intent, a commitment to perform, a vow to deliver
sannyāsa dīkṣā	formal process of permission and initiation of a seeker into sannyāsa, by the Guru
sansthan	institution, establishment
śānti-pāṭha	a prayer or mantra chanted — at the beginning and end of every worship, spiritual discourse, or yajña — for peace, harmony and cooperative conduct of the worship. It ends with invoking peace thrice: within oneself, in one's external environment, and in the many relationships one has with the world.
śāstras	sciences derived from scriptures, referring to the science of religion
satsaṅga	in the company of one's Guru or participating in an assembly of people all of whom are seeking the highest Truth
sattva/sāttvika sādhanā	— the predominance of the pure and spiritual; hence, spiritual processes that are pure and divine
Sepoy Rebellion	India's First War of Independence, or the Great Rebellion against the British in 1857
sevak	devotee, worker, servant
śilpī	sculptor
Śrāvaṇa	the fifth month of the Hindu year, beginning in late July and ending in the third week of August
śravaṇam	devoting the ears to the hearing of spiritual knowledge; a prescribed spiritual practice/process
śreyas	wise, good, hence of the intellect, as opposed to the emotional and impulsive (see preyas)
Śrī Raghunath	another name by which Lord Rāma is known — the head of the Raghu dynasty
svādhyāya	self-study of scriptural texts; prescribed spiritual process, or sādhanā
svayambhū	that which appears by itself, not made by man

T

tapas — from the root word 'tap,' meaning fire; intense effort applied by seekers to achieve their goal

tīrthakṣetra — pilgrimage sites

Trivarga — the Doctrine of Trivarga, comprising of 'dharma, artha, and kāma,' declaring the supremacy of dharma over artha (wealth) and kāma (every type of desire)

V

vairāgya — dispassion, indifference

vānaras — has, over time, come to mean monkeys; in the *Rāmāyaṇa,* refers to the forest-dwelling humans, with monkey-like features, who helped Rāma defeat Rāvaṇa

Vanvasi Ram — reference is to the personality of Rāma on being exiled to the forest for fourteen years

vāsanās — inborn dispositions and motivating urges deep in the unconscious; the impressions formed in the personality when one acts in the world with egocentric desires

vibhūti — the sacred ash left behind by the special wood that is burned during a fire worship, or homa; considered holy and placed on the forehead as a blessing

viṣayananda — joy from objects, viṣaya

Viṣṇu-sahasranāma-arcanā — the attributes and glories of Viṣṇu as spoken by Bhishma in the form of 1,000 names, to Yudhishthira. The Lord is worshiped with an offering of these 1,000 divine names.

Y

yajña prasāda — blessing at the successful completion of a yajña

Yogīṣa — the King of Yogīs, Śrī Nārāyaṇa. (*Nāma* 850 – *Viṣṇu-sahasranāma*)

yuga — the name of an epoch or era within a four-age cycle

TRANSLITERATION AND PRONUNCIATION GUIDE

In the book, Devanāgarī characters are transliterated according to the scheme adopted by the International Congress of Orientalists at Athens in 1912. In it, one fixed pronunciation value is given to each letter; f, q, w, x and z are not called to use. An audio recording of this guide is available at www.chinmayamission.com/scriptures.php. According to this scheme:

	sounds like		*sounds like*
a	o in son	ḍh	dh in a*dh*esive
ā	a in f*a*ther	ṇ	n in u*n*der*
i	i in d*i*fferent	t	t in *t*abla
ī	ee in f*ee*l	th	th in *th*umb
u	u in f*u*ll	d	th in *th*is
ū	oo in b*oo*t	dh	dh in Gan*dh*i
ṛ	rh in *rh*ythm*	n	n in *n*ose
ṝ	**	p	p in *p*en
ḷ	**	ph	ph in *ph*antom*
e	a in ev*a*de	b	b in *b*oil
ai	i in del*i*ght	bh	bh in a*bh*or
o	o in c*o*re	m	m in *m*ind
au	o in n*o*w	y	y in *y*es
k	c in *c*alm	r	r in *r*ight
kh	kh in *kh*an	l	l in *l*ove
g	g in *g*ate	v	v in *v*ery
gh	gh in *gh*ost	ś	sh in *sh*ut
ṅ	an in *an*kle*	ṣ	s in *s*ugar
c	ch in *ch*uckle	s	s in *s*imple
ch	ch in wit*ch**	h	h in *h*appy
j	j in *j*ustice	ṁ	m in i*m*provise
jh	jh in *Jh*ansi	ḥ	**
ñ	ny in ba*ny*an	kṣ	tio in ac*tio*n
ṭ	t in *t*ank	tr	th in *th*ree*
ṭh	**	jñ	gn in *g*nosis
ḍ	d in *d*og	'	a silent 'a'

* These letters do not have an exact English equivalent. An approximation is given here.
** These sounds cannot be approximated in English words.

Patrons and Contributors

Grateful acknowledgement and special thanks is given to the following:

DAVID & MARGARET DUKES

| TORONTO, ONTARIO, CANADA |

JANGA & SHASHIKALA REDDY

| SAN MARINO, CALIFORNIA, USA |

SANTOSH & GAYATHRI BHAGWATH

| SUGAR LAND, TEXAS, USA |

SHALINI SAHNI

| OTTAWA, ONTARIO, CANADA |